Black
Silent
Majority

MICHAEL JAVEN FORTNER

Black
Silent
Majority

The Rockefeller Drug Laws
and the Politics of Punishment

 Harvard University Press

Cambridge, Massachusetts, and London, England 2015

First printing

Library of Congress Cataloging-in-Publication Data

Fortner, Michael Javen, 1979–
    Black silent majority : the Rockefeller drug laws and the politics of
punishment / Michael Javen Fortner.
        pages cm
    Includes bibliographical references and index.
    ISBN 978-0-674-74399-1 (alk. paper)
    1. Discrimination in criminal justice administration—New York (State)
2. African American criminals—New York (State)   3. Drug control—
New York (State)   4. African Americans—New York (State)—Social
conditions.   5. Middle class—New York (State)   I. Title.
HV9955.N7F67 2015
364.1'3365089960730747—dc23

                                                            2015012136

For Curley

Contents

Preface

I HAVE NEVER BEEN INCARCERATED. But my brother has—for a long time. I have never been stopped and frisked. Yet as a black man I know how it feels to be watched. I know how it feels to scare strangers for no reason. At the same time, I know crime and the toll it takes on communities. Growing up in Brownsville, Brooklyn, during the height of the crack epidemic I watched as the drug trade killed people and destroyed families. I remember addicts knocking on my door hawking electronics, clothes, and sometimes food they stole from neighbors. I remember sleeping with my wallet under my pillow just in case addicts in my family became desperate for a hit in the midnight hour. I remember the sound of crime. All New Yorkers grow accustomed to the din of sirens, but you never really make peace with the clatter of gunshots. You never get used to violence and insecurity. Criminal acts that show up only once in data sets—if they show up at all—can have lasting impacts. I was only a couple of years old when one of my brothers was stabbed to death. I do not remember him, but the pain and sorrow of that day stayed in my home like accumulated dust.

Over the past twenty years, activists and academics have valiantly come to the aid of the nation's prison population. With perspicacity and passion, they have drawn attention to the ways racism has corroded the administration of criminal justice, and they have awakened us to the insidious consequences of mass incarceration. We are now witnessing some of the benefits of these noble efforts. Entrepreneurial lawyers continue to set the innocent free. Politicians as ideologically opposed as Attorney General Eric Holder and Senator Rand Paul are fighting to end mandatory minimum sentences for nonviolent drug offenses. Private prisons, the malignant cancer on the criminal justice system, are now in decline. Like the prophets of old, these advocates, experts, and public officials "preach good tidings unto the meek," "bind up the brokenhearted," "proclaim liberty to the captives, and the opening of the prison to *them that are* bound."[1]

These great works notwithstanding, our new American dilemma is Janus-faced. There are those who have endured the inequities of the penal system, and there are those who have suffered the unfairness of crime. This second face deserves a fair hearing. I started this project because the literature on mass incarceration neglected the voices of working- and middle-class African Americans dealing daily with drug addiction and violent crime and their aftermath. Few scholars have taken stock of their views. In an essay entitled "Listen to the Black Community," Glenn C. Loury wrote, "The young black men wreaking havoc in the ghetto are still 'our youngsters' in the eyes of many of the decent poor and working-class black people who are often their victims. The hard edge of judgment and retribution is tempered for many of these people by a sense of sympathy for and empathy with the perpetrators." But that's not what I heard. I remember a community at war with itself—not in the bloody, violent sense, but war as a state of constant conflict between opposing and seemingly irreconcilable interests and values. Working- and middle-class families like mine were not deeply invested in civil rights or the politics of race. Of course, particular moments—the murder of Michael Griffith in Howard Beach, Queens, in 1986 and the shooting death of Yusef Hawkins in Bensonhurst, Brooklyn, in 1989—awakened deep feelings of racial solidarity, but in between the ethnic conflagrations that occasionally engulfed the city, I remember black folks constantly worrying about keeping their children, homes, and property safe. These working- and middle-class families did not express much "sympathy for and empathy with the perpetrators" of crime in the neighborhood. I recall hearing "That's what he gets" every time one of "our youngsters" was arrested. I recall hearing about fathers calling the cops on sons and mothers throwing daughters out onto the street. I remember that from the pews of my Pentecostal church sanctified working- and middle-class African Americans distinguished between saints and sinners. They certainly believed that salvation was free for drug users and dealers, but salvation was always a choice—a test of individual morality and fortitude—because these iniquities were rooted in the soul rather than social structure. These saints had no compunction about beseeching police or calling forth prisons for their own salvation when junkies and pushers became a cross too heavy to bear.[2]

Black Silent Majority is neither a memoir nor a polemic. It is a scholarly history of drug policy development in New York State from 1944 to the passage of the Rockefeller drug laws—the nation's most consequential and devastating narcotics control legislation—in 1973. It systematically gathers a mélange of materials to adjudicate between contending explanations of crime policy formation. Drawing on a diverse collection of sources, it documents the existence of a black silent majority, a phenomenon insufficiently explored in histories of the 1960s and 1970s, social scientific studies of African American politics, and narratives of mass incarceration. My own experiences prompted me to investigate the role that African Americans played in crime policy development.

Whether my memories are representative of the views of millions of working- and middle-class African Americans trapped in dangerous urban ghettos and whether these voices shaped drug policy in New York State are empirical questions that this book pursues. These are controversies than can be resolved only by listening to the black community and tracing the legislative histories of drug policies.

I hope advocates and scholars continue to lay bare the bewildering immorality of the criminal justice system and its blatant inhumanity. However, I wrote this book to redeem the agency of black people who are portrayed, at best, as backbenchers to history, treated either as hostages of white supremacy or as the collateral damage of neoliberalism. I wrote this book to recover the voice of the "invisible black victim." While the literature on mass incarceration has correctly highlighted racial discrimination within the criminal justice system, it has unnecessarily discounted the hurt and terror of those who clutch their billfolds as they sleep, of those who exit their apartments and leave their buildings with trepidation, and of those who have had to bury a son or daughter because of gang activity, the drug trade, or random violence. I pray that one day we can proclaim liberty to the captives of violent crime and open the prison to which residents of Brownsville, the South Side of Chicago, and urban minority neighborhoods across the country are bound. My fervent wish is that we can bind up those brokenhearted by crime.[3]

Black
Silent
Majority

Introduction

"The Reign of Criminal Terror Must Be Stopped Now"

"LADIES AND GENTLEMEN," Governor Nelson Rockefeller announced, "this is an unusual press conference." On January 23, 1973, five Harlem civic leaders joined New York's governor in the state capital's ornate Red Room to voice their support for Rockefeller's proposal for new, punitive antidrug measures. During his annual message to the legislature a few weeks earlier, the governor had proposed mandatory life sentences for individuals convicted of selling *any* amount of "hard" drugs, including heroin, cocaine, and hashish. He had also advocated life sentences for individuals convicted of violent crimes while under the influence of such drugs. Now five leaders from the nation's most prominent black neighborhood—Rev. Oberia D. Dempsey, pastor of the Upper Park Avenue Baptist Church; Glester Hinds, founder of the People's Civic Welfare Association; Dr. George W. McMurray, pastor of the Mother African Zion Church; Rev. Earl B. Moore, pastor of St. Paul Baptist Church; and Dr. Robert W. Baird, a white physician and the founder of the Haven Clinic for drug addicts—were standing alongside the Republican governor and endorsing his plan.[1]

The proposed drug laws had stoked the ire of white liberals. The *New York Times* took Rockefeller to task, complaining, "Governor Rockefeller's proposed crackdown on the addiction problem as outlined in his State of the State message is little better than a politically attuned harangue that threatens to make a bad situation worse." The *New Republic* was incredulous: "The 19-year old Brooklyn boy who sells a co-worker the resin of marijuana (hashish) and the Queens housewife who lets her neighbor buy a few of her diet pills (amphetamines) would be treated by the law no differently than the multimillion-dollar heroin dealer: all would get life sentences with no hope for commutation. That's not justice; it is ignorance." The New York Civil Liberties Union (NYCLU) warned that the law "represented a frightening leap towards the imposition of a total police state." At a hearing on the governor's proposal, Kenneth P. Norwick, legislative director of the NYCLU, inveighed against the program's seemingly capricious barbarism: "The New York Civil Liberties Union is unalterably opposed to each and every aspect of the Governor's proposed legislation, which we believe to be demonstrably inhumane, unworkable, unconstitutional and essentially irrelevant to the problem to which it is purportedly addressed." For white liberals, the drug laws were both ideologically unpalatable and inconsistent with their understanding of this policy problem. The laws would never solve the problem of drug addiction and trafficking but instead would simply lead to the unjust incarceration of many people.[2]

They were right.

Given liberals' hostility toward the proposed laws and the widespread belief that they would lead to the mass incarceration of small-time pushers and drug addicts from predominantly minority neighborhoods, the appearance of five Harlem leaders at the governor's press conference was unexpected. Yet Dempsey insisted that their presence was quite proper. "I do not hesitate to say that no people in the State of New York have felt the impact of drug addiction and crime more than we have," he declared. "We are from Harlem and from other ghettos in the City of New York and so we have come today because we felt that we had a right to come, that a great moral issue is involved." According to Dempsey, drug dealers and abusers alike had abandoned middle-class values and threatened the lives and liberty of those who faithfully abided by them. While considering the dealer's iniquity and skulduggery troubling in itself, Dempsey also held pushers responsible for the violence, disorder, and insecurity caused by drug users trying to finance their next fix. In a searing indictment of pushers, Dempsey plumbed the depths of their immorality:

> The hard drug non-addict pusher is cruel, inhuman and ungodly. He knows that he's afflicting his victims but he doesn't care. He knows that he's committing genocide but he doesn't care. He knows that he's creating fear and panic, but that is what he wants, to keep the people afraid so that he can operate. He knows that he's committing a murder a minute through overdoses, homicides, all kinds of physical assaults committed by his slave addicts upon innocent, hard-working people, but he doesn't care.

He added, "The non-addict pusher knows too well that his slave hard drug addict pushers are violating the constitutional rights of blacks and whites daily. Freedom of worship, a cherished right, and the right to work and earn a living have been, since the beginning of time, the most honored rights among human beings." Drug addicts were hurting "hardworking people" who could not enjoy the fruits of their labor because addicts were stealing their property and jeopardizing their safety. Addicts were assaulting the natural rights of workers, merchants, and "god-fearing people."[3]

Imposing life sentences on both the "hard drug non-addict pusher" and his "slaves" seemed excessive and cruel to many white liberals. But the Harlem leaders who joined Rockefeller acknowledged the laws' harshness and even seemed drawn to it. "I don't think the governor went far enough," Hinds confessed. "It should be included in his bill as capital punishment because these murderers need to be gotten rid of completely." Responding to those who thought him "a little too harsh," McMurray insisted that if the pusher was left on the street "because of sympathy, he's going to kill you, he's going to kill me. Then he's going to kill himself." McMurray added, "Where someone says, 'What you going to do with the poor little boy who is not 21 years of age? You mean you're going to send him up for life?' Yes if this is his choice, then let him go for life." McMurray reasoned that spending life in prison could help pushers become "productive citizens." "There are many things to do in prison," he quipped.[4]

Amid their forceful advocacy, the leaders practiced a bit of linguistic chicanery. Dempsey and the others heaped opprobrium mostly on the "non-addict pusher." They considered "addict pushers"—individuals who sold illegal narcotics to support their habit—"slaves" of big drug dealers. But Rockefeller's proposals would not make this distinction: they placed master and slave in the same legal category. This tension was not lost on the assembled reporters. One asked Dempsey if he would "rather see the bill draw that distinction as far as the penalties." Dempsey's reply, focused on the threat of all drug traffic, collapsed the moral boundaries separating master and slave. "I would rather it stand as it is," he responded, "because I'm more concerned about the drug getting into the hands of your daughter or my daughter or my son or somebody else's daughter than I am worrying who actually sells the hard drug. Who sells it really doesn't matter to me because of the fact it is just as deadly, just as poisonous, just as harmful as if the hard drug non-addict pusher sells it as it would be if the addict drug pusher sold it. I draw no distinction." Although they acknowledged the differing motivations and impulses of "pushers" and "addict-sellers," these Harlem leaders wanted both expelled from the community.[5]

Some were suspicious at the sight of African American leaders—
civil rights activists and social reformers—promoting the patri-
cian governor's proposal to accelerate the imprisonment of young
black males and expand a police state in Harlem. Black state senator Sidney Von Luther protested, "When he rounded up some
ministers and other leaders to support him, he created a stacked
deck; many of those people have gotten money from the Governor
to run the very drug programs that have failed to solve the problem."
Woodrow Lewis, a black assemblyman from Brooklyn, lamented
that Rockefeller had divided the black community by using these
pastors as "[p]uppets and instruments in the creation of hysteria."
Lewis charged that the governor never consulted leaders who
accurately reflected the desires of the city's African American community. Even Joseph Persico, a Rockefeller aide and speechwriter,
believed, at one point, that the governor had expertly manipulated
some black ministers to engineer the passage of his drug program.
In the proposal for his biography of Rockefeller, Persico wrote that
the wily governor had called "in the chits" of Harlem pastors "whose
churches had benefited from Rockefeller family bounty."[6]

But while Rockefeller dubbed the event "unusual" and critics
looked askance, the alliance on view that day was hardly unprecedented. Four years earlier, the Anti-Crime Committee of the New
York City branch of the National Association for the Advancement
of Colored People (NAACP) had issued a report that presaged the
angst expressed by Harlem's civic leaders in the Red Room and
the support they afforded Rockefeller's punitive drug laws. The
NAACP's 1969 report described "measures which can and must
be taken at once to meet and master the challenge of the hoodlum
element." At a news briefing on the document, Vincent S. Baker,
chairman of the branch's anticrime committee, blamed the culture
in Harlem, saying, "There are people known to cheer when some
offender rushes from a store. . . . They seem to have the idea that
these are some sort of 20th Century Robin Hoods. With the hoods,

we agree." Baker stated that, although the NAACP would continue to confront police brutality, "it is not police brutality that makes people afraid to walk the streets at night." Police brutality, he intimated, was being "superseded by criminal brutality."[7]

The NAACP's report began and ended with a simple yet urgent plea: "The reign of criminal terror in Harlem must be stopped now." In between, it described a dire situation, asserting, "The lives and property of the people are in constant danger by day and night. This is true whether they are black or white, male or female, young or old. Indeed the old, the weak, the handicapped are the special prey of marauding hoodlums." The report declared that "the economic, civic, religious and social life of the community is being strangled," with residents in constant fear of being mugged and burglarized and refusing to leave their homes at night so as not to "tempt fate." Foreshadowing the 1973 comments from Dempsey and others, the NAACP's report highlighted the dangers that crime, particularly drug trafficking and addiction, posed to "hardworking people" and black civil society. The report depicted "marauding hoodlums" as threats to working- and middle-class African Americans' life chances and lifestyles.[8]

The report did not heap moral opprobrium only on "hoods." With a keen sociological eye, it also identified the complex structural origins of crime and crime-related problems. It admitted "that such social evils as white racism, unemployment, underemployment, family breakdown, inadequate education and substandard housing must be successfully attacked if there is to be a long-term solution of the crime problem." Still, this sociology did not assuage fears or alleviate anxieties. Immediately after this analysis, the document pressed its main point: "But the reign of criminal terror must be stopped now. For the decent people of Harlem, this issue is as crucial as any other. This is quite literally a matter of life and death." Terror rather than sociology informed the committee's policy recommendations. The committee advocated life sentences for all illegal drug sales. Its prescriptions for murder were similarly pitiless. In 1965, Rockefeller, although a supporter of capital punishment, had signed a bill abolishing the penalty except in cases involving the murder of police officers. Consequently, in the absence of the death penalty the report recommended a mandatory sentence of at least thirty years for first-degree murder. Of course, the proposed punishment for drug sales was harsher than the proposed punishment for murder; the pusher was, after all, the root of all evil.[9]

The following month, Baker, the NAACP committee chairman, testified before the State Joint Committee on Crime and reiterated these views. According to a digest of his testimony, he championed the severe sentencing policies recommended in the report, adding that drug pushers "should be subject to indefinite imprisonment until they reveal [the source of their drug supply]" and that mugging should be punishable with a minimum five-year term, with no time off for good behavior or possibility of commutation. Baker appeared unconcerned with the potential consequences of these sentencing proposals. Although he acknowledged that such sentences would create an overcrowding problem in prisons, he felt that early release of these "hoodlums" caused much more serious problems to innocent citizens. "The avowed purpose of these recommendations is to rid the streets of these criminals," he said. He also seemed uninterested in the racial consequences of aggressive policing strategies and maintained that people of Harlem favored "such measures as police saturation and use of the 'stop and frisk' law." Baker dismissed the protestations of other African American leaders, insisting that a reckless minority of community figures had misled white politicians and the public about black public safety concerns. "The silent majority in Harlem," he asserted, "would welcome a police order to get tough."[10]

Baker and the five Harlem civic leaders who stood with Rockefeller were not alone. They were leaders within a broader, grassroots, anticrime social movement bubbling up from the streets of Harlem and black communities throughout the United States. In 1968, Roy Wilkins, the legendary leader of the NAACP, witnessed the toll crime was taking on African Americans and heralded the growing movement against it. "It is too early to raise a victory cry, but a reaction is setting in that could make the demand for order far louder than the emotional call to race—right or wrong," he wrote. He reported that the "millions of [law-abiding] colored citizens (and these include all grades, not just the loosely-labeled middle class) are beginning to stir against the hoodlums and criminals." By 1974, this movement had intensified and spread. Roy Wood, a National Black Network radio commentator, urged a united effort in combating crime, saying, "I think when the criminal element of our communities becomes so bad and brazen that Black people are no longer safe on the streets . . . it is time to rally decent, self-respecting Black people together for nationwide action against Black on Black crime." Jesse Jackson, who once railed against the "law and order" rhetoric of Republican politicians, declared, "We must be tough on crime. Handguns ought to leave. Dope pushers mush be dealt with severely, and the streets must be made safe for normal citizens." That same year, Andrew Barrett, executive director of the NAACP's Chicago chapter, said, "Blacks have always been concerned about crime, but hesitated to crusade because of the negative meaning of . . . law and order. . . . But the situation is so bad that action is the only thing left." In 1976, Robert L. Woodson, director of the National Urban League's administration of justice division, remarked, "[Frank Rizzo] won with black votes in Philadelphia because he was talking about short-term solutions—more cops, locking up the youths, restoring the death penalty. And the people are more afraid of crime in the streets than the racism of a Rizzo."[11]

Working- and middle-class African Americans in cities like Chicago, Los Angeles, Detroit, Philadelphia, Memphis, New Orleans,

Washington, D.C., and Atlanta activated the black institutions that had been tested in the struggle for racial equality and also formed new groups to affirm "traditional black values" and end "the reign of criminal terror" in their communities. Leaders and everyday folk tapped their discontent and drew from the well of black middle-class morality to make sense of urban crime and formulate appropriate responses. Specifically, they shifted focus from structural problems to individual behavior. In 1967, an African American business owner in Baltimore opined, "It's been said that poverty is the cause [of crime], but many of us come from the ghetto, from poor homes and have not turned to crime." By the early 1970s, this sentiment had become commonplace. In 1976, Joe Gardner, an official at Chicago's Woodlawn Organization, the "voice" of the predominantly black and crime-plagued neighborhood, confessed that while activists like him used to "stress underlying causes like poverty and racism[,] rising crime rates had forced them to tell it like it is." While members of the black silent majority believed in the structural origins of crime in the abstract, the violence in their communities forced them to prioritize public safety over economic and racial inequality. It drove them to rally and rail against "hoodlums" instead of seeking reform of society.[12]

In New York, the black silent majority achieved its greatest legislative victory with the passage of what became known as the "Rockefeller drug laws"—a set of statutes only slightly less punitive than the proposals the governor had initially offered. While white liberals fought for rehabilitation and smarter policing strategies focused on large-scale drug dealers, the black silent majority supported the regulation and removal of the poor, whom they blamed for urban blight and violence in the streets. After tilting the discursive terrain in the direction of racial equality during the struggles of the civil rights movement, working- and middle-class African Americans tilted it in favor of punitive crime policies and against economic justice for the urban black poor. As a result, the black silent majority created an important opportunity for the ambitious governor to achieve his own goals and laid the groundwork for mass incarceration. This book tells that uncomfortable story.

A CURIOUS THING HAPPENED AFTER THE CIVIL RIGHTS MOVEMENT ended. Many African Americans, who had just won new freedoms, found themselves captured once more after the 1970s. Numerous young black men were caught in the throes of the modern carceral state, a term used by scholars to describe the set of organizations and capacities employed by the government to administer its monopoly on violence and maintain order within its borders. Since the early 1970s, the American prison population has increased by more than 500 percent, and the United States today boasts the highest incarceration rate in the world. African Americans are incarcerated at nearly six times the rate of whites, and Hispanics are incarcerated at almost twice the rate of whites. Mass imprisonment harms the life chances of racial minorities by limiting the employment opportunities of ex-felons. It hinders democracy, as felon disenfranchisement has diminished the electoral power of African Americans and altered political outcomes.[13]

Studying drug policy formation in New York State during the 1960s and early 1970s helps uncover the origins of mass incarceration and its indisputable disastrous consequences. First, mandatory-minimum drug sentences are the keystone of the modern carceral state: they allow for the policing and prosecution of relatively minor crimes and guarantee lengthy sentences for individuals convicted of these offenses, and both factors populate and propel the growth of prisons. Accordingly, many scholars have attributed mass incarceration to President Ronald Reagan's "war on drugs" and the passage, with bipartisan support, of the Anti-Drug Abuse Act of 1986, which imposed severe mandatory-minimum sentences for the sale and possession of drugs, including marijuana.

The law also notoriously imposed heftier sentences for possession of crack cocaine, which affected mostly people of color, than for possession of powder cocaine, which mostly affected whites. Even so, this legislation is not the most significant moment in the history of American crime policy. The number of individuals in state penal institutions rose slowly in the immediate postwar period, climbing from 115,011 in 1945 to 181,396 in 1973. Then the state prison population more than doubled, increasing from 196,105 in 1974 to 470,659 in 1986. Thus mass incarceration was well under way before Reagan launched his inglorious war. Second, then, New York's Rockefeller drug laws, passed in 1973, represented a critical juncture in the historical development of the carceral state. They were the first of their kind, and, in the decade following their passage, forty-eight states enacted their own antidrug laws with mandatory-minimum sentences, instigating the rapid rise in the number of individuals imprisoned in state institutions before 1986. Therefore, identifying the origins of mass incarceration in the United States demands studying the politics of punishment in New York during the 1960s and early 1970s.[14]

Third, New York State provides an especially suitable venue for answering recent calls to trace crime policies over a longer time span so as to better understand what specifically changed in the politics and administration of criminal justice to spur modern mass imprisonment. The heroin trade accelerated after the end of World War II, and the federal government, through the Bureau of Narcotics, initiated an aggressive campaign against illegal narcotics shortly thereafter. Congress also acted. In 1951, it passed the Boggs Act, which increased penalties for drug violations and imposed mandatory-minimum sentences for simple possession of heroin, cocaine, and marijuana. In 1956, Congress ratcheted up the punishment when it passed the Narcotics Control Act, expanding penalties established in the Boggs Act and enacting the death penalty for some drug offenses. After World War II, New York State, more than any other state, witnessed a dramatic rise in heroin addiction, particularly in black neighborhoods like Harlem. In 1947, Col. Garland H. Williams, district supervisor for the Bureau of Narcotics, labeled New York City a "haven" for drug addicts and "the center for dope traffic in America east of the Rocky Mountains." District Narcotics Supervisor Boyd Martin described it as the "cancerous heart of the heroin traffic." City ports, organized crime, and criminal networks in Harlem aided the precipitous rise in heroin trafficking and addiction in black communities. "By the mid-1950s," David T. Courtwright reports, "the modal addict profile was that of a young black male . . . in his twenties." Despite punitive federal policies and the concentration of addiction within black communities, New York State took a unique approach. In 1962, the legislature responded to New York City's drug crisis by passing the Metcalf-Volker Act, which permitted voluntary commitment to a mental health facility for addicts charged with felony or a drug possession. The law, as Eric C. Schneider explains, "marked a high point of liberalism, a notable retreat from the criminal justice model established by the federal government in the Harrison Act (1914) and reaffirmed in the Boggs (1951) and Narcotics Control (1956) Acts." Thus the question is: What happened between the late 1940s and early 1970s to precipitate the passage of the Rockefeller drug laws, which repudiated the lofty principles embodied in Metcalf-Volker? The answer, this book maintains, was the mobilization of working- and middle-class African Americans against "the reign of criminal terror in Harlem."[15]

Others have offered alternative explanations. Michelle Alexander's *The New Jim Crow: Mass Incarceration in the Age of Colorblindness* documents with brutal clarity the ways in which punishment has perpetuated racial inequality in the post–civil rights era. She situates the carceral state within the teleology of American racism and treats mass incarceration as another logical step in this history. According to Alexander, white supremacy is durable and determined; after political forces dismantle one system of racial domination, another one quickly takes its place. There was slavery, then there was Jim Crow. Next, she argues, came mass incarceration— the new Jim Crow. For Alexander, the rise of the modern carceral state after major civil rights achievements was not curious. These victories were its cause: a "backlash" among whites worried about their position within the racial order triggered the deployment of the police and prison system as a new method of control.[16] Other accounts connect the rise of the carceral state to the ascendance of neoliberalism. The shift from the industrial society of the "Fordist-Keynesian order" to the "information society" of neoliberalism displaced American workers, particularly urban African Americans. A confluence of events closed off the labor market to the urban black poor: technological advances decreased the number of labor-intensive jobs, globalization replaced unionized labor in the United States with low-cost workers in other countries, and the information-based service-sector economy required higher educational levels and skills. According to Loïc Wacquant, the modern prison system arose to control this surplus labor. Like Alexander, Wacquant attributes mass incarceration to broader structural forces, but within this framework it is the invisible hand of the market rather than the uncompromising rule of white supremacy shackling racial minorities. And these economic forces were just as unrelenting and just as cruel.[17]

Despite the popularity of such theories, their elegant simplicity compromises their descriptive force and explanatory power. They mask more than they expose. In both accounts, crime victims are rendered invisible. African Americans are more likely than whites to be victims of crime, but both theories highlight white resentment while ignoring black agony. Both theories denude black politics of purpose and power. They depict African Americans either as victims of an unyielding racial order, one diminished during the mid-1960s but not deterred, or as useful casualties of the inescapable resolution of economic crises. The assessment of black politics in both models is the same and simple: it lost. *Black Silent Majority*, however, takes black agency seriously. To be clear, acknowledging black agency in a process does not mean assuming blacks had total control of its outcome. Instead, it means systematically studying the role that black politics played in the formation of crime policies. It also means deconstructing the very notion of "black interests" and allowing for the possibility of class conflict. Scholars have been slow to recognize forms of black class conflict in the post–civil rights period. Michael C. Dawson, for instance, concedes the increasing significance of class in the life chances of African Americans but insists that "systematic manifestations of these class divisions in the political arena have been difficult to find." Dawson offers the theory of "linked fate" to explain this paradox, arguing that, because middle-class African Americans and the black poor share a history of racial discrimination, the black middle-class relies on their racial identity rather than class status to understand their individual self-interests. "Linked fate," however, ignores the fact that values operate as interpretative frames that individuals use to understand their material interests and their relationship and obligation to others. Within urban communities across the United States, working- and middle-class African Americans differentiate between "us" and "them," between "decent families" and "street families." And "decent families" do not believe that their fate is linked with the fate of "street families." In fact, they are committed to forging a future that they trust will be different from and brighter than the one "street families" will choose.[18]

This is not to ignore the progressive potential of working- and middle-class African Americans. Rather, it is to recognize that there are moments when working- and middle-class African Americans condemn the urban black poor *and* moments when they come to the aid of the "truly disadvantaged." This dynamic is hardly new or unusual. Morality has always been a double-edged sword in American politics, at times inspiring reform movements and at times animating reactionary politics. As James A. Morone documents in *Hellfire Nation: The Politics of Sin in American History*, this duality dates back to the Puritans, who bequeathed two moral traditions to the nation: "One . . . touts personal responsibility. Sinners impoverish themselves and diminish their community. . . . The alternative tradition, the social gospel, shifts the emphasis from the sinner to the system. . . . Social gospel solutions reverse the focus: rather than redeem the individual, reform the political economy." Still, questions remain: When do Christian soldiers embrace their "social gospel," and when do they backslide? When does reform end and punishment begin?[19]

Black Silent Majority argues that the political aims of black middle-class morality vary according to the nature of threats to their social position. At the turn of the twentieth century, entrenched racism engendered the "politics of respectability," which emphasized "reform of individual behavior and attitudes both as a goal in itself and as a strategy for reform of the entire structural system of American race relations." Fearful of the "white gaze," "righteous" middle-class African Americans sought to curtail behaviors among the poor that would perpetuate stereotypes and undercut middle-class claims of equality. In *The Condemnation of Blackness: Race, Crime, and the Making of Modern Urban America*, Khalil Gibran Muhammad supplies an illuminating example of this dynamic with his discussion of James Stemson, "a [black] Philadelphia race-relations reformer and local crime fighter." In 1910, Stemson's League of Civic and Political Reform published a handbill titled "Appeal to Self-Respecting Colored Citizens." It addressed those who were embarrassed by the "rowdy, ruffianly, blatant, foulmouthed, corner-lounging, dive-infesting elements among them." In order to eliminate this "stigma," the League encouraged people to "report every such crime against decency." After Rudolph J. Blankenberg was elected mayor in 1911, Stemson sent him "Appeal to Self-Respecting Colored Citizens" and wrote, "The colored people of this, and every other large city, furnish far too large a quota of venal [and] vicious . . . characters." He asked for the newly elected mayor's aid in the "suppression of this element." Contrasting the conservative response of African American reformers like Stemson to "black criminality" to the progressive response of white reformers to immigrants, Muhammad argues, "[U]nlike black reformers, white progressives did not endure the personal pressure to define their respectability or right to middle-class standing as a negation of working-class culture." Blessed with power, money, and social standing, white reformers did not depend on the perception of white immigrants. On the other hand, many middle-class African Americans, believing that racial stereotypes based on the behaviors of the black poor hampered their own progress, privately disciplined disadvantaged members of the race or publicly disavowed them in order to gain entrée into white society and achieve the benefits of American citizenship.[20]

This book argues that the structural and ideological context of postwar American society engendered different reactions to "black criminality." The expansion of rights and opportunities for working- and middle-class blacks lessened the salience of the "white gaze"; their citizenship no longer rested on the benevolent attitudes of whites. Simultaneously, the disappearance of industrial society and the persistence of racial segregation segmented the urban black class structure into the employed and unemployed and compelled them to live together. The chronic joblessness of the urban black poor and concomitant "ghetto-related behaviors" conflicted with the material interests (e.g., property values), life chances (e.g., personal safety and children's futures), and ethics of working- and middle-class black families. By the 1960s, work, indigenous black morality, and common threats posed by the actions of the unemployed had united working- and middle-class blacks into a coherent status group, defined less by differences in wages and wealth and more in terms of shared worldviews, aspirations, and despair. Drawing on the class-based values sustained within black civil society, working- and middle-class African Americans responded to the perceived public safety threats posed by the unemployed by sharpening the boundaries between "us" and "them," between "citizen" and "criminal." They turned to punishment.

Meanwhile, by the postwar period, the racial notions of white reformers had been transformed. They no longer fixated on black inferiority and increasingly embraced structural explanations for social problems in African American communities. Their position within the racial order shielded them from the tragic consequences of deindustrialization and the concentration of poverty. Spared by segregation and unencumbered by the dangers of mean streets, white liberals turned their moral outrage on political economy rather than people. They tried to expand the "us" and provide an array of rights and services to the downtrodden, including drug addicts and criminal offenders. In New York in 1973, they lost.[21]

Working- and middle-class African Americans' dread of urban black crime and suspicion of the urban black poor were deeply consequential. But African American activism alone was not decisive. While it is important to recognize the agency of African Americans, it is equally important to realize that black politics occurs within a polity composed of governmental organizations that can operate autonomously of societal forces. Rev. Oberia Dempsey did not begin demanding aggressive action against pushers and junkies in 1973; his crusade began in the early 1960s. Roy Wilkins witnessed the stirring of "law-abiding" "colored citizens" against crime in 1968, and Vincent Baker sounded a clarion call for extreme punishment in 1969, but Rockefeller proposed his punitive drug program only in 1973. On the recommendation of law enforcement officials, the state's bar association, medical and public health officials, and liberal interest groups, the governor routinely vetoed bills imposing extreme criminal sentences for drug trafficking during the late 1960s. Rockefeller himself had struck a very different tone in his state-of-the-state address in 1970, when he announced, "We must continue to reach out, to experiment with new methods of treatment and rehabilitation." On the advice of liberal state legislators, medical and public health officials, and interest groups, the governor continued to expand the state's rehabilitative resources. Despite the anguished pleas of the black silent majority during the late 1960s, New York State refused to enact harsh criminal penalties for drug possession.[22]

So what changed? Another strand of the mass incarceration literature draws attention to a fundamental historical shift in the dominant "causal story" animating criminal justice policymaking: the emergence of the "new penology." This evolution entailed the replacement of discourses of clinical diagnosis with the language of risk, a shift from rehabilitation to control, and the use of techniques that target "offenders as an aggregate in place of traditional techniques for individualizing or creating equity." In short, the new penology "is about identifying and managing unruly groups." David Garland's pioneering work on modern crime policymaking profiles the policy activists, practitioners, and administrators who are so crucial to the formation and implementation of this new causal story. He is also interested in change: the turn from "criminologies of the welfare state," which assume the "perfectibility of man," to the "culture of control," which assumes the imperfection of man and emphasizes the importance of restrictions and restraints. Garland argues that the normalization of greater insecurity and risk in modern society prompted the shift from penal welfarism to criminologies of control. He is also careful not to claim that these changes occurred "naturally." Instead, he argues that developments in the sociopolitical world created pressures for the selection of new criminological ideals and strategies. Escaping the reductionist reasoning of the "new Jim Crow" thesis and arguments about neoliberalism, Garland's "soft structuralism" creates space for historical contingencies and ideological contradictions. This theoretical space, however, is underspecified, and the relationship between the bureaucratic field of crime control and the sociopolitical environment is unclear. In order to clarify the field's relationship to the sociopolitical environment, this book adopts Hugh Heclo's concept of "issue networks," which emphasize the ways certain ideas, rationalities, practices, and technologies become established within and are perpetuated by independent coteries of public officials and "policy activists" that share a knowledge base "having to do with some aspect (or, as defined by the network, some problem) of public policy." The concept of the issue network has an additional benefit: the actors within a network possess crucial resources—organizational capacity, reputation, and interest group resources—that give them leverage during conflicts with elected officials and social groups.[23]

The ideas and capacities of issue networks, however, best explain incrementalism and periods of stability in crime policymaking. Alone, they do not provide a compelling theory for sudden and dramatic policy change, particularly the monumental move from criminological approaches that underscored the perfectibility of man to the culture of control. John W. Kingdon's theory of policy change is useful here. He argues that the conjuncture of three processes, or "streams," can incite dramatic policy shifts: problem recognition, the formation and revision of policy proposals, and politics. Problem recognition refers to the process by which social problems occupy the attention of political officials. The policy formulation process encompasses the work of issue networks and outside groups who populate the "policy stream" with solutions to social problems. The political stream includes elections and partisan or ideological shifts in the electorate or legislative bodies. Kingdon argues that politicians, when convinced of the seriousness of an issue, reach into the "policy stream" for reasonable policy options that will serve their reelection interests or achieve other goals.[24]

Informed by Garland and Kingdon, this book discusses both stability and change in drug policy in New York State. It traces the evolution of the ideas and practices of the state's narcotics control issue network and examines how the network was able to achieve periods of autonomy during which it advanced criminologies of the welfare state. This book considers electoral imperatives and party politics in order to explain the implementation of the new penology. It argues that media attention and the activism of social groups forced political officials in New York to deal with drug addiction and crime. At these critical moments, liberals in the state's narcotics control issue network and the black silent majority supplied contrasting solutions for the state's drug problem. The former, based on their professional knowledge and moral sensibilities, espoused criminologies of the welfare state. The latter, based on its own experience and values, endorsed the culture of control. Depending on the configuration of electoral, partisan, and ideological imperatives, Rockefeller selected policy approaches that advanced his own electoral ambitions from the early 1960s until 1973.

THE PROMINENT SOCIOLOGIST LEE RAINWATER ONCE STATED, "The first responsibility of the social scientist [is to] 'tell it like it is.'" This phrase from the black vernacular, Rainwater explains, signals the intention "to strip away pretense, to describe a situation or its participants as they really are, rather than in a polite or euphemistic way." "'Telling it like it is,'" he adds, "can be used as a harsh, aggressive device, or it can be a healthy attempt to face reality rather than retreat into fantasy." This book attempts to "tell it like it is." Reviewing the public and private papers of more than two dozen elected officials and scores of documents from legislative committees, public and private agencies, and interest groups, this book exposes how a network of liberal white do-gooders and bureaucrats, guided by professional expertise and moral indignation and aided by their reputations and organizational capacities, instituted and faithfully guarded the old penology. It reveals how institutional rivalries and insufficient resources led to policy failures that eventually eroded confidence in criminologies of the welfare state. This book also describes the black silent majority, a phenomenon previously unexplored in histories of the 1960s and 1970s, social scientific studies of African American politics, and narratives of mass incarceration. This book draws on a variety of social statistics to lay bare the devastating effects of deindustrialization and racial segregation—the social milieu that gave life and purpose to the black silent majority. Through the exploration of surveys, interviews, letters, editorials, cartoons, and plays, this book uncovers how working- and middle-class African Americans made sense of a world crumbling around them—one they fought hard for, one they were losing.[25]

But describing situations or participants as they really were is no simple task. Reconstructing the politics of the past and recovering the actual sentiments of marginalized peoples pose significant methodological and interpretative difficulties. It is possible that the materials used to tell this story are themselves products of power, constructed to validate the modern prison system and the racial inequality it perpetuates. Consequently, this book analyzes what James C. Scott termed "public" and "hidden" transcripts. In the face of domination, people may defer and dissemble. They may perform, "speaking the lines and making the gestures [they know] are expected of [them]." The public record may be skewed. All the real action and honest appraisals may take place backstage, beyond the bourgeois public sphere and the regulating force of white supremacy. Public African American pleas for punishment may have been performances crafted for the benefit of the white gaze, a genuflection to power rather than a genuine expression of the heart. Accordingly, this book inspects multiple black discursive spaces with varying levels of visibility to the white public, and it analyzes stories, metaphors, and everyday talk in order to capture as fully as possible the indigenous framing of drug addiction and crime.[26]

Some readers may be tempted to find heroes and villains in this story, but they do so at their own peril. Despite the role that values play in this narrative, the actors and actions in this book elude simple moral judgments. Advocates of robust democratic action will find in the black silent majority a deep republican ethos and a vibrant participatory zeal, although the illiberal ends to which working- and middle-class African Americans directed this civic energy might dishearten. Civil libertarians will probably applaud the lengths to which reformers and bureaucrats tried to protect the rights of drug users and criminal offenders. At the same time, these readers might be dismayed by moments when white liberals ignored black voices and minimized their grievances. Additionally, this book is neither an indictment of Nelson Rockefeller nor an apologia. In this tale, he is simply a politician—a perceptive and enterprising one caught in an evolving political order. At one moment, American politics pushed him to be a great defender of racial liberalism and criminologies of the welfare state. At another, the changing dynamics of partisan play made him a patron of punishment.

Black Silent Majority is not about the morality of the criminal justice system in the United States. Mass incarceration represents a glaring and dreadful stain on the fabric of American history. The carceral state is unfair, demeaning, and destructive. Yet its true origins are unknown; the jumbled roots of this pernicious system still need to be dug up and unraveled. That is the purpose of this book. By "telling it like it is," this book tries to bring to light the complexities of crime policymaking and solve one particularly

vexing puzzle: why the carceral state, this nation's most ignoble institution, appeared after the monumental civil rights victories of
the 1960s, this country's most noble moment. It finds that mass
incarceration had less to do with white resistance to racial equality
and more to do with the black silent majority's confrontation with
the "reign of criminal terror" in their neighborhoods. It was not a
coincidence that African American activists, who had been foot soldiers in the long and bloody struggle for black rights, stood with
Nelson Rockefeller in the Red Room to laud his drug proposals.
That press conference was not unusual at all.

Rights and Wreckage in Postwar Harlem

THE HISTORY OF POSTWAR HARLEM is an uneven one, a story of both spectacular triumph and astonishing turmoil. After the "New Negro" collapsed under the weight of the Great Depression, Harlemites stood tall. They persevered and fought. From the 1930s until the 1960s, the community had served as a key organizational node in the national civil rights activist network, and local leaders marshaled the civic resources of the nation's black cultural capital to achieve important legal protections in New York State and secure a degree of economic progress. Yet these victories did not serve as a bulwark against broader structural transformations. Lingering residential segregation, exploitative and absentee landlords, and the increasing disappearance of work generated a variety of ills that undermined this historic community's vibrancy, abraded its civic infrastructure, and frayed its social bonds. By the mid-1960s, Harlem was no longer in vogue. It had become, in the words of Kenneth Clark, a "dark ghetto."[1]

Few things so poignantly and publicly captured the tone and pulse of Harlem's postwar challenges as *Dope*, a play written by

Maryat Lee in 1951 at the request of the East Harlem Protestant Parish. Sponsored by Jackie Robinson, Borough President Robert Wagner, a popular disk jockey named Dr. Jive, the famed African American comedian Nipsey Russell, and Willie Bryant, the "Mayor of Harlem," the one-act play, performed in open lots on the streets of East Harlem, portrayed a day in the life of a heroin addict. Robinson introduced the play by saying, "The story tonight is about Louie. Louie grew up on a block like this. This is his home. He lives here. We all know guys like him. Some people say Louie's no good. They think he had what was coming to him. Maybe that's true, and maybe it's not. But let's see just what did happen on a certain evening, not long ago." On that "certain evening" Louie's relationship with Porse, his dealer, spirals out of control. Porse is a slick, unfeeling predator. Louie is the unwitting victim of his cruelty, though not of his merchandise. In fact, at the start of the play, Louie defends heroin during a conversation with Hum and Marc, two inquisitive eighteen-year-olds. When Marc mentions that he heard "junk" "takes ten years off ya life," Louie asks, "Well, who wants ta live a hundr'd years 'round here?" He then tells the two curious youths, "It turns ya on. Everyday life is dull, oncet ya take it. Ya don' know how dull it is. Ya feel great—free—free, yea, like a bird way up there—like a God damn kite in a cloud—yea, that's what it is. No Troubles!"[2]

But the junk eventually brings trouble. After learning that Porse turned his sister Celee into a junkie, an angry Louie tries to quit and convince Porse to stop dealing to her. Porse reacts by taunting him with the drug. And Louie gives in. He gets high. But coming off the high, he gets sick, suffering withdrawal symptoms, guilt, and acute sadness, and once again tries to quit. Porse once again taunts him: "Louie, ya're a junkie 'n' ya sister is a junkie." This time, however, Louie resists. They fight. Louie dies. The moral of the story is clear: just say no to drugs, for junkies find redemption only in death.[3]

Yet this tragic morality play is about more than saying no to drugs. It is also about Harlem, depicting the community in despairing terms: a place where ne'er-do-wells accost decent people and nefarious characters target innocent individuals. Porse preys on the weak and defenseless; he manipulates addicts like Louie into luring children at candy stores and schools into the drug life. Residents suffer the behavior of all manner of malcontents. At one point, a drunk even "stumbles across the stage." Soon, the drunk returns and "assails an imaginary passerby or two, wanting some company."[4]

The play also illuminates how some residents of the community interpreted these problems. A woman carrying "a sack of groceries" and Kareen, a little girl with her, walk by Louie. Seeing him, the woman sighs, "Things is jus' gettin' too bad." After the little girl sees him, the woman says, "Kareen, come along, ya hear me!" and then yells, "Kareen! Get away from there!" The little girl tells the woman, "Mama, I jus' wanta see if he's sick." To which the woman responds, "He sick all right. Now jus' min' ya own business." After the little girl presses, "Mama, he sick," the woman says, "What he done to himself? Jus might as well be dead—poor Jesus. C'mon, Kareen! Kareen!" Another woman is equally harsh. After Louie complains about being "trapped," she says, "You should a thought a that a long time ago." "Suddenly a little sad," she tells him, "Boy, ya waited a long time to fin' this out. It's happened, honey. Ya cain' pull away from junk. It'll get ya. Ya been too long. You shoulda known better in the firs' place." Like these women, many people in Harlem ostracized people on the junk. They felt little sympathy for them. People like Louie were captives of their own sinfulness rather than unsuspecting casualties of society.[5]

Dope captivated Harlem. People flocked to the play. Lee recalled of opening night, "The street was blocked off and crowded, people jammed on fire escapes. About 2,000 people standing against each other, pushing around the stage so that the poor actors had to beat onto stage like it was a subway at rush hour." One evening, audience members "got up on the stage to dance during a party scene" and "hissed at the hero when he started to take a fix," and "an old woman junkie begged the hero not to take the drugs, telling him to look at her, see what dope had done to her." *Jet* reported that, because of the play, "dope pushers went into brief hiding and narcotic sales declined," and the "term 'junkie' became a term of derision among neighborhood youngsters." "Dope was on the defensive," the African American weekly pronounced. Much less sanguine, it also confessed, "Gradually, though, the dope salesmen regained their boldness and peddling resumed on the same scale."[6]

Part of Harlem's postwar history has already been told, but other stories still need to be heard. Gilbert Osofsky's *Harlem: The Making of a Ghetto* and Kenneth B. Clark's *Dark Ghetto: Dilemmas of Social Power* both provide canonical accounts of the wreckage, powerfully explicating the structural origins of the social problems represented in *Dope*. Yet there is also a story about newly won freedoms and how the beneficiaries of these triumphs made sense of the juxtaposition of rights and wreckage. Peering into the nooks and crannies of Harlem's black public sphere from the 1920s until the late 1960s reveals how working-class and middle-class activists and residents framed and negotiated postwar prosperity and problems.[7]

DURING THEIR SOJOURN TO HARLEM IN THE 1920S, WEALTHY whites discovered jazz. They heard the blues. They met the New Negro. The Harlem Renaissance was more than a cultural bacchanal for white and black artists and the city's petit bourgeois. It was also political. With the white gaze in mind, African American activists and intellectuals sought to use art to expose the humanity of African Americans and champion the intellectual achievements and worth of the New Negro. Black Brahmins and bohemians fervently believed that notions of black inferiority represented the greatest impediment to racial equality, the most formidable constraint on their liberty. James Weldon Johnson, one of the architects of this movement, proclaimed, "The status of the Negro in the United States is more a question of national mental attitude toward the race than of actual conditions." "And nothing," Johnson insisted, "will do more to change that mental attitude and raise his status than a demonstration of intellectual parity through the production of literature and art."[8]

For Harlem's poor, actual conditions mattered as much as white respect and bonhomie. As Osofsky documents, this community needed urban renewal as much as a cultural renaissance. Racial segregation and economic exploitation cultivated a host of social problems, including disease, juvenile delinquency, and adult crime. "All of the ingredients for ghetto-making were in evidence in the 1920s," the historian Nathan Huggins writes. "Yet, in those years few Harlem intellectuals addressed themselves to issues related to tenements, crime, violence, and poverty. Even *Opportunity*, the magazine of the Urban League and social work among Negroes, did not discuss urban problems as much as it announced the Negroes coming of age." In 1940, Langston Hughes, Harlem's great bard and one of the stars of the renaissance, reflected, "The ordinary Negroes hadn't heard of the Negro Renaissance. And if they had, it hadn't raised their wages any." Even for those who thrived, the moment did not last. Hughes asked, "For how could a large and enthusiastic number of people be crazy about Negroes forever?" He added, "But some Harlemites thought the millennium had come. They thought the race problem had at last been solved through Art plus Gladys Bentley." Moreover, the Great Depression devastated Harlem, exhausting the resources of white patrons and increasing economic insecurity for people already in desperate financial straits, and racism within the real estate market solidified the racial boundaries of this ghetto. Alain Locke, the movement's "publicist," lamented that the Harlem that emerged during the 1930s was "a nasty sordid corner into which black folk are herded." He confessed, "There is no cure or saving magic in poetry and art for . . . precarious marginal employment, high mortality rates, civic neglect."[9]

After the Great Depression, whites left Harlem, but the prepotency of their gaze persisted. Concern for white "mental attitudes" and indigenous values profoundly shaped how middle-class blacks responded to social problems caused by economic dislocation and racial segregation, especially crime. In early November 1941, a spate of crimes ranging from theft to murder, committed mostly by young black males in lower Harlem and the area immediately north of Central Park, caught the attention of white politicians and the media. The press labeled it a "crime wave." A writer with the *Daily News* entitled an accusatory column "Listen, You Harlem Kids." In an editorial entitled "Tragedy in Harlem," the *New York Times* insisted, "We need more police protection in areas where such crimes occur. We may be appalled at the youth of the criminals, but they must be run down and placed where their viciousness will no longer endanger the public." Contemplating potential questions about the structural context of the "young gangster," the *New York Times* stated, "It is hard to reform a youth already hardened in criminal ways. Some youngsters may be so twisted mentally that they will never grow into good citizens."[10]

Many middle-class African Americans took umbrage at the coverage, dismayed by "sensationalized" crime stories that relied on and perpetuated racial stereotypes and ignored the structural problems. The editorial office of the *New York Age,* the influential black newspaper, was "deluged with letters [about the 'crime wave'] from readers in all walks of life and from both races." One writer stated, "The present so-called 'Harlem crime wave,' or other localized manifestations of crime or vice, even regardless of their causes, are no more reflective of the Negro character than they are of any other racial or national group." The *New York Age* maintained, "Work for all is the biggest need to curb juvenile delinquency in Harlem." The title to a 1941 Claude McKay essay got straight to the point: "New Crime Wave Old Story to Harlemites: Poverty Brings Prostitution, 'Muggings,' Robberies."[11]

The NAACP was incensed. In early November, Roy Wilkins, editor of the *Crisis*, wrote to the head of the organization, Walter White, "I feel that it might be a good thing if the board at its meeting this afternoon issued a statement on the 'crime wave' which the newspapers have created in Harlem." Wilkins added, "I do not know how the Board will feel, but the performance of the New York *Times* on this topic constitutes some of the most shameless racial slander and incitement to distrust and hatred between the races that has been in any New York paper for many years." The following day the NAACP board of directors released a statement acknowledging the problem and lambasted the coverage: "We condemn and deplore these crimes. But New York needs to wake up to the conditions that bring such gangs into being." The organization highlighted employment:

> First of these is jobs. Let those who may be indulging in smug condemnation of the Negro stop and ask themselves if they may not be partly responsible. The majority of defense and private industries in the New York area have slammed the door of employment in the face of Negroes. "Door key children," so called because they go to school with the keys of their parents' apartment tied on strings around their necks, roam the streets of Harlem after school hours while both parents work at poorly paid menial tasks in a desperate effort to pay the exorbitant rents and high prices for inferior goods which Negroes have to pay in Harlem.

Referencing the main character in Richard Wright's *Native Son*, who is turned into a murderer by the poverty and racism of 1930s Chicago, the statement continued, "These are the children who are being made by society into desperate Bigger Thomases." The following month, *Crisis* reported that blacks were angry because "newspapers have not concerned themselves with law-abiding citizens who hate crime, who want protection, and who want to do something about present conditions." It also noted, "The people of Harlem, the respectable, hard-working, everyday citizens, want something done about discrimination in employment so that a father can support a family and rear children to be good citizens instead of hoodlums."[12]

As Harlem's crime problem persisted, the media kept the same narrative alive and middle-class African Americans in New York City and throughout the country kept rejecting it. In January 1943, a column in the *Afro American*, Baltimore's popular black newspaper, observed, "One finds an unhealthy paradox in such respectable papers as the [*New York Times*], where splendid editorial attacks on [Jim Crow] appear in the same issue carrying hysterical front-page scareheads about a press-created 'Negro crime wave.'" In late March, black and white clergy and law enforcement officials in New York City issued a statement after a closed meeting, saying, "There is no crime wave in Harlem." At a press conference following the meeting, Rev. John Johnson, a black police chaplain, said, "I feel that Harlem crime has been overemphasized." At a meeting of the Harlem committee of the Community Service Society, Edward S. Lewis, executive secretary of the New York Urban League, denounced "top-flight social work leaders" for not speaking out against "erroneous mugging stories appearing recently in newspapers." In early April 1943, the *New York Times* published two crime stories side by side. One discussed the rape of a seventeen-year-old white woman by a theater manager and seven white youths; the other reported on two "22-year-old 'muggers'" convicted of stealing $8.75 from a sixty-year-old man. African American activists complained that the paper devoted more attention to the "alleged 'mugging.'" The NAACP charged that the venerable newspaper had "gone to fantastic lengths in an attempt to fasten a crime wave on

Poster announcing an anticrime meeting, 1943. (Courtesy of the Library of Congress.)

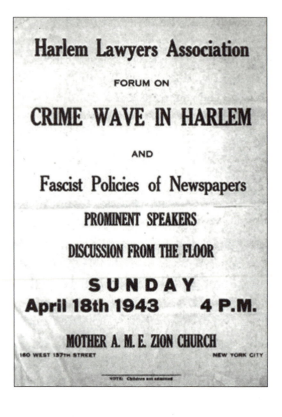

Harlem Lawyers Association

FORUM ON

CRIME WAVE IN HARLEM

AND

Fascist Policies of Newspapers

PROMINENT SPEAKERS

DISCUSSION FROM THE FLOOR

S U N D A Y
April 18th 1943   4 P.M.

MOTHER A. M. E. ZION CHURCH
160 WEST 137TH STREET   NEW YORK CITY

NOTE: Children not admitted

the Negro community." In mid-April, the Harlem Lawyers Association held a public forum at Mother African Methodist Episcopal (AME) Zion on the "fascist policies of newspapers."[13]

When the "crime wave" narrative returned in 1943, many middle-class African Americans continued to treat it as an impediment to their pursuit of racial inequality. In May 1943, the *Afro American* published "The Truth about Crime in New York's Harlem," which disputed stories about "a cooked-up crime wave" that "occupied the front page space in most of New York's daily papers." In addition to challenging the substance of press accounts, the article drew attention to their consequences: "Crime waves indicate a very serious problem. When they are limited to any minority race they reveal flaws in the pattern of life of a whole people. In peacetime such stories increase the separatism between peoples. In wartime they unbalance national unity and hamper the war effort by splitting interracial cooperation." Kenneth Clark told the paper, "The crime wave is an excuse for continued denial of rights. Why give 'rights' to a half-ape who is sub-human and who will probably break up delicate instruments in a factory."[14]

At the same time, working- and middle-class African Americans were growing concerned about public safety and felt the need to do more to curb juvenile delinquency. In February 1943, Walter White invited several prominent Harlem leaders to a "frank, off-the-record discussion of the crime situation in Harlem." While expressing consternation with the media and emphasizing the economic origins of crime, White told invitees that residents of Harlem "do not appear to be doing what we can locally in addition to our campaign against what is being done to us." White then described the problem:

> A prominent Harlem citizen told me yesterday that he, though well-known in Harlem, is actually afraid to go out after dark into any side street for fear of being robbed or mugged. A hard-working mother living in Harlem River Houses accompanies her young son each Saturday morning to the Roosevelt Theatre to protect him from being attacked and robbed by sixteen and seventeen-year-old boys armed with switchblade knives. Prostitution and abnormal sexual practices among grammar school and high school children appear to be alarmingly present.

Connecting the crime threat to the struggle for civil rights, White wrote, "All of these and many other conditions are having a most disastrous effect outside of Harlem in increasing feeling against Negroes."[15]

At the meeting, some attendees, animated by middle-class notions of reform, focused on the structural origins of crime and called for action by private and public social service agencies. Responding to his invitation, Hulan Jack, Harlem's assemblyman, wrote, "[S]ociety has denied the youth of Harlem a chance to live as a normal citizen." "I pray," he said, "for a united front of the citizens of Harlem to demand that Harlem be given equality among the communities that comprise the City of New York." At the meeting, Dr. George H. Sims, pastor of Union Baptist Church, said, "Poverty is the greatest cause of [delinquency]. There are no institutions for Negro delinquents other than Warwick [a juvenile correctional facility], since other institutions refuse Negro children." Judge Charles E. Toney, one of the first African American judges in New York City, commented, "We must consider psychology behind the entire crime situation. Negroes have been mistreated, discriminated against to such an extent that they are hostile to any police discipline."[16]

Sensing a real criminal threat, some attendees expressed consternation and drew on indigenous values to blame individual behaviors. Some criticized the community for downplaying the crime threat and ignoring the dangers of juvenile delinquents. Ludlow Werner, editor of the *New York Age*, whose pages lambasted the mainstream media's "crime wave" narrative, argued, "The citizens of Harlem should realize that there is a serious delinquency problem and should stop making excuses for it." He added, "When we look at the actual picture, white newspapers which play up the crime situation have treated us decently." Elmer Carter, a writer and Republican politician, unapologetically said:

[T]he situation in Harlem calls for drastic action on the part of decent colored citizens and . . . squeamish, half-hearted appeals to Negroes intent on criminal acts is not enough. . . . I'm in favor of giving the police the green light to rid Harlem of its criminals and of throwing the fear of God and the nightstick into that group of young men to whom no appeal can be made on the basis of decency, or pride, or anything else. . . . I do not overlook the necessity of a constructive approach and the slow process of education, but in the meantime citizens, particularly their leaders, must impress upon the Police Department its desire and its willingness for that department to invoke severe and extraordinary efforts in order to make Harlem safe at least for its own citizens.

Similarly, some claimed that social institutions, particularly families, were failing to instill proper values into troubled youths. Mrs. Alexander said that her sorority, Delta Sigma Theta, had tried to reach out to the parents of "delinquent children" but failed. She and another attendee advocated for corporal punishment in schools, but this idea was met with "considerable opposition."[17]

While both actual experiences with crime and indigenous values shaped the discussion, the influence of the white gaze was still operative. Fearing that their "candid" opinions would perpetuate racial stereotypes and harm their pursuit of equality, these leaders retreated to the safety of the Harlem YMCA to hold the "off-the-record" meeting. Not willing to concede the seriousness of Harlem's crime problem, Adam Clayton Powell Jr., pastor of the Abyssinian Baptist Church, told White, "The conference is alright if—You recognize that adult crime has decreased during the past year. That [juvenile delinquency] among Negroes has not increased as fast as it has among whites. That we do not consider [delinquency] separate and [distinct] from that of whites." As in 1941, the structural analyses black reformers made in defense of the urban black poor were also formulated to guard against claims of black inferiority that also plagued the black middle class. Even individuals worried about crime were still preoccupied with white perceptions of Harlem's citizens. Like Elmer Carter, some attendees called for aggressive policing, but not just to improve public safety in black neighborhoods: they also hoped that this action would help whites to distinguish between black criminals and decent black citizens. Photographer James Allen felt "that [the] important thing was to dispel the idea Harlem citizens don't want police protection." Allen hoped that the group would formulate "a definite platform" to be "released to the public to show that Harlem is for the [strictest] enforcement of the law." The confab concluded with White suggesting that "Negroes, as citizens, should guard against defending Negro criminals, no matter how guilty they are."[18]

Crime continued to plague Harlem, middle-class African Americans continued to downplay the issue, and others were becoming convinced that the community needed to take more aggressive steps against crime. "True there is juvenile delinquency and crime in Harlem, but where is there not juvenile delinquency," conservative African American writer George S. Schuyler contended. Others were not as ambivalent. In June 1944, White held a meeting of Harlem's civic leaders and prominent residents to discuss strategies for preventing a repetition of the riots that had occurred the summer before. They discussed a variety of issues, including the community's gang problem, debated several measures, and decided to take their proposals to Mayor Fiorello La Guardia. A few days later, a jarring headline appeared in the *New York Times*: "Powell's Church Wars on Hoodlums; Favors Stronger Measures by Civil and Military Police in Negro Communities." Powell had stolen their thunder. Before their meeting, the board of deacons at the Abyssinian Baptist Church had adopted a formal resolution expressing concern about increasing criminal activity in black communities: "We have always used legal, peaceful, non-violent forms of direct social action to secure, protect and extend our rights. We are specifically mindful of the threat to our gains, our security and our lives that this lawlessness and violence represents. . . . We therefore do earnestly desire to go on record as being opposed to all lawlessness and violence, especially that which tends to increase tensions between races. In stating this we state it for the vast majority of the Negro people of this city." At first, middle-class leaders vigorously disputed the Harlem "crime wave" narrative circulated in the mainstream media. Then, after discussing and acknowledging criminal activity in the community, they called for more aggressive law enforcement in order to separate themselves from "negro criminals" and protect the legitimacy of their claims of racial equality.[19]

As the 1940s came to a close, middle-class leaders and residents faced a new crime problem: heroin. The postwar recrudescence of the heroin trade hit Harlem particularly hard. Because of entrepreneurial white and black gangsters, heroin flowed through Harlem's streets and coursed through the veins of some of its celebrities and many of its residents. In June 1951, James R. Dumpson, a prominent black social worker, told a U.S. Senate panel that in Harlem drug dealers "are pushing as you would push legitimate business." He reported that "peddlers" were leaning against school walls waiting to "pass the goods to girls as they go into schools." Statistics confirm Dumpson's description. That same year, Dr. Paul Zimmering, head of the boys' ward in Bellevue's Psychiatric Division, and his associates reported that from 1941 to 1950 the number of individuals admitted to the Psychiatric Division for either heroin or morphine addiction averaged twenty per year. From 1940 to 1948, no adolescents were diagnosed as having a drug addiction. In 1949, one adolescent was diagnosed with addiction, and that number rose to six in 1950. During the first two months of 1951, sixty-five boys, from fourteen to twenty years old, and nineteen girls were admitted with a heroin addiction. All but twenty-two of their patients were black or Puerto Rican.[20]

Something changed around the time *Dope* opened. This time the people of Harlem did not consider narcotics trafficking and juvenile addiction fictional concerns. To them, drugs were a serious issue. It is around this moment that addiction piqued the interest of Rev. Oberia D. Dempsey. He recalled in 1972, "It was about twenty-two years ago when I saw a youngster out there die from an overdose. At that time, it wasn't a good thing to talk about narcotics, because nobody would even discuss it." In his graphic bildungsroman *Manchild in the Promised Land*, Claude Brown remembered, "The slang was always changing for heroin. They called it duji or shit or poison. After about 1952, nobody called it horse any more. I always referred to it as the shit plague." Within black civil society, African Americans drew on their experiences and morality to explain this "shit plague." Black periodicals frequently published dramatic articles about big drug busts, sensational profiles of "good" people gone "wrong," or sorrowful accounts of "one youthful victim" who "paid with his life for his folly." In 1951, the *New York Age* published a letter a teenager had written Willie Bryant about the mounting problem:

> I am the young man who called you last night to offer my services in helping to reduce the drug addiction among teenagers. Tonight I viewed the body of a [schoolmate] and I think your audience would like to hear the story of his tragic and untimely death. Last July 28 this young man succumbed to an overdose of Cocaine. This tragic story can happen to you or your teen-age son or daughter. Unless we all get together young and old alike and try to stamp out this evil that is destroying our youth there will be no future to look forward to. I think that it is a wonderful idea to send these [youngsters] to the hospital . . . but for everyone who enters the hospital for the cure there are two more getting the habit. We must stop the sources.

In 1951, Langston Hughes wrote, "Harlem is bugged with dope. In spite of the cops, even school kids are using dope. Addicts are jerking and scratching and dozing and muttering and behaving

more weirdly in public places these days." A year later, the ac-
claimed poet observed, "On the streets of Harlem the Zombie-eyed
junkie is not an uncommon sight. Certainly, Negro communities
are plagued with enough problems without the addition of a
growing narcotics evil." Thus by the early 1950s, African Americans were now willing to discuss drug addiction and trafficking
in Harlem. Much less worried about the white gaze, black Harlemites were not ambivalent. They spoke openly about the unique
challenges heroin addiction was posing to individuals and the
community.[21]

The indigenous characterizations of the problem and the prescriptions did not stay within the black public sphere. Black Harlemites injected their frames and proposals into the broader public
sphere and made their grievances known to white officials. During
hearings on narcotics addiction and trafficking held by the U.S.
House of Representatives' Committee on Ways and Means in 1955
and 1956, Harlem's representative Adam Clayton Powell brought
the community's views to Congress. Representative Howard Baker
(R-TN) asked, "Congressman Powell, to what do you attribute the
big increase in addiction in Negroes?" Powell responded, "I don't
know, I will tell you frankly, because sociologists say it is due to
the slums; it is due to that, but Negro people in New York City are
much better off now than they were when I first started going to
Congress." Powell emphasized black advancement, saying, "We
have broken through nearly every roadblock; we are working
everywhere; we are making equal wages. There are more slum-
clearance projects built, being built, and money appropriated to be
built, in my congressional district than any other congressional district in the United States."[22]

Despite his well-known proclivity for self-promotion, Powell's
statement was about so much more than the pork barrel projects he
had managed to secure for Harlem: it was about broad and positive
changes taking place in the community. That same year, Laymond

Robinson, an African American reporter for the *New York Times*, wrote about both Harlem's travails and its optimism. He began by reviewing the community's growing pains: "In the years between the start of World War I and the end of World War II, Harlem changed from a melting pot into the city's boiling pot. It became a turbulent area of decaying tenements, chronic unemployment, dirty streets, racial classes, poor schools, high rents, jazz music and noisy politics." According to Robinson, Harlem's decaying form then found fresh vitality: "However, in the last ten years, and particularly in the last five, Harlem has been a community on the upswing—economically, politically, socially, and physically." To substantiate this rosy depiction, Robinson listed a series of positive outcomes: "Employment is up; business is good; a large-scale slum clearance program is under way; streets are cleaner; new schools have gone up and others planned; youth centers have opened; a new savings institution has been established and another is under construction; new churches are planned and others have been renovated; a new city market is to be built; new stores and shops have sprouted every where; and Harlem's citizens enjoy a growing political power." "In short," he concluded, "the community is riding a wave of optimism."[23]

The hopefulness was not simply a figment of the imagination of politicians and journalists. It was shared by everyday folk. In 1951, the *New York Age* published a poignant exchange between two residents, Mr. Samuel Jasper Johnson Sr. and a young man. "Brother Johnson" was a "composite Harlemite": "He is 43, a Baptist, lives in a third-floor apartment on an east-west street somewhere between 125th and 140th Sts., and he works downtown as a shoe repair man." His wife is a member of the Pastor's Aid Society at a "leading" AME church in the community. His daughter works as a cutter for a millinery manufacturer, and his son will be entering City College. At a park, Johnson overheard a young man complaining to his girlfriend about the state of black New York.

"Orating," the young man declared, "Negroes ain't nowhere—at least in New York. . . . Look at those dumps down there. . . . They're talking about another general rent increase. Negroes control less than half of the property in Harlem, and the banks own more than half of that half." In the middle of his tirade, Johnson interrupted, "I know you aren't talking to me, but I could set you right on some of those things." Then he proceeded to set the young man "right": "When my parents brought me up in 1919 (that's the year the tobacco crop failed in Forsythe County), Negroes were getting a toehold in Harlem. Most confectionaries on Seventh Ave. wouldn't even serve you, and waiters and Pullman porters were top money people, except for undertakers like Rodney Dade and a few others. You couldn't find a Negro doctor in Harlem Hospital unless he happened to be a patient, and a Negro with a pushcart was a pioneer." After pausing briefly, Johnson continued, "Son, we've got nine judges on the bench. We were begging for jobs as court janitors when I put on my first long pants. We have a congressman now. . . . When I was your age all the Negroes working in stores on 125th St. were porters and maids, and Samuel Jesse Battle was the only Negro policeman and Wesley was the only fireman." Johnson ended this impromptu history lesson by saying, "Boy, we've come a long way and we're not going to stop." At the core of the enthusiasm expressed by Brother Johnson and others was an energetic ethos that celebrated Harlem's agency: the belief that the people of Harlem themselves had wrested progress from the jaws of discrimination and degradation and had begun building a new existence and forging a new fate.[24]

Furthermore, African Americans in New York not only had won important civil rights; they had also begun to enjoy economic freedom. The number of African American professionals in the metropolitan area rose dramatically from 1950 to 1960. The number of accountants and auditors increased by 220 percent, from 242 to 775. The number of engineers increased by 134 percent, from 225 to 527. The number of teachers increased by 125 percent, from 1,596 to 4,020. The number of physicians increased by 56 percent, from 392 to 613. The number of lawyers increased by 55 percent, from 225 to 527. Some of the largest absolute gains occurred in the fields of nursing and social services. The number of nurses increased by 90 percent, from 3,583 to 6,831. The number of individuals employed as social workers increased by 146 percent, from 1,352 to 3,085. Moreover, the African American proportion of the total number of individuals employed as nurses or social workers climbed from 1950 to 1960: "Negro nurses, who ten years before made up 10 per cent of the profession, accounted for 57 per cent of the profession's ten-year increase. And in the field of social work, Negroes contributed nearly two-thirds (64 per cent) of the net increment in workers, though they had comprised in 1950 only 11 per cent of those employed in that field." Finally, historian Martha Biondi reports that "[from] 1940 to 1950 the earnings of Black workers tripled, with a substantial number meeting the income eligibility of home ownership suggested by [the Federal Housing Administration]. They gradually gained access to more residential space, although the initial homesteading of the city's Black working and middle classes proceeded on a segregated basis." In a 1955 essay on black political consciousness published in the *Nation*, John O'Kearney wrote, "The Negro, 15,000,000 of him throughout the country, each wanting equality of opportunity as one of his civil rights, is constantly aware that in this prosperous national household his victuals are mainly the left-overs from the white man's plate." Then, in an abrupt twist, O'Kearney noted, "Of course, things aren't quite as bad as they used to be; there was a time in Harlem, before the riots of 1943, when the whole length of 125th Street . . . had no more than a handful of Negro-owned shops manned by Negro workers. Boycotts and a day of violence have changed that. City jobs as policemen, firemen, teachers, clerks, have opened to the Negro. He drives buses and runs subway trains, and there are scores of other jobs, formerly in the white's preserve, now available to him."[25]

Civil rights and economic opportunity erected a "consumers' republic"—"an economy, culture, and politics built round the promises of mass consumption"—in the ghetto. In 1955, E. Franklin Frazier famously described the "conspicuous consumption" of the "black bourgeoisie," but postwar economic expansion and equal rights also augmented the purchasing power of working-class African Americans. Beginning in the 1940s, businesses began hiring marketing firms to study the spending habits of black consumers. In 1952 the *Amsterdam News* hired a marketing firm to survey the "purchasing, readership and brand preferences" of "the New York City Market," which had "intrigued both local and national advertisers and left a confused picture for many others who might otherwise be interested in this market." In 1952, Associated Publishers released *Quick Facts about Selling the Negro Market: Where the Most Changes Are Taking Place; A Handy Guide for National Advertisers and Advertising Agencies.* In 1953, *Time* proclaimed, "The signs of Negro prosperity are everywhere. On the rooftops of Manhattan's Harlem grows that bare, ugly forest of TV antennae which has become a new symbol of middle-class achievement." It reported that on "Harlem's Lenox Avenue, Cadillacs are so commonplace that nobody turns to look at them any more (a situation which one resourceful driver met by having his Cadillac's top painted a gay plaid)." The magazine also noted, "There are signs that the Negro has begun to develop a large, strong middle class. Some Negro leaders, in fact, believe—and they do not consider it a bad thing—that the Negro is turning into the nation's new Babbitt." Because of these visible signs of racial change, John H. Johnson, the publisher of *Jet* and *Ebony*, proclaimed, "Every Negro is a Horatio Alger. . . . His trek up from slavery is the greatest success story the world has ever known."[26]

To understand the evolution of the indigenous framing of Harlem's drug trade, it is important to juxtapose this cautious optimism with the seemingly inexplicable rise in drug addiction and trafficking. Because of the political and economic achievements of the 1940s and 1950s, the force of the white gaze began to wane, and material interests and class-based values started to define how Harlemites understood black criminality. Because of improved social and political conditions, some were less likely to blame delinquency and addiction on structural conditions. Back in 1944, Ludlow Werner said that, while economic conditions and the lack of recreational opportunities made it hard for young people to become "decent and upright citizens," "[t]hat picture is changed now." He explained, "There are numerous recreational places . . . [and] the picture has improved to such an extent that anyone who wants to work now can find a job." Consequently, Werner insisted that there was no excuse for "anti-social" behavior. Although Powell either minimized Harlem's crime problem or emphasized racial explanations for it during the 1940s, he reiterated Werner's views in 1955. As *Dope* makes clear, working- and middle-class Harlemites believed junkies were victims of their own character flaws. Still, at this point, drug addicts did not represent a threat to the community. Instead, working- and middle-class African Americans treated junkies as they did other forms of urban blight: as something disturbing but ignorable. Because addicts were threats more to decency than to decent citizens, some working- and middle-class African Americans, driven by their Christian principles, had some sympathy for them—even though, as *Dope* depicts, this compassion was in short supply.[27]

Drug dealers, however, were an entirely different matter. Not only did they create the nuisance of the "Zombie-eyed junkie," but community members associated them with gangsters and violence. As such, the pusher constituted a real menace that warranted greater policing and imprisonment. Toward the end of his 1955 testimony, Powell placed great weight on the presence of "dope pushers." He surmised, "It is a fact that our high schools, junior high schools, and elementary schools in the Negro area during the lunch period and after-school period are just thronged outside with pushers. This is where they are trapped. They are trapped between there and home." After listing the various social services and programs his community center offered and delineating how recreational activities could prevent young people from succumbing to addiction, Powell stated, "But when they don't have anything to do the drifters become susceptible to the pushers." "What is the meaning of the term 'pusher'?" Baker asked. "The pusher is a salesman," the Harlem representative replied. "The pusher is the problem. If we can get that man or that woman, and oftentimes there are teenagers, too, who push in order to get free drugs for themselves, if we can get them . . . if we can nail them with the stiffest penalty possible, not to increase the penalty for those who use it, but to increase the penalty for those who push, we will have broken the bottleneck."[28]

While many white public safety and health officials stressed the need to extend available rehabilitative services to pushers, Powell demurred. He did not consider the pusher a victim of broader structural forces. According to him, the pusher chose his lifestyle: he decided to be a menace, so he deserved extreme punishment. Powell endorsed the Boggs Act of 1951, which did not distinguish between "dope peddlers" and "addict-pushers," and, as such, criminalized addiction. White liberals opposed the legislation. Emanuel Celler, a representative from Brooklyn and a supporter of civil rights, assailed the law, saying, "If penalties are made too severe and judges are put in a strait-jacket, grand juries will refuse to indict and petit juries will refuse to convict." The *Washington Post* opposed the law on both practical and moral grounds: "[The Boggs bill] deals indiscriminately with the vicious drug peddler and the pathetic victim of addiction. And it takes away from Federal judges the discretion they need to handle these cases wisely and humanely. The mandatory minimum sentences imposed by the

Boggs bill are bad in principle; they are also bad when applied in this field where a distinction ought always to be observed between the vice and its victim." Whereas white liberals and middle-class Harlem leaders and residents once espoused structural explanations for criminal behavior, their views began to diverge in the 1950s. Driven by their middle-class values and reformist politics, white liberals continued to believe in the perfectibility of man. Informed by their experiences and values, middle-class leaders and residents in Harlem increasingly embraced methods of control.[29]

By the beginning of the 1960s, Harlem had changed. The community that Powell described with cautious optimism in the mid-1950s was almost gone, nearly swept away by the ebb of Fordism and the flow of social pathology. In 1960, one of seven or eight adults in Harlem was unemployed, while the unemployment rate for the entire city was half that. The disappearance of work hit Harlem's youth particularly hard. Twice as many young black males were out of work compared to young white males. For young black women, the gap was even larger: their unemployment rate was two and a half times higher than the rate for young white women. The job situation was poor, though not for everyone. The proportion of white-collar workers in Harlem increased from 34.1 percent in 1950 to 36.9 percent in 1960, then to 46 percent in 1970. At the same time, the proportion of blue-collar workers decreased from 38.9 percent in 1950 to 37.0 percent in 1960, then to 29.5 percent in 1970. Working- and middle-class African Americans also benefited from public sector employment, secured by vigorous black activism. So, as the slow end of Fordism undercut the job opportunities for uneducated African Americans, the growing service sector and public sector afforded some working- and middle-class African Americans additional employment opportunities.[30]

This economic dislocation, along with racial segregation, compounded the struggling community's social problems. At the beginning of the 1960s, on nearly every key measure of social disorder, the patterns in Harlem were far worse than the citywide average: Harlem's juvenile delinquency rate and the proportion of Harlem residents on Aid to Families with Dependent Children were more than double and Harlem's rate of venereal disease for young people was more than triple the rate for the city. Not only did Harlem's juvenile delinquency rate hover well above the city average from 1953 to 1962, but it also climbed dramatically over that period. All of Harlem's individual health areas witnessed extremely high rates of juvenile delinquency during the early 1960s—double or nearly double the city average, which had also risen. Rates of drug addiction followed a similar trajectory. Four years after *Dope* premiered in Harlem, addiction began to wane, then the number of drug users in Central Harlem spiked in 1959. In 1961, the rate was almost eight times the city average. While Central Harlem's share of the city's total number of habitual users fell to around 23 percent, it still stayed extremely high for one neighborhood. Most of the addicts in the United States resided in New York City, and most of them lived in Harlem. Most drug-related deaths in New York City took place in Harlem, and most of the victims were black.[31]

Statistics tell only part of the story, however. In 1960, James Baldwin was much less sanguine than Powell and others about the progress of the 1950s. He wrote, "There is a housing project standing now where the house in which we grew up once stood, and one of those stunted city trees is snarling where our doorway used to be. This is on the rehabilitated side of the avenue. The other side of the avenue—for progress takes time—has not been rehabilitated yet and it looks exactly as it looked in the days when we sat with our noses pressed against the windowpane, longing to be allowed to go 'across the street.'" Baldwin observed, "The people in Harlem know they are living there because white people do not think they are good enough to live anywhere else. No amount of 'improvement' can sweeten this fact. Whatever money is now being earmarked to improve this, or any other ghetto, might as well be burnt. A ghetto can be improved in one way only: out of existence."[32]

Three years later, Baldwin's cynicism had turned into despair. In an interview with Kenneth Clark in 1963, he said:

> I was born in Harlem, Harlem Hospital, and we grew up—the first house I remember was on Park Avenue, which is not the American Park Avenue, or maybe it is the American Park Avenue. . . . We used to play on the roof and in the—I can't call it an alley—but near the river—it was a kind of dump, a garbage dump. That was the first—those were the first scenes I remember. . . . And when I look back on it—after all it was nearly forty years ago that I was born—when I think back on my growing up and walk that same block today, because it's still there, and think of the kids on that block now, I'm aware that something terrible has happened which is very hard to describe. . . . I was raised by families whose roots were essentially . . . Southern rural and whose relationship to the church was very direct because it was the only means they had of expressing their pain and their despair. But twenty years later the moral authority which was present in the Negro Northern community when I was growing up has vanished. And people talk about progress, and I look at Harlem which I really know—I know it like I know my hand—and it is much worse there today than it was when I was growing up.[33]

There were a number of ways in which Harlemites could have interpreted this decline. A 1966 congressional hearing on the "federal role in urban affairs" shed light. Ralph Ellison, author of *Invisible Man,* reminisced about Harlem's halcyon years, when the area was "a glamorous place, a place where wonderful music existed and where there was a great tradition of Negro American style, Negro American elegance," when the "great European and

American composers were coming there to listen to jazz—Stravinsky, Poulenc," and when some "of Orson Welles' best efforts which led to his fame were being produced there." Ellison then blamed the neighborhood's deterioration on economic and racial segregation and the "crisis of optimism" fostered by the slow pace of change. Claude Brown and Arthur Dunmeyer, a friend Brown met in reform school, gave an alternative account. They wove a bewitching yarn about the baneful behaviors of the black underclass. Rather than addressing the "crisis of optimism," Brown and Dunmeyer drew attention to culture and behavior. They talked about "crooked cops, the numbers game, prostitution." Dunmeyer testified that his mother became a prostitute in order to feed the family. Brown admitted, "I was selling dope—heroin—at 13." Interpreting the testimony, a *New York Times* reporter described the Harlem ghetto as "the world of the child watching his father slit another man's throat. Of mothers who go to bed with the butcher to get pork chops for her children. Of a boy who turned dope pusher at the age of 13. The world of the wino and the back yard crap-shooter, of the 12-year-old mother and the cop hater, the world of southern Negroes who went north looking for streets paved with gold and found them paved with garbage."[34]

Rev. Bill Jones of Brooklyn took great exception to Brown and Dunmeyer's testimony. Invoking the traditional politics of respectability, Jones was concerned about how their portrayal would affect race relations. He sent a telegram to the committee asking to testify on behalf of the "hardworking, decent people, who make up the backbone" of the city's black communities and who were "unfairly stigmatized" by Brown and Dunmeyer's testimony. Jones conceded the accuracy of their general description of urban life but criticized them for not acknowledging hardworking black people. He wrote, "Granting that Claude Brown clawed his way out of the concrete jungle of the slums to become a one-book, best-selling author, granted that dope, prostitution, gambling and other evils exist in the ghettos of Harlem and Bedford-Stuyvesant section of Brooklyn but we feel duty bound to stand up for the industrious people that make up the backbone of these communities." According to Jones, black New York had become a city of two tales: one in which the community's "industrious people" persevered and one in which poverty destroyed the lives of everyone else. And like previous Harlem activists, Jones emphasized the structural roots of the community's problems: "But the answer to this complex problem lies not in the further degradation of the residents of these communities. It lies in fact in the desperate measures that have to be taken on the federal level via massive transfusion of government funds to help these people lift themselves from the abyss of poverty in the midst of plenty."[35]

Several residents echoed these sentiments. Assemblyman Percy Sutton opined, "There's much that is wrong with Harlem: massive poor housing, massive unemployment, substandard schools. However, there are also many good people who are working hard to improve conditions in Harlem. . . . I cannot buy the statement of those who say Harlem is a jungle. It sells newspapers, attracts attention to these things, but Harlem is not a jungle." Mrs. Mildred Allen of 125th Street worried that the testimony would "cause a gloomy picture to become gloomier in the minds of prejudiced men." Others were more blunt. One employee of Harlem Youth Opportunities Unlimited (HARYOU), a social service agency founded by Kenneth Clark, stated, "[Claude Brown is] a liar. All of our women here in Harlem are not prostitutes and all of our men here do not eat dope. . . . [Brown] forgot to tell the investigating committee about the countless scholars we have here in bad schools and the young people here who go to college and become great and highly respected in all walks of life." Rev. Millard A. Stanley, pastor of the Bethelite Institutional Baptist Church, remarked, "Isn't that a horrible mess? Why would they lie like that? I'm getting fed up with this kind of thing. What they said isn't true; it certainly doesn't apply to most people in Harlem." John Smith of 126th Street called Brown "a fool": "He's only low rating his own people. Leave this for others to do. We must find and play up the many, many positive sides of Harlem."[36]

Other residents supported Brown and Dunmeyer. Miss Aileen Jeffries thought that Brown had "dramatized the situation" but noted that her life "has been Middle Class" and that she had some insight into the world "those people" lived. Mrs. Bernice Simms of West 121st Street was more specific about "those people": "A lot what was said by Claude Brown and Arthur Dunmeyer is true. In some cases men and women consider it a badge of honor in going to jail and prostitution is a profession to a number of women. It may be difficult to swallow but a great deal of the statements [attributed] to them is true." "It's true. Positively," Miss Wilhelmina Adams insisted.

> It's an element that you [the reporter] and others have never seen. You have not come in contact with this hard core grass roots element. So few have been called upon to tell about the life among this element. I have had to be among those people, and I often wonder why I have never been called to talk about it before any governing body who could help. Of course none of us like to hear the truth, but the truth comes out sooner or later. . . . Prostitution is running rampant. Muggings are common. I was mugged. It's quite an element. And it's true, positively true.

Mrs. Miller of 125th Street declared, "I think Brown and Dunmeyer were right. It's time someone brought out the facts about Harlem. The middle class Negro is a minority, the rampant poverty-ridden element are in the majority." Ultimately, the deteriorating condition of Harlem caused Mrs. Miller and others to articulate a new interpretation of the social problems that had plagued Harlem since the arrival of the New Negro. Unlike Jones, many expressed little concern for white attitudes or race relations. Unlike Ellison, many did not attribute Harlem's problems to poverty or racism. Mrs. Miller and others maintained that the attitudes and behavior of the urban black poor posed serious risks to the life chances and lifestyles of working- and middle-class African Americans.[37]

Mrs. Miller was not in the minority. In 1966, the polling agency Kraft, Inc., hired and trained Harlemites to interview members of the community, reasoning "that a respondent living at 119th Street and Lenox Avenue, for example, would 'unload' more freely to an interviewer from 121st and Madison; and, in turn, the interviewer might more readily understand and communicate with a respondent from his or her neighborhood, or near neighborhood." The "everyday talk" interviewers encountered corroborates Mrs. Miller's assessment. In her discussion of Harlem's troubles, one respondent expressed great resentment toward people on welfare: "[Harlem is] too crowded. This is because welfare dependents are breeding too fast. These welfare dependents should also be placed in a neighborhood by themselves instead of in projects with decent working class men and women. They build slums wherever they go." Echoing the dual concerns of housing and public safety, a thirty-year-old woman stated, "Problem? Poor housing. People live in rat holes. These houses aren't safe, and they need guards. We're not protected. We can't find the Police Department when we need them. Need more protection." She added, "Never can find police in a crisis. Drug addicts! Winos! The terrific concentration influences the kids. They lay on the stoops and stairs. Them, and rats and roaches. Just corroded with them. Landlord don't fix things, ceilings fall in." One sixty-five-year-old "loquacious" woman complained about almost everything—everything, that is, except racism. She complained about her neighbors: "The people down under me here in that apartment that raises hell all night. The man upstairs coming down to your window and peeping in my window." She complained about her landlord: "The landlord won't paint or fix anything. The landlord, but he's money-hungry." She vilified welfare recipients: "Then welfare people lay around and look pitiful for the next two weeks. Them mothers need to do something. They ought to cut out the welfare altogether. They ought to make him pay back some of that money. . . . What the hell," she said. "We need help."[38]

By the 1960s, working-class, middle-class, and urban poor African Americans had become enmeshed within a calamitous and deepening social morass produced by residential segregation, the loss of labor-intensive work, and unscrupulous landlords; but instead of blaming social and economic forces, working- and middle-class African Americans, motivated by fear and advised by indigenous values, inveighed against the poor. They blamed the community's downfall on individual behavior, the self-indulgent, irresponsible actions of the disadvantaged, rather than racial or economic inequality. The interviews Clark's researcher William Jones conducted on the streets of Harlem vividly convey these attitudes. Jones asked one woman, "What about employment? Are there a lot of unemployed men around here?" She responded, "Just those that don't want nothing. You have to consider the dope addicts. But the people who have families, they are working trying to do something. If they're not holding down steady jobs, they're out trying to make a dollar. Except for the people that don't want to do anything and are not going to do anything." When questioned about people hanging around her block, another woman complained, "I don't know anybody and they don't act right. I know all the men. They don't work. None of them. All the way down to the station, when I go to work, they stand on the corner and they pick at people. All the men. All the women you see going to work and all the men you see on the corner. They even disturb the teachers going to the schools."

The opinions expressed by this woman were not unique. Jones asked a sixty-three-year-old married man, "What do you see for the future of Harlem?" The man, a resident of Harlem for forty years, responded, "Well, I tell you one thing, peoples that want to do something for themselves, it's all right. But eighty per cent of the peoples around Harlem here, especially the men situation, they don't want to work and they don't want to do anything." Jones pressed, "Well, you said before there isn't any jobs. Do you think that might be the case? Maybe they want to work but they can't find a job?" The man answered, "Well, some of them want to work and a hundred—eighty per cent don't want to work, especially the men situation." Jones asked, "So you're saying that the men situation is so bad that you don't see any future for Harlem then, huh?" "Not right now," the man replied.

Another Harlem resident, Sonny Jim Gaines, offered his own structural theory:

> Me . . . Sonny Jim Gaines, here's how I feel about the whole situation about Harlem. . . . I feel because they talk about the rehabilitation about 114th St. You can take any street . . . all streets are the same thing. What has happened is this. . . . They have invoked, and pressed, and constantly pressed upon the Blacks here in [America, Negroes in Harlem], or in any ghettos where Negroes congregate. They want dope to flow in here. They don't want Negroes to stand up. . . . They don't want Negroes to be human beings. . . . [T]hey want Negroes to be as subservient and humble in every form that there is life.

Gaines contended that white racism created great hardship in Harlem. He believed dope was part of a larger white strategy to oppress African Americans and maintain white supremacy. At the same time, he considered the dominant negative perception of Harlem a result of lies and distortions from sensationalized stories in the media. For Gaines, roaches, poor living conditions, and the lack of social programs were the real culprits of social disorder, not junkies.

To test his theory, Gaines periodically stopped strangers on 114th Street and asked for their opinions on junkies while Jones observed. Unfortunately for Gaines, the everyday talk he facilitated did not confirm his theory. He stopped two young girls, one seven and the other eight, and asked, "Has any of these fellows that use dope here bother you?"

One girl responded, "No."

"Do you feel 'fraid coming in your hallway?"

"No."

"Have you ever seen any roaches? Do this scare you more than seeing a dope addict sleeping in your hallway, blocking your way to go upstairs. What frightens you more? The rats, the roaches or the dope addicts in the block? What frightens you more? Speak your mind."

One girl responded, "I don't know."

Gaines then stopped a young man: "Are you scared to walk in this block?"

"What do you mean, what time of day?" the man replied.

"Any time of the day? Are you scared to walk in your own block?"

"Not now, but when I first moved around here I was."

"Why, because you was a stranger? Now that you belong are you afraid of anyone in this block?"

"No."

"Because you figure what? Why are you not afraid?"

"Because I know most of the people in the block. The only time I'm afraid is when I see a few new people come around here, the junkies or the dope addicts."

"And what are you afraid about the dope addicts?"

"Well you know . . . most times I stop."

"But has any dope addict that you've been afraid of approached you?"

"No."

"Why are you afraid of the dope addicts?"

"Well a friend of mine, I know his sister was going in the hallway, she used to live around here, and I know she was robbed."

Displeased with the man's responses, Gaines repeated a question he asked the young girls: "Are you more afraid of dope addicts than you is of rats and roaches and broken walls, and ceiling falling down and running water, and gas that's leaking? What are you afraid of most? Dope addicts or the living conditions?"

"The living conditions."

Again, trying to teach Jones how people in the ghetto make peace with addicts and manage local dangers, Gaines asked the man, "Would you say from proof, that most people have been robbed don't know who robbed them? Whether they're dope addicts or good citizens. Would you say that?"

"Yes."

Gaines also stopped George Walker, who introduced himself by saying, "I myself is a drug addict." His own substance abuse notwithstanding, he offered a very critical assessment of drug addicts, and his comments, about himself and other addicts, emphasized individual character flaws. About himself Walker remarked, "Been using the stuff for 15 years. I never broke in nobody's apartment. I work, and I do other things for people to take care of my habit. I never raped nobody, I got a decent woman. She don't use narcotics. I do. They can lock me up today, tomorrow or the next day. Up until I get ready to get up off it I won't stop. Up until then they can lock me up."

Trying to regain control over his study, Jones interjected, "What do you think about the program?"

Walker responded, "The program, what they're doing here is just a waste of time. The simple reason why I said that you dig the projects that they build now man, they put the wrong people in there."

"What do you mean they put the wrong people in there?"

"They put people that don't want nothing out of life. That don't care nothing about life. . . . Them projects ain't 10 years old yet. . . .

[T]hey piss in the hallways, wine bottles in the hallways, windows are broken out, and any apartment you go in you can find holes in the walls."

"Well, why do you think they don't want to do nothing?" Jones asked.

"The individual themselves that don't want to do anything."

"Why is he like this?"

"Why is he like this? I'm gonna tell you why. The way that they treat the poor man, he considered nothing. The addict he's nothing. But they should try to get next to an addict, and find out where he's at. It's something in addict's mind that make him use that stuff. Because he sleeps in basements, he sleeps on rooftops, he do this, he steals, he burglarizes, he do that. Not all of them but the majority of them do. Now that's where it's at. Now what they should do is spend some money and try to find out where the addict is really at. Because I'm an addict myself, and I don't know where I'm at. I got a decent woman, I got a nice woman. Don't indulge in life whatsoever. She look at me. . . . She say daddy why you keep sticking that thing in your arm. I don't know myself why . . . but its something upstairs that I can't find out myself."

Vexed by his results, Gaines persisted. He stopped two young boys, "Let me ask you a question. Are you afraid of the fella who said he's a dope addict?"

One boy responded, "No."

"Why you not afraid of him?"

"I ain't scared of no dope addicts."

"Why?"

Not willing to appear weak, the boy answered, "Cause I'm brave enough to protect my own myself."

"But have anybody ever bothered you?" Gaines pressed.

"No, I know them all."

"Would you say they were nice people in their hearts OR not nice people?"

"They nice in their heart . . . cause he helped me with my bicycle one time."

Jones interjected, "Let me ask this. . . . What do you think about the conditions in the block?"

The other boy responded, "I'm moving I'm glad of that . . . but it's real bad."

"What are you moving from?" Gaines interrupted.

"The bad house and the junkies."

"The bad house and the junkies. . . . Now let us take every thing in its perspective. What about the housing problem?"

"It's bad."

Jones then asked the other boy, "How do you feel about this block?"

"I'm scared about this block."

Gaines probed, "Why?"

"Cause there's dope addicts hang around here and everything."

"You said they didn't bother you."

"They hang around this block and everything."

"Maybe you want to change your mind. Do they bother you?"

"They stand around on the corner . . . putting bottles in the hallways."

"You ever hear your mother or father say they tried to bother them?"

"Yes."

"What did they say?"

"That this block is pitiful the way these junkies hang around here bothering people and everything."

Some time after this exchange, Gaines stopped a woman and said, "Tell me madam what are you afraid of when you come into this block?"

"Junkies naturally," she replied.

Frustrated by her answer, Gaines prodded, "Let me ask you something, did a junkie approach you?"

"No."

Sensing her sentiments may have been the result of sensationalized news stories, Gaines inquired, "Are you more afraid of what you read in the papers, or what you've personally experienced?"

"What I've experienced I imagine."

"What did you experience?"

"I've had my bag snatched from me but it wasn't in this block."

"When they snatch your bag, and you compose yourself, the bag is stolen, etc., do you feel as though they're sick or just generally bad people?"

"I don't care anything as far as them. . . . I was hurt myself."

Gaines peppered the woman with more questions, desperately trying to solicit responses that would validate his theory. At one point, he asked, "Would you say that your children are treated more viciously by dope addicts or by the policeman?"

"My children aren't touched by either," she stated.

At another point, Gaines inquired, "Would you say that living conditions would clean up dope addicts?"

"Living conditions clean up dope addicts . . . not hardly."

"In order words, do you feel as though there should be a thing on the council of New York on the Mayor to do something for these people are sick. Do you see them as sick or vicious people?"

"I'd rather not say."

"Do you think they should have a clinic for them?"

"If they're willing to help themselves."[39]

When Gaines fostered a lively dialogic space removed from the white gaze, he and Jones unexpectedly stumbled across a stunning level of class conflict on the streets of Harlem. By asking leading questions and pushing residents to explain and defend their positions, Gaines thought he would get beyond superficial complaints and find a foundational racial solidarity. He believed residents would express sympathy for users—even consider junkies "good citizens." He did not succeed. When people reported their fear of drug users, Gaines asked whether addicts were scarier or worse than roaches, rats, broken walls, collapsed ceilings, gas leaks, or the police. But his respondents rated drug users the greatest evil. And, according to them, they were not sick; they were just bad. His respondents felt besieged by junkies. Addicts did not just offend decency; they threatened the decent. Junkies endangered the newly acquired consumer goods of the "nation's new Babbitt" and jeopardized the future of their children.

As he had during the 1950s, Langston Hughes powerfully captured the indigenous construction of drug addiction during the 1960s. In Hughes's column in the *Chicago Defender,* Jesse B. Simple is a "Harlemite whose bailiwick is Lenox Ave., whose language is Harlemese, and whose thoughts are those of black Harlem." While Hughes depicted the "Zombie-eyed junkie" as a pitiful, relatively hapless figure a decade before, his Simple stories describe them as menaces that threaten working- and middle-class Harlemites and their consumer goods. One column features a heart-wrenching story about an altercation between an addict and his mother. The son frequently steals items from his home, and, after finding pawn tickets in his dresser drawer, the mother buys them back. Then the son's habit worsens: "One fix a day does not do him no more, neither two. Seems like he needs more and more money to feed the pushers." One day the mother catches the son removing her fur coat from the closet, "her one and only fur coat that her husband worked hard to pay for." After tussling over the coat, the son lets go. The mother then sits in an armchair and cries. As she wiped her eyes, the son came "out of the kitchen with a clothesline, sneaked up behind his mama, threw [a rope] around her, and tied her up in the chair—with the hard knots behind her back so there was no way for her to get loose." He stole the coat.[40]

Because of the threat to property and person that addicts posed, they became objects of moral indignation rather than beneficiaries of Christian charity. As a result, middle- and working-class African

Americans demanded removal rather than reform. In 1964, Simple asks, "What can I carry to guard against the junkies who need thirty dollars for a fix?" He complains, "Junkies should be able to tell by looking at me that I don't have any money. But a junkie in need will steal even the widow's mite." He then proposes that the city "start a Junk Fund to take care of poor junkies and pay for their fixes, so they don't have to rob old ladies and stick up cabbies." Simple's advocacy of the "British system," methadone maintenance, grew out of a sense of threat—fear of the addicts rather than compassion for them. Even so, Simple prefers more drastic approaches: "I would also (was I the mayor of New York) have me a Junkie Catcher's Wagon and go around New York gathering up all the junkies and getting them nice pads to cop a nod in—but far away from peoples who do not use junk, in someplace like Mississippi." He defends the proposal by suggesting, "Junkies would not mind being down in Mississippi because neither Jim Crow nor police dogs nor bombs bother dope addicts at all. A junkie does not care and is not bugged by anything in this world so long as he has his junk." Simple ends his ruminations in dramatic fashion: "A reservation for the goofy, an island for the winos, a new land for the teen-age subway slashers—palm trees, wide-open spaces, nice happy places—for all the un-nice, upset, disturbed, hopped-up, wine soaked people who cannot and do not and will not and *won't* act nice on their own accord in New York—and who is driving the rest of us crazy. Help, Mayor! Help! Help!"[41]

WHILE STYMIED BY THE LIMITATIONS OF ART AS A POLITICAL strategy during the 1920s, Harlem's middle-class leaders and residents still believed that their fates were inextricably linked to white "mental attitudes" during the 1930s and 1940s. Consequently, they viewed the "Harlem crime wave" stories plastered throughout the mainstream media in 1941 and 1943 as a significant threat to progress. Concerned that black crime would validate ideas about black inferiority and in turn hurt race relations, Harlem leaders framed the issue as a media concoction or even racist propaganda. To the extent that they acknowledged the problem, they proposed structural explanations for it and insisted that expanding employment and recreational opportunities would curb juvenile delinquency and other criminal activity.

As "hardworking" mothers and other "citizens" began to report their victimization and express their frustration, African American leaders retreated to hidden spaces within the black public sphere to debate and formulate solutions without supplying fodder for bigots and unscrupulous reporters. In the 1940s, their analysis struck a markedly different tone; there the critical edge of black middle-class morality cut deeply. While they did not dismiss the structural origins of criminal behavior, they emphasized individual attributes and character and blamed the lack of discipline and moral teaching on families and schools. Now, facing the dual threats of white racial attitudes and black criminal behaviors, these middle-class leaders and residents decided to invite aggressive policing into their community and publicly resolved to do so. They believed that greater policing would increase public safety. They hoped that public declarations would distinguish them, "negro citizens," from "negro criminals" and thereby maintain the legitimacy of their *unique* claims for racial equality. By the 1960s, working- and middle-class African Americans began to invite police and aggressive policing into Harlem to regulate the behavior of a larger group of individuals. They began to view junkies, alcoholics, welfare recipients, and teenage dropouts as sources of insecurity rather than risks to good race relations and began to advocate for their punishment and removal.

To understand the emergence of these punitive impulses, it is important to trace the arc of Harlem's transformation from the 1940s until the 1960s. Published in 1971, Gilbert Osofsky's second edition of *Harlem: The Making of a Ghetto* included a new chapter, "Retrospect: The Enduring Ghetto." This brief new essay compares 1960s Harlem to late nineteenth-century and early twentieth-century Harlem, the central focus of the original book. Osofsky finds that postwar Harlem had not fully escaped its inglorious past:

> At first glance the worlds seem hardly comparable. The most obvious distinctions appear to be the radical changes in Negro status and in race relations that have taken place between the Jacksonian era and the America of Watts, Newark and Detroit. It is my thesis, however, that despite seeming transformations, some of which I shall describe, the essential structure and nature of the Negro ghetto has remained remarkably durable since the demise of slavery in the North. There is an unending and tragic sameness about black life in the metropolis over the two centuries.

Osofsky concludes, "What has in our time been called the social pathology of the ghetto is evident throughout our history; the wounds of centuries have not healed because they've rarely been treated. By all standard measurements of human troubles in the city, the ghetto has been with us—it tragically has endured." In a very broad sense, the ghetto certainly endured. Many of the factors that define the modern ghetto, specifically segregation, concentrated poverty, and social ills, persisted over time. But the "radical changes in Negro status and in race relations" meant that the tragedy of 1960s Harlem assumed an essentially different quality.[42]

Osofsky's analysis suffers two analytic flaws. First, he ignored the 1950s. Because of this, the optimism that pervaded much of Harlem during that decade escaped him. According to many working- and middle-class African Americans, Harlem experienced a new renaissance in the 1950s. Blacks in New York had begun to live the American dream. While the "millennium" still had not come, working- and middle-class African Americans lived in the fresh comfort of the hard-fought rights of citizenship and hard-earned consumer goods. Second, Osofsky based his assessment of 1960s Harlem on the claims of Malcolm X and Kenneth Clark, two leaders not favored by large swaths of New York City's black community. By not rigorously interrogating the hidden and public transcripts created within multiple spaces in the black public sphere, he missed a significant feature of 1960s Harlem: class conflict.

In contrast, Clark's ethnographic study encompassed various spaces within Harlem's public sphere, particularly street corners, restaurants, and bookstores. Based on the everyday talk his researcher initiated, Clark concluded that the "pathologies of the ghetto community perpetuate themselves through cumulative ugliness, deterioration, and isolation and strengthened the Negro's sense of worthlessness, giving testimony to his impotence." This conclusion best applies to Harlem's poor. His interviews with drug addicts and the unemployed reveal how racial domination and underemployment cultivated nihilism and loneliness and engendered self-destructive behaviors. Clark's conclusion, however, barely captures the worldview of Harlem's working- and middle-class residents. Many felt that the "wounds of centuries" had been partially treated and partially healed by their industry and probity. From the 1940s until 1960, signs of change had begun to sprout up from the concrete terrain. Opportunities and access were expanding. Black businesses were popping up everywhere. African Americans were integrating public sector jobs and New York City's political class. Moreover, according to many in Harlem, these advances were not gifts from whites but hard-fought victories achieved by the determination and rectitude of black people. "Every Negro [was] a Horatio Alger." They were citizens. They were consumers. They were masters of their own fate.

Some scholars have illuminated the ways black consumerism undermined the formation of a black middle-class critique of American capitalism, but they have missed the ways the consumers' republic in the ghetto instigated class conflict in black communities. Because of racism in federal housing policies and local real estate markets, working- and middle-class African Americans, unlike their white counterparts, could not enjoy the fruits of postwar American citizenship out on the suburban frontier. They were stuck in the ghetto, or nearby, and had to face all the social problems associated with concentrated poverty, especially the postwar rise in drug trafficking and addiction. As the decline of Fordism exacerbated Harlem's social problems, working- and middle-class African Americans began to feel surrounded by "un-nice, upset, disturbed, hopped-up, wine soaked people." They did not blame the "cumulative ugliness [and] deterioration" they experienced on racism or economic restructuring. They blamed the urban black poor. In churches and clubs, these new citizens and consumers blamed their insecurity and misery on the poor—people who, Simple maintained, "cannot and do not and will not and *won't* act nice on their own accord." Moreover, fear of the white gaze did not incite this resentment; their day-to-day encounters with junkies, pushers, "winos," "hoodlums," "bad kids," "ladies of the night," and "welfare dependents" did. Working- and middle-class Harlemites were also deeply concerned about housing, which they interpreted in both structural and behavioral terms. In terms of the former, they blamed absentee and exploitative landlords for dilapidated buildings. In regard to the latter, they blamed the poor and junkies for the insecurity and poor quality of life within those neglected structures. While they reviled landlords for nonworking elevators, they feared riding those elevators with "vagrants," "hoodlums," and junkies. While they lambasted landlords for poor upkeep, they blasted "winos" for urinating in the hallways and bashed "bad kids" for loitering. They berated junkies for risking their personal safety and property.[43]

Mrs. Miller from 125th Street was right: the "middle-class negro" believed that he or she was in the minority. This, however, will not last. They will stop considering themselves members of a beleaguered and forgotten population. They will no longer be close-mouthed or reticent. Working- and middle-class African Americans will voice their distress and resentment and introduce into the political environment a behavioral alternative to structural theories purported by white liberals. Powell's embrace of the Boggs Act foreshadowed the conflict between liberalism and the moral sensibilities and material interests of working- and middle-class African Americans that would define drug policy development in New York from the mid-1960s until the passage of the Rockefeller drug laws in 1973. White liberals in New York would not focus on individual character, instead drawing attention to the structural origins of criminal behavior. Meanwhile, many African American activists in New York, who believed their life chances had been improved by newly won local and national civil rights victories and for whom crime and vagrancy represented threats to the perceived improvements in their life chances, would dismiss the significance of social programs (or a lack thereof). Many working- and middle-class African Americans would not, as the *Washington Post* proposed, observe the distinction between "the vice and its victim." As one of the women in *Dope* told Louie, "You shoulda known better in the firs' place." Pushers and junkies were the architects of their own demise and the main source of the insecurity felt by working- and middle-class Harlemites. So the black silent majority will soon mobilize on behalf of polices that resembled Simple's far-fetched "Junkie Catcher's Wagon." They will lobby for a "reservation for the goofy."

2

Black Junkies,
White Do-Gooders, and
the Metcalf-Volker Act
of 1962

HIS NAME WAS CHARLIE REED. This "medium-sized, bow-legged, freckled-faced, light-brown Negro boy of sixteen" from Harlem was a recovering heroin addict and the subject of "Sixteen," Eugene Kinkead's long 1951 profile in the *New Yorker.* Charlie's friends introduced him to heroin, or "horse." He enjoyed it. It empowered him. Relaying the drug's euphoric high to Kinkead, the teenager said, "You're relaxed. And you ain't got a care from here to Brooklyn." Charlie's mother noticed the mood changes. Asked how she could tell when he was high, she shared, "Right off, he seems happy. . . . Wants to dance. Comes around and kisses. Says 'Mom, I love you.' " Yet happiness was just one emotion. Horse also made Charlie feel powerful: "A cop can come up to you and talk to you, and you won't get nervous or anything. When you're on marijuana and a cop comes up to you, you're leery and you want to run. But not on horse. You talk right back to him."[1]

Kinkead, puzzled by Charlie's life and by teenage addiction in general, sought the counsel of community leaders and public officials. He interviewed Rev. J. Archie Hargraves, an African American minister and a cofounder, along with two white ministers, of the East Harlem Protestant Parish (EHPP), a community organization engaged in a mixture of ministry, social work, and community organizing. Hargraves, who had been mentoring the sixteen-year-old, attributed Charlie's addiction and the area's drug problem to environmental factors. He characterized East Harlem as a place where "[p]overty, love and ignorance are all mixed up." Describing Charlie's block, he told Kinkead that it was "part of a wretched area in which the police records show an alarming incidence of narcotic addiction. Six-story cold-water tenements, their fronts fretted with moldering fire escapes, line both sides of the street, except at a point in the middle of the block where the city has torn down one of the most decrepit buildings, leaving a makeshift play lot that is strewn with debris." The minister also drew attention to "broken homes": "Up here [in Harlem], society tends to be matriarchal in the less prosperous families. That is, couples live together and have children, and sometimes they're married and sometimes they're not, but almost always the man is a transient or a weakling and the lease of the apartment is in the woman's name. She gets the relief check, too, and tries to hold the family together."[2]

Curious about the services available for teenage addicts, Kinkead contacted a series of white middle-class reformers at a number of agencies that had intervened in Charlie's life. After a cop arrested Charlie for possession, Kinkead met Sylvia J. Singer, the New York County assistant district attorney who prosecuted the case in youth court. Singer encouraged the court to allow Charlie to plead guilty to a violation of the Youthful Offender Law and send him to Bellevue, a public hospital, for observation. The court complied. Dr. Paul Zimmering, who had twice treated Charlie, lamented the limited resources available for teenage addicts: "[W]e don't have the ideal setup here at Bellevue for the treatment of narcotics cases. . . . Fortunately, it's temporary. We expect something better soon, in the way of a new hospital on North Brother Island, in the

East River. Meanwhile, we're just having to do our best with existing municipal hospital facilities in handling the rash of teenage drug cases that the city has been confronted with during the past year or so." Meanwhile, Charlie relapsed.[3]

In 1962, Governor Nelson Rockefeller, siding with the old penology, signed Metcalf-Volker into law. Attuned to the struggles and backgrounds of addicts like Charlie, the law drew on a discourse of clinical diagnosis rather than risk and permitted users charged with possession of illegal narcotics to elect either prison or treatment. With Metcalf-Volker, white reformers secured passage of legislation that "provided a new approach to the drug problem," one that "[moved] in the direction of treating addiction as an illness rather than a crime." Rockefeller said it himself: "It is a measure designed to save hundreds and ultimately thousands of young narcotics addicts from a life of enslavement to drugs by offering medical treatment instead of prison." He explained, "Addicts are most often adolescents and young adults who are victimized before they are old enough to appreciate the tragic consequences. Many who have no place to turn for guidance and help are driven to criminal activity to support their habit." Reform groups and liberal newspapers across the state applauded the measure. "New York State is first with a law to help drug addicts," read the full-page advertisement New York's *Journal-American* purchased in the *New York Times* to praise Rockefeller's signature on the legislature (and to tout their role in its enactment). Nevertheless, while the passage of Metcalf-Volker was a monumental victory, reformers had been calling for such a policy for quite some time. Even before ADA Singer successfully convinced the court to treat Charlie's addiction as an illness rather than a crime, white reformers were advancing criminologies of the welfare state. They had been emphasizing the structural roots of addiction and urging the legislature and every governor of New York State, from the end of World War II until

1962, to establish sufficient hospital facilities for drug users. What changed?[4]

JUST AS TURN-OF-THE-CENTURY WHITE POLITICIANS AND reformers attacked social maladies plaguing immigrants huddled in the tenements of bustling cities, a new breed of white activists began to tackle the ills bedeviling African Americans stuck in urban ghettos during the 1930s and 1940s. White social workers, civic leaders, and public officials joined their black middle-class counterparts to highlight the perfectibility of the urban black poor and promote penal welfarism. In 1942 the Subcommittee on Crime and Delinquency of the interracial City-Wide Citizens' Committee on Harlem, cochaired by Adam Clayton Powell Jr., pastor of Harlem's Abyssinian Church, and Algernon D. Black, a Jewish "liberal social critic" and leader at the New York Society for Ethical Culture, released a report on the community's budding delinquency problem. While drawing attention to the character flaws of young criminals and calling for the cooperation of "self-respecting and law abiding" citizens, the document stressed the structural roots of youth crime: "A Negro boy may become a burglar because his mother is working every afternoon and evening and must leave him neglected; and the mother may be compelled to work because some white employers discriminate against the boy's father by refusing to employ Negroes." It added, "The slum, a broken family, the great increase of migration of certain sections of the South, insufficient educational opportunities, and the lack of vocational training—all these and a hundred other factors may aid in the creation of a Negro criminal."[5]

Given this ideology, it is no surprise that white reformers and liberal politicians condemned the Harlem "crime wave" narrative promoted by newspapers in the early 1940s and echoed the critiques leveled by middle-class black activists. In late November

1941, Dr. Robert W. Searle, executive director of the Social Service Bureau of the Magistrate Courts, convened a conference in Harlem to discuss the "so-called 'crime wave.'" These articles prompted Vito Marcantonio, the leftist U.S. representative, to call an emergency meeting of the Harlem Legislative Conference, which comprised over 200 civic, religious, labor, and fraternal organizations from the community, in early November 1941. In his invitation to the NAACP's Walter White, Marcantonio called the stories "attacks against the Negro people of Harlem." At the meeting, Stanley Isaacs, Republican borough president of Manhattan, remarked, "I hope the city will realize that crime has been committed against Harlem as well as in Harlem." According to Isaacs, these offenses included overcrowding and unemployment. On November 8, 1941, Magistrate Anthony F. Burke, while presiding over a bail hearing for four African American youths charged with robbery, said that the recent outbreak of crime in Harlem was "not entirely a police situation, but more a social and economic problem." Morgan Dix Wheelock, trustee of the Children's Aid Society and the chairman of the Harlem City-Wide Citizens' Committee, attributed the criminal activity to the fact that African Americans were the "last hired and first fired."[6]

While the postwar drug trade threatened the security of working- and middle-class African Americans, it provided white reformers an opportunity to practice their social gospel. Two groups in particular epitomized these ideological sensibilities: the East Harlem Protestant Parish and the Welfare Council. In 1948 three alumni of Union Theological Seminary, Donald Benedict, George Williams Webber, and J. Archie Hargraves, founded the EHPP. Funded by Baptist, Congregational, Methodist, and Presbyterian denominations and the New York City Mission Society and informed by their Christian principles, the EHPP labored in the "concrete vineyard" to empower residents and help them improve conditions in their communities. In 1950 the EHPP initiated an antinarcotics ministry that supplied counseling and social services to those suffering from drug addiction; it remained a central player in this policy arena for the next thirteen years. In December 1950, the Welfare Council of New York City, an umbrella group composed of public and private social work agencies in the city, formed the Committee on the Use of Narcotics among Teen-age Youth to study the origins and extent of teenage addiction in the city, review relevant laws and propose any necessary statutory revisions, evaluate available medical facilities, and develop a preventative education program. The committee quickly cultivated ties with state officials and other civic organizations and became a key node in the state's growing narcotics control network.[7]

Although this network of local public officials, civic groups, and medical professionals espoused many of the same beliefs of their Progressive Era predecessors, they escaped their racial trappings. Describing East Harlem, the parish mission statement read, "The greatest tragedy in East Harlem is not the lack of possessions, but the absence of hope and vision which challenged the people to fight against environmental conditions. The problems in this area grow greater each year." Sylvia Singer, now head of the Welfare Council's Committee on the Use of Narcotics among Teen-age Youth, urged that "narcotic addiction be made a reportable disease, much as tuberculosis is, instead of [a] crime." The committee doubted that racial minorities were predisposed toward addiction, even as most hospitalized and incarcerated drug addicts were nonwhite. In 1951 Raymond M. Hilliard, the executive director of the Welfare Council and the former commissioner of welfare for New York City, unequivocally proclaimed, "The color of one's skin does not promise exemption from narcotics." In 1951 and 1952 the Committee on Public Health Relations of the New York Academy of Medicine held a series of meetings titled "Drug Addiction among Adolescents." In the introduction to the published conference proceedings, Frank Fremont-Smith, the medical director of the organization funding the meeting, wrote, "What has developed . . . is a much clearer recognition that drug addiction in adolescents must be seen as one symptom of the serious deprivations suffered by many children living in large and crowded cities." A study by Zimmering and several collaborators made this point more emphatically. All but one of the patients studied over a three-year period were "Negroes or of Puerto Rican descent," and the study concluded that these subjects "all suffered psychologically from the discriminatory practices and attitudes directed against their racial groups." The researchers explained, "All of our addicts have come from the Harlem area. This section of New York City is notorious for its poverty, intense congestion, filthy slums and high delinquency rate."[8]

In contrast, working- and middle-class African Americans considered drug addiction a crime problem rather than a public health concern. They were much less focused on environmental conditions than on an environment inhabited by pushers, prostitutes, and pimps. *Jet* found law enforcement wanting and harangued white politicians for allowing viciousness and vice to creep into black communities, crying, "Despite efforts of the Kefauver committee to root out the confidence men, policy operators, bookies, hustlers, and bootleggers who infest these Negro areas, overloads of these vice-ridden neighborhoods continue to elude the Federal dragnet." An item in Jack Dalton's gossip column in the *New York Age* in late 1950 powerfully evinced the same angst: "Harlem dope peddlers are becoming amazingly bold. If you were to look into the window of that 117th Street and Seventh Avenue restaurant any afternoon, you are likely to see users, men and women, in a state of stupor or sleeping off their jags. Once inside, you'll notice the sly exchange of the stuff for cash or stolen property." In June 1951 Earl Brown, Harlem's councilman and head of the Manhattan Neighborhood Improvement Association, held a mass meeting—or, as the *New York Age* called it, a "rally for dope war"—at the Golden Gate Ballroom to "bring home the seriousness of the widespread narcotics influence to the community-at-large." Nearly 1,000 people attended. In fact, people had to be turned away by police because the venue had reached its capacity. After several public officials addressed the crowd, local PTA president Pat Brown asked the first question: "Why doesn't the District Attorney protect the people who 'turn in' pushers?" "We do," the DA responded. The audience jeered. Three years later, William Bryant, the "Mayor of Harlem," disc jockey, and one of the sponsors of *Dope*, advocated treatment for teenage addicts and praised Police Commissioner Francis H. W. Adams for his recent " 'dragnet' movement to rout out undesirables and rid the streets of vagrants who might well be potential rapists or crime-committers."[9]

For their part, white reformers continued to lobby for more hospital facilities for all addicts, but capacity constraints and the federal push for more punitive measures frustrated their attempts to secure more treatment resources. In early 1947, days after a federal drug raid in Harlem, representatives from national and local law enforcement and public health agencies met at police headquarters in Manhattan to discuss the city's heroin problem. Led by Police Commissioner Arthur Wallander, the group promulgated a policy that would have compelled "drug addicts to submit to a cure" instead of imprisoning them. The specific language of the proposed ordinance stated that drug addicts "shall be sentenced to prison for a term not less than required for a medical cure and not more than a year." It would have given judges the ability to sentence drug addicts to probation if they agreed to enter treatment in a government facility. Yet neither New York City nor the state operated facilities that could have accomplished these goals. Consequently, the group proposed using the federal hospital in Lexington, Kentucky, to implement the policy.[10]

Capacity constraints also prevented local reformers from securing state action. A few weeks after the conference at police headquarters, State Senator Walter J. Mahoney introduced a bill that followed the logic of the proposed ordinance. But after its passage, Governor Thomas E. Dewey vetoed the bill, criticizing it for criminalizing addiction. "This bill would make every drug addict a criminal," his veto message read. "It is not directed at the criminal narcotics traffickers in narcotic drugs. It ignores completely the contributions of modern medicine and modern psychology in the evaluation of the deep-seated personal maladjustments of those unfortunates who succumb to drug addiction." Two years later, the Federal Bureau of Narcotics convinced Mahoney to introduce the measure again. And again the governor vetoed the legislation, calling it premature. The stated rationales notwithstanding, a more concrete concern also animated the vetoes. Both times the Department of Health advised the governor to reject the bill, believing it lacked sufficient capacity to execute the law. Years later, Samuel Levine from the Federal Bureau of Narcotics remembered, "Bills [creating more hospital facilities] were passed by the Legislature in 1947 and 1949, but the governor vetoed them because the State didn't have the institutions or the money to build them."[11]

Despite early setbacks, reformers mobilized their network of civic associations, public officials, and medical professionals on behalf of more hospital facilities in the early 1950s. Mayor Vincent R. Impellitteri, who assumed office in late 1950, did not know much about the city's narcotics problem and did not take it very seriously. Eventually, reformers swayed the new mayor, convincing him to establish the Committee on Drug Addiction to study teenage drug abuse. When announcing the new committee, the mayor assayed, "While there has been some increase in the distribution and use of drugs, notably in some depressed areas of the city, the situation, I was assured, is under control and not one to cause alarm." He went on to say, "However, I believe that an ounce of prevention is worth a pound of cure, and therefore I have appointed this committee to look into the picture thoroughly and provide me with a first-hand account, together with statistics and a program of procedure to combat this evil."[12]

Unbeknownst to the mayor, civic leaders and public officials had already been studying the problem and had already formulated policy prescriptions. A month after the mayor's announcement, the

United Parents Association called on the city to "set up a curative center for the treatment of young people who have become the victims of the narcotic racket." The Welfare Council's Committee on the Use of Narcotics among Teen-age Youth submitted a complete program to the mayor's committee. The proposal primarily advocated for more treatment facilities and an end to sending noncriminal addicts to jails. That same year, Manhattan District Attorney Frank Hogan issued a report that reiterated the facts and prescriptions highlighted by the Welfare Council and other groups: "[I]t is obvious that criminal prosecution neither spares the community nor cures the addict." "Control and rehabilitation of [addicts] cannot be accomplished through the criminal law," Hogan claimed, "for he is definitely a public health problem, a 'Typhoid Mary' who should be subjected to compulsory quarantine until cured." Hogan then outlined his three policy recommendations: (1) enacting stiffer penalties for "dope peddlers"; (2) amending the Sanitary Code to rescue "the youthful addict by declaring him a menace to public health and permitting his confinement and cure without criminal prosecution"; and (3) initiating comprehensive study of the state's narcotics problem in hopes of formulating "a state program for the treatment and cure of addicts."[13]

In July 1951, the Mayor's Committee on Drug Addiction unveiled an interim report that reflected the consensus of white reformers while acknowledging the capacity concerns of public officials. After surveying the extent of the problem, the report encouraged federal authorities to expand their efforts to curb the international drug trade and advocated increases in federal and state penalties for the possession and sale of illegal narcotics. Although the committee supported minimum penalties, it opposed "drastic punishment such as death or life imprisonment." This position did not represent a moral objection; it reflected practical concerns. Based on their expertise, members of the committee felt that "extreme penalties . . . might lead to nullification or seriously impair the certainty of punishment." Experience told them that juries would acquit instead of giving out "extreme penalties." Additionally, the report advised rehabilitation for teenage addicts. Keenly aware of the organizational and political challenges of creating new institutions and services, it proposed expanding existing public and private programs and encouraged the federal government to open "as soon as possible" the narcotics treatment hospital planned for New York.[14]

Coming up against formidable local impediments, local reformers took their measures to Albany, and they and their allies in the media pressured the legislature to act. In January 1951, Senator Seymour Halpern, a liberal Republican from Queens who worked closely with the Welfare Council of New York, introduced several narcotics control bills. One established a Bureau of Narcotics Control in the State Department of Health. Another proposed a temporary investigative committee to study the problem. One bill set up a state institution for the rehabilitation of drug addicts, and one transferred certain state hospital facilities from the Department of Mental Hygiene to the Department of Health to expand the treatment capacity. One proposal introduced a mandatory minimum sentence for individuals convicted of selling drugs to minors; one provided for the noncriminal confinement of addicts upon the certification of two physicians; and one required that voluntary commitments last at least six months unless the individual is cured. A few weeks later, Halpern and Assemblyman Frank Mullen met Miles F. McDonald, the Brooklyn district attorney, representatives from the district attorneys of Manhattan and the Bronx, and officials from the State Health Department to write legislation that would curb teenage addiction. The group agreed that facilities for the rehabilitation of underage addicts were needed "at once," supported the imposition of stiffer penalties for possession with the intent to sell to minors, and called for a new state commission to study the problem. Still, the group did not resolve key questions:

"where to locate the pilot institution for rehabilitation of minors and whether the project should be conducted by the state or by New York City, with state aid." Legislators balked at the costs, and state bureaucrats resisted accepting responsibility for the execution of a policy outside of their organization's central mission and without sufficient funds.[15]

While efforts to create a state rehabilitation program faltered, revisions to the penal code proposed by district attorneys moved easily through the legislative process. About a week after the meeting between state legislators and district attorneys from New York City, the legislature tasked Nathaniel L. Goldstein, the state attorney general, with investigating New York's narcotics problem and passed the narcotics study proposal and two bills increasing penalties. The first of the two bills amended the penal code to treat individuals who give away narcotics the same as individuals who sell narcotics, and it increased the maximum penalty for selling narcotics from ten to fifteen years. The second bill imposed indeterminate sentencing for possession of illegal narcotics, mandating that an individual convicted of possession be sentenced to anywhere between two and ten years in prison. As Richard G. Denzer, ADA for New York County, explained, the bill made the "evidence test" more realistic by not requiring evidence of sales or possession of large quantities of drugs, both of which major pushers had successfully avoided in the past. Supporters of the second bill also insisted that the measure did not criminalize addiction. Defending the law, the governor reasoned, "The amounts specified in this section are sufficiently large so that persons convicted under it will in almost all cases be sellers rather than mere users."[16]

Although reformers could not convince the legislature to finance the construction of new hospital facilities, the mayor and governor capitulated somewhat to their demands by supplying additional capacity that exploited preexisting resources. Mayor Impellitteri unveiled a plan for a hospital for teenage addicts. The plan, initiated by the Board of Estimate—the governing body of New York City composed of the mayor, the comptroller, the president of the City Council, and the five borough presidents responsible for budget and land-use issue—entailed the refurbishment of Riverside Hospital on North Brother Island in the East River and a staff of 200 to provide "appropriate care, treatment and follow-up service to teen-aged drug users." The Board of Estimate appropriated over $700,000 for the endeavor. In November, Governor Dewey outlined the state's new approach to addiction: it would offer financial aid to private hospitals and social welfare agencies that offered rehabilitation and aftercare services to drug addicts. As the *New York Times* opined, "Governor Dewey is known to believe that any program involving new withdrawal facilities for addicts is out of the question now when aroused public opinion and humanitarian motives demand immediate action." The paper reported that the governor was convinced that "such action would also put a heavy strain on an already tight budget and might very well be precluded by shortages of materials needed for defense production." The following month, Dewey and Impellitteri, because they wanted "to do as much as government can do to save children who have fallen victim to drugs," decided to combine city and state resources to expand the plan for Riverside Hospital. The revised project included the construction of a school and gym as well as 306 full-time and 97 part-time staff. The new plan also increased hospital capacity from 150 to 200 beds.[17]

Public outrage eventually forced the legislature to act. The "frightening testimony" and "shocking revelations" at Attorney General Goldstein's public hearings, which were broadcast on the radio, caused a stir across New York State and intensified public pressure. A *New York Times* editorial claimed that the hearings uncovered and dramatized "some ugly, sickening facts about the use of narcotics by teen-agers." After noting slow but steady progress in enforcement and education measures, the article ended by stressing, "One glaring deficiency is the lack or shortage of facilities for treatment and rehabilitation of young addicts. When it meets again in January the Legislature will have plenty of evidence on which to build a program for better coping with this dirty business of narcotics." Two days later, the paper, reflecting further on the hearings, affirmed their "arousing effect." It also castigated local officials, saying that the hearings had "shown the ineffectiveness if not negligence by the New York City administration in dealing with the drug traffic." Right after the hearings concluded, Dewey announced the formation of an experimental rehabilitation program at Bedford Hills. The following year, he signed five narcotics control bills Goldstein authored based on his investigation. Promoted by white reformers in New York City, one bill mandated compulsory treatment, rehabilitation, and aftercare for drug users under the age of twenty-one, and another initiated a high school antidrug education program. The three other bills targeted drug dealers: one imposed a mandatory sentence of fifteen years to life for third-time offenders; one reduced the amount needed for simple possession; and one allowed state and local authorities to confiscate automobiles or aircrafts carrying illegal drugs. It is important to note that the tougher penalties were less a knee-jerk reaction to hysteria than an attempt, based on the advice of law enforcement officials, to overcome the capacity issues and judicial discretion that caused court proceedings to fall short of the objectives of laws already on the books. The limited ability of the state court system to try all cases involving drug offenses forced prosecutors and judges to accept pleas to lesser offenses, which, according to Goldstein and others, undermined the desired deterrent effect of existing law.[18]

From the end of World War II until the end of the Dewey administration, white reformers and working- and middle-class African Americans kept drug addiction on the public agenda but secured limited policy changes. White reformers and law enforcement officials agitated for more rehabilitative resources for the "innocent victims" of the drug trade and practical sentences for dealers who would seek to corrupt youngsters like Charlie Reed. In contrast to this consensus, working- and middle-class Harlemites pleaded with the police to expand their campaigns against pushers and other progenitors of vice. Nevertheless, because African Americans neither played a crucial role in the various special narcotics investigations and committees nor participated in any of the private conferences that produced most narcotics control legislation during the early 1950s, these policies reflected the ideas, ideologies, institutional interests, and political influence of the white middle-class members of the state's narcotics control network. To be clear, these reformers rarely got their way: capacity limitations routinely forestalled the development of a robust medical response. Even so, the issue network successfully secured incremental increases in the number of hospital beds, and Frank Hogan and other law enforcement officials leveraged their expertise and reputation to prevent dramatic shifts in criminal sentences that they believed would criminalize addiction and undermine their efforts to achieve successful prosecution of pushers.

Discouraged by the intractability of the city's narcotics problem and the ineffectiveness of previous policy interventions, city, state, and federal officials spent the greater part of 1955 investigating this issue. In May 1955, Deputy Mayor Henry Epstein submitted to the Board of Estimate a study of juvenile delinquency that drew attention to the troubling effects of drug abuse. Yet Epstein did not suggest new policy solutions; he simply placed hope on Riverside Hospital. Like his predecessor, the new attorney general of New York State, Jacob Javits, filed a report on the state's narcotics problem in September 1955. Because of high recidivism rates, he argued, the state should "establish compulsory after-care clinics and link them directly to our Parole and Probation system" and "[a]ddicts released from prison should be required to take treatments at these clinics over a prolonged period under penalty of suspension of parole or probation." Additionally, the attorney general proposed a "State 'Watchdog' Agency" to serve as "a center for statistical evaluation and planning." He also advocated coordination across all levels of government in order to boost state capacity, including "creating more facilities jointly with neighboring States through inter-State compacts," enabling "the Federal government to take more State addicts into its hospitals providing the States absorb the care costs of their patients," and holding a national conference to "re-organize the presently disjointed fight against narcotics."[19]

Despite a growing narcotics problem, multiple investigations, and public pressure, drug policy continued along the same trajectory. Once again the issue network failed to attain substantial rehabilitative resources, but it obtained its preferred revisions to criminal sentences. In a special message to the legislature in 1956, Governor Averell Harriman announced that he would include a $160,000 appropriation in his supplemental budget for an experimental treatment facility in New York City. The center would be attached to a teaching hospital and would treat 120 patients a year. Although the legislature approved the appropriation that year, no teaching hospital would accept the grant. Many hospitals did not want their institution associated with drug addicts. So the funds remained unspent from 1956 to 1958. In early 1956 a bipartisan group in the Assembly introduced a bill drafted in conferences with representatives from the State Narcotics Control Board, the New York Police Department, the Kings County district attorney, and the New York County district attorney that incorporated the recommendations of the commissioner's report. The bill included the following elements: an increase from five to seven years in the minimum sentence for individuals convicted of selling narcotics to minors and an increase from two to five years in the minimum sentence for individuals convicted of selling to adults; a reduction in the amount of drugs in possession necessary to establish the intent to sell; and an increase from two to three years in the minimum sentence for illegal possession without the intent to sell. The first element sought to deter drug peddling rather than punish drug addicts. In April, Governor Harriman signed a bill that mandated that an addict with a prior conviction for possession be sentenced to a minimum of six months. This measure tried to provide sufficient time for rehabilitation. Another measure mandated that addicts be given treatment as a condition of their probation. The problem: the law supposed the existence of a cure that did not exist, and it supposed the presence of services that neither the state nor the city provided. To the extent that such services existed, they were reserved for juveniles. And they were paltry.[20]

Then the state's narcotics problem worsened. The number of habitual users rose from 1,637 in 1955 to 4,006 in 1960. The number of narcotics deaths in New York City climbed from 30 in 1940 to 199 in 1960, and the number of narcotics deaths of individuals between the ages of fifteen and nineteen climbed from 0 in 1940 to 15 in 1960. Making matters worse, in 1958 Anna M. Kross, commissioner of the New York City Department of Corrections, ordered that prisons would no longer accept voluntarily committed drug users. Although she believed in rehabilitation, Kross felt that her department lacked the capacity to provide these services. During a 1954 conference on addiction, she told Sylvia Singer, "There's only one thing that I need: money! . . . If I had the money, I could go along with you 100%. And [it] doesn't have to be city money. . . . [T]here's no use kidding ourselves. There is no city money available. Period! We don't need to waste any time." Four years later, after damaging reports of overcrowding and prison riots, Kross finally decided to end drug treatment programs in order to make room for inmates.[21]

Upset, activists remained undeterred. In the past, delay tactics and institutional obstacles had caused rehabilitative schemes to die. But this time was different. The rehabilitative model had acquired new energetic allies. Since the creation of the EHPP, the organization had been aggressively tackling East Harlem's narcotics problem, and, due to the leadership of Rev. Norman Eddy, the organization's antidrug activities expanded in the mid-1950s. Born in Connecticut and educated at Yale, Eddy fled the "postwar world of middle-class Protestant religion and country club comfort" to enter the ministry and live a life of service. In July 1958, at the height of the controversy surrounding Commissioner Kross's decision, the EHPP's Narcotics Committee and the Greenwich Village Association's Committee on Narcotics established the New York Neighborhood Council on Narcotics Addiction (NCNA) to plan and coordinate efforts. Edwin Fancher, cofounder of the *Village Voice,* used the pages of his newspaper to publicize the city's drug problem and advocate for reform, and he assumed the chairmanship of the new organization. Although an umbrella group of multiple community groups, the council was still just one node in the dense network of reformers devoted to the hospitalization and rehabilitation of drug addicts. In February 1959 around 400 civic leaders, religious leaders, medical professionals, and social workers attended a conference on narcotics addiction sponsored by the Community Council of Greater New York and the New York Society for Ethical Culture. Conferees pinpointed the need for a medical approach.[22]

The EHPP and other civic associations provided the state's narcotics issue network the political leverage it needed to enact its preferred policies. In March 1959 the EHPP's Narcotics Committee sponsored a march to publicize the inadequate facilities available to drug users. Around 200 people took part in a silent prayer demonstration outside of Metropolitan Hospital. Two days later, Robert Low, the mayor's health adviser, announced that the Department of Hospitals would work with state officials to explore options at a state hospital, specifically Manhattan State Hospital on Ward's Island. Still, the EHPP remained dissatisfied with the pace of progress and the unresponsiveness of local officials, particularly those within the Department of Hospitals. Consequently, the parish wrote Mayor Robert F. Wagner Jr. to protest the shortage of treatment facilities and to seek a meeting with him. Carrying a cross of gold and signing hymns, 200 people joined the parish at a demonstration outside of City Hall and the Department of Hospitals at the end of April. The next day the mayor agreed to meet with representatives of thirty church groups. A month later, Wagner unveiled the "most ambitious [anti-drug] program in history," "a milestone in the evolution of governmental approaches to the problems of addiction." The grand appraisal notwithstanding, it represented the city's first serious attempt to develop an antidrug policy consistent with the long-standing proposals embraced by activists, public officials, and medical professionals. The program included new small units within city hospitals and cooperating medical schools for the hospitalization and rehabilitation of young and adult drug addicts and a research program devoted to finding a cure.[23]

Local activists also secured victories at the state level. In March 1959, Assemblymen Sidney H. Asch, a Democrat from the Bronx, and MacNeil Mitchell, a Republican from Manhattan, followed the recommendations of the NCNA and cosponsored a bill to create more space within mental hospitals "for the care, cure and rehabilitation of narcotics addicts." On November 5, 1959, Governor Rockefeller, standing before 1,000 representatives of 221 members of the Federation of Protestant Welfare Agencies' Board Members Institute, announced the formation of the Special Task Force on Narcotics Addiction. The governor charged the task force with "recommending specific steps which can be taken by the state within our budgetary capacity towards the solution of this grave problem." Rockefeller's administration also established a small experimental center, a fifty-five-bed unit in Manhattan State Hospital on Wards Island, that would accept voluntary commitments. In mid-March 1960, the New York Senate passed the Mitchell-Asch bill. The measure appropriated $500,000 to the state's Department of Mental Hygiene for additional hospital beds for drug users.[24]

The passage of Mitchell-Asch testifies to the influence of the statewide coalition of reformers that Reverend Eddy and others built. Initially, the legislation had encountered some resistance. The state's budget director advised the governor to veto it, commenting, "Although drug addiction has been a problem for years, it is our understanding that there really is no accepted method of treatment and cure. The speed with which a narcotic addiction program is developed will be dictated by the results of the research program established last year at the Manhattan State Hospital. The hospitals would be greatly handicapped at this time if required to treat this type of patient." After the measure stalled in the Assembly, Reverend Eddy activated supporters. As the Department of Mental Hygiene's report on the measure stated, "This bill is strongly supported by church and community groups particularly in New York City." Explaining their support for the measure, Eddy released an open letter that read, "Your support, your action in the next three days, may put an end to the suffering of thousands of our most neglected citizens. . . . Men and women come to us daily in the throes of withdrawal with no place to turn." In early April, the United Neighborhood Houses of New York, Inc. wrote the governor. Reminding Rockefeller of the association's political reach, Helen M. Harris, the organization's executive director, stated, "On behalf of the United Neighborhood Houses, the federation of 50 settlements in Greater New York's most troubled neighborhoods, I want to express our enthusiastic support for the Mitchell-Asch Bill. . . . We feel confident of your approval." Feeling the pressure, the Assembly eventually passed the legislation. Rockefeller signed the bill on April 14.[25]

Interest group mobilization and heightened public concern gave advocates for a comprehensive antidrug strategy a fighting chance in the early the 1960s. Toward the end of 1960, Senate Majority Leader Walter J. Mahoney, sensing the public pressure, grew frustrated with "the stalling by the Department of Health and the Department of Mental [Hygiene]." Given the difficulties of having multiple agencies execute the anti-addiction plans of the legislature, Mahoney drafted a plan that placed a director of narcotics control within the governor's office to coordinate and focus the state's resources—spread across multiple agencies—on the state's narcotics problem. The senate majority leader met with the heads of the Department of Health, the Department of Mental Hygiene, the Department of Labor, and the State Parole Board to discuss his bill. Concerned about the establishment of a new agency that would compete and interfere with their own, the commissioners did not like what they heard. In fact, they "sat in stunned silence." At a follow-up meeting, the agency heads criticized the bill. At a third meeting, an agitated Mahoney told them, "If the combined brains of this group can't come up with a suitable piece of legislation, I'll pass a bill without you next week, and I'll get the governor to sign it." After Mahoney stormed out, one commissioner drolly remarked, "Well, I guess we'd better get to work." And work they did. The "Rules bills" they authored established a bureau of drug addiction within the Department of Mental Hygiene to coordinate activities across agencies and called for separate hospital facilities to which addicts would be admitted upon court certification.[26]

As the commissioners drafted their proposal, a rival bill wound through the Assembly. At a conference in August 1960, Richard H. Kuh, assistant to Frank Hogan and a representative of the State District Attorneys Association, unveiled a new legislative proposal establishing a civil commitment program that would allow a person arrested on narcotics charges to elect hospitalization rather than incarceration for not more than three years, with a subsequent two-year probationary period. Upon successful rehabilitation, the criminal charges would be dismissed. Kuh also indicated that "[t]here would be similar civil commitment of persons arrested for other crimes if an underlying narcotics addiction was responsible for their perpetration" and claimed that a proposed federal law would provide $25 million a year over a four-year period for the construction of hospitals. Berkowitz-Volker, a version of Kuh's proposal introduced in the legislature, would have allowed individuals facing a criminal trial to take a diagnostic examination, and, if the examination revealed a substance abuse problem, the judge would have the power to commit them to a hospital for one to three years.[27]

Despite the groundswell for a robust antidrug program, conflicting ideas and institutional interests—"professional bickering"—among members of the issue network scuttled this effort. Berkowitz-Volker passed the Assembly 143 to 4 but died in the senate. Yet important members of the issue network disapproved of the measure. Reverend Eddy argued that it prioritized hospital beds for addicts convicted of crimes and complained that the bill "does not provide for beds before arrest." Worried about capacity constraints, Paul Hoch, commissioner of the Department of Mental Hygiene, informed Senator George R. Metcalf, chairman of the Senate Committee on Public Health, that there "are insufficient facilities available and we are not ready to give any effect to this legislation. . . . When more facilities are available and can be staffed and more is known about drug addiction and its treatment, the admission base for patients will be broadened." Given these misgivings, he suggested "that [Berkowitz-Volker] be killed in your committee." For all of these reasons, the bill died in committee. After Kuh's legislation went down in defeat, he turned against the Rules Bill, ensuring its downfall. Afterward Senator Metcalf sent Kuh an angry letter: "Now it is clear . . . that once the State District Attorney's Association found itself thwarted, it prepared a memorandum in stern opposition to the Rules Bill. . . . I may as well tell you that I dislike such surreptitious dealings."[28]

In 1951 public attention was not enough to overcome capacity constraints; in 1959 interest group mobilization augmented popular concern and helped produce Mitchell-Asch. After efforts at a comprehensive program floundered in early 1961, pressure mounted. In 1962 civic organizations like the New York State Council of Churches and the EHPP escalated their lobbying efforts. The governor's staff noticed whenever the *Journal-American*'s "blood pressure" was "up again" on this issue, and it was high in 1962. The progressive newspaper initiated several letter-writing campaigns to encourage all the state's elected officials to pass significant narcotics control legislation. Additionally, Governor Rockefeller faced reelection in 1962, and, with the fight against drug addiction at the top of the agenda, he needed to sign a bold bill. Thus all the stars were aligned for a dramatic shift in the state's drug program. Members of the issue network simply needed to agree on a proposal.[29]

Political exigencies and the preferences of the governor compelled members of the issue network to make certain concessions. Everyone quickly realized that they needed to put together an omnibus bill combining aspects of Berkowitz-Volker and the Rules Bill. This meant that the final legislation would have to include voluntary commitment for arrested and nonarrested addicts and a new organizational entity to administer the state's narcotics control program. But disagreements persisted. At an October 6 meeting, the members of the issue network spent most of the time debating which office would coordinate the state's antinarcotics efforts. Representatives of the District Attorneys Association advocated for an independent agency within the executive branch. Kuh argued that that concept had two advantages: an independent agency would have no other responsibility and could focus on addiction, and it would have the "authority to impose its will on people in other departments," which would help resolve coordination problems in the patchwork of narcotics control programs in New York State. Agency heads viewed those benefits as threats. A new independent bureau would compete with others, specifically the Department of Health and the Department of Mental Hygiene, for scarce resources and attention and would undermine their autonomy. Besides Kuh and the agency heads, few others were that invested in this particular issue, and, after Commissioner Hoch informed them that the governor opposed a new agency, the group quickly abandoned that idea and agreed to establish a narcotics office within the Department of Mental Hygiene.[30]

Funding for the new program instigated another conflict. At the suggestion of Senator Metcalf, the legislation did not specify a funding level. This fact was not lost on some legislators. Senator Frank J. Pino stated, "I would like to say that this bill is just a step in the right direction. I emphasize the word 'just' because it is not an adequate step in the right direction." He continued, "Nowhere in this bill is there any appropriation of money for the implementation of the very pious expressions of intentions. True, the bill for the first time enunciates a very important principle that we should treat narcotics [addicts] as sick people. But, a careful reading of the bill will show that the commitment of these addicts is dependent upon the availability of beds. Nowhere in the bill is provision made for the beds." This was no accident. The architects of the bill designed it this way to avoid the potential political obstacles that attaching a specific appropriation would engender. Kuh initially balked, commenting, "Appropriations of several millions will undoubtedly be required. If the massive approach such as we have outlined is contemplated it would be in the neighborhood of ten million dollars." Although he conceded that "it is easier to get a general bill through rather than one that deals with specifics in great detail," he also noted, "It is also possible to get a general bill that gives us nothing." In response, Metcalf cautioned, "I can testify that it is always advisable in introducing legislation not to be specific[;] otherwise you get involved in rather elaborate logrolling. . . . The smart thing to do is to phrase things broadly and let the administrative department which is to be given the responsibility carry the ball from then on."[31]

In the end, intense deliberations, gubernatorial leadership, and interest group mobilization turned a rare opportunity into a major policy achievement. Members of the state's narcotics control network overcame their policy disputes and bruised feelings and negotiated a bill that, at the level of principle, remained faithful to the dominant causal story attached to the state's heroin epidemic ("criminal prosecution neither spares the community nor cures the addict") and that, in practical terms, represented a compromise of the goals and interests of key actors in this issue network. Senator Metcalf remarked, "I think it be obvious to all of us here that none of these gentlemen [who spent eight months deliberating on this measure] had the bill that he probably wished he could have, but, in effect, this is a bill which represents their combined thinking." The governor's office also intervened at critical moments to protect Rockefeller's interests and settle lingering disagreements. Though important, concession and accommodation did not guarantee the success of Metcalf-Volker. Activists in New York City rallied civic organizations across the state in support of the program. (Metcalf joked, "I didn't know there were so many Presbyterian churches.") The *Journal-American* also flexed its muscles by initiating a letter-writing campaign for the bill. The measure eventually passed both chambers unanimously.[32]

Although no black expert or activist participated in the meetings during which the issue network ironed out the details of Metcalf-Volker, many African Americans greeted the new law warmly. At this point, many Harlemites supported rehabilitation. In early 1961, the Health Committee of the Harlem Neighborhoods Association, a umbrella group of local community groups, insisted that the area needed "[s]pecial public health services in Harlem for alcoholics, drug addicts and sufferers of social diseases." Sharing this sentiment, Harlem's assemblyman Lloyd E. Dickens applauded the Metcalf-Volker Act, and he asked the governor to establish a narcotics hospital in Harlem. African American senator James Lopez Watson voted for the bill because of its "recognition that addicts are sick people and diseased people," and he warned that without the new measure the state would have to spend "hundreds and hundreds of thousands of dollars—if not millions and millions of dollars on [law enforcement] in terms of people who become unemployable and people who steal and rob in a community."[33]

This support notwithstanding, working- and middle-class African Americans had begun to craft an alternative to the frame developed by the state's narcotics control network. The contrasting perceptions of a 1961 documentary speak to this cresting tension. Early that year, WCBS-TV aired an hour-long exposé entitled *Junkyard by the Sea*, which featured interviews with current and former drug users as well as members of the state's issue network, including Anna Kross and Reverend Eddy. The *New York Times* praised the documentary's compassionate portrayal of addicts and its sensitivity to structural causes: "Like some other television studies of narcotics and their users, this program included interviews with the unfortunate victims of the habit. But here sensationalism was not the purpose. The discussions were conducted intelligently and served to establish compellingly the realization that present facilities for meeting the problem are woefully inadequate." "The cameras," it noted, "ranged from prison to hospital to a Harlem street where, in the midst of poverty and despair, drug addiction is flourishing." While the *New York Times* commended the depiction of the "victims" of this scourge, the *Amsterdam News* portrayed drug users themselves as the scourge: "How the community is handling the problems of its 20,000 to 30,000 'junkies' will be the subject of [a] special one-hour documentary." The film, according to the *Amsterdam News*, took "viewers into neighborhoods where 'junkies' are as numerous as the children playing in the streets."[34]

This was quite a reversal for both papers. During the early 1940s, the *New York Times* published "sensational" stories that hyped the "crime wave" in Harlem, while black periodicals like the *Amsterdam News* spurned the "crime wave" narrative and accused the *New York Times* and other mainstream newspapers of trafficking in offensive stereotypes. By the early 1960s, drug addiction had begun to provoke conflicting reactions. The *New York Times* review of *Junkyard by the Sea* evinced the old penology: it considered the drug addict a victim of broader social forces, and the policy model it derived from that causal story ordered medical treatment rather than punishment. The write-up in the *Amsterdam News* validated the new penology by referencing the ubiquity of junkies and highlighting the risk they posed to the community. The *New York Times* emphasized equity and individualized the problem, quoting at length a statement from an incarcerated drug user that "betrayed her hopelessness." The *Amsterdam News*, on the other hand, addressed drug users in the aggregate, simply calling them "junkies," a term that never appears in the review in the *New York Times*.

The mind-set of the *Amsterdam News* was representative of the general mood of Harlemites. While working- and middle-class African Americans did not oppose expanding rehabilitation resources for young drug users, they were adamant about the need for aggressive policing. In 1959 the *New York Age* declared:

> The AGE asks no leniency for the criminals, the recidivists, the junkies, dope pushers, muggers, prostitutes, or pimps. Clean out this scum—and put them away as long as the law will allow. . . . The AGE does not seek less use of the nightstick or fewer arrests of Negroes or even less policemen in Harlem. What it does seek, however, is more use of the nightstick on the trespassers and criminals in our society, more arrests of the loiterers and crap-game organizers and more policemen to protect the majority of citizens in Harlem who are, despite all the trials of living here, law-abiding and God-fearing human beings.

At a public hearing organized by the state Democratic Party to hear proposals for the party's platform in 1961, Mark Southall, the Democratic leader of Harlem, insisted that the community was "slowly and surely becoming a cesspool of the dreadful narcotics racket and disease." He asserted, "Irreparable harm is being done to the community. . . . Churches are constantly being robbed by addicts and property is being destroyed. . . . Ministers and other citizens of the community are being mugged, beaten and robbed by addicts, who also are guilty of rapes, pickpocketing and many other crimes, daily and nightly." In March 1962 representatives of Southall's Trojan Democratic Club presented Governor Rockefeller with a petition signed by 5,000 Harlem residents that complained that residents had been "surrounded by the disastrous toll and effects of drug addiction, as well as the free and easy use of dope and narcotics," and were "desirous of eliminating and eradicating the use of dope and narcotics and the illegal traffic of drugs in our City, and the elimination of all the undesirable effects accompanying the same." The signatories resolved that "the State laws against the illegal sale and distribution of dope, drugs and narcotics be effectively tightened and the punishment for violation thereof be made more stringent and severe." That same year, Howard E. Jones, candidate for the Assembly, pledged that, if elected, he would "introduce legislation establishing a 20-year to life sentence for anyone convicted of selling drugs to teenagers," and he backed an "all-out war in Harlem against the evil of the narcotics menace."[35]

WHITE REFORMERS IN NEW YORK FINALLY WON A DRAMATIC change in narcotics control policy in 1962, but they did not have an easy go of it. It took some time. More than a decade after Manhattan District Attorney Frank Hogan called for "a state program for the treatment and cure of addicts," Richard Kuh, his ADA, helped author such a program. More than a decade after the Welfare Council's Committee on the Use of Narcotics among Teen-age Youth began holding conferences, gathering evidence, writing reports, and lobbying political officials for an approach that treated addiction as a disease rather than a crime, the EHPP and NCNA built a statewide coalition of interest groups that won passage of a law consistent with that ideal. Capacity constraints regularly prevented the enactment of a comprehensive drug addiction program. From the early 1950s until the beginning of the 1960s, New York State frequently established fact-finding commissions to study the problem. The purposes of all these investigatory committees were questionable as a policy consensus around rehabilitation rather criminalization had emerged early in New York. Nonetheless, these panels did not require great expenditures or much capacity, and they offered politicians the ability to claim credit. Elected officials responded to policy constraints in other ways as well. At moments of intense public pressure, mayors of New York City and governors of New York State either reorganized preexisting resources or secured modest appropriations to increase the number of hospital beds for drug users. Every time a comprehensive rehabilitative scheme passed the legislature, New York governors, on the advice of budget directors and agency heads, vetoed those bills. Instead, governors and other elected officials constructed public statements that minimized the state's or city's role in fighting drug addiction and trafficking and stressed the appropriateness and necessity of federal action to avoid blame and justify inaction.

Revising the penal code, however, proved to be a much easier lift. Elected leaders generally deferred to law enforcement officials on revisions to criminal sentences. The expertise and influence of Hogan and others made modifying the penal code a relatively easy exercise. Moreover, they were able to ignore popular punitive impulses and defy the wishes of federal actors. Local law enforcement officials consistently rejected federal pleas for dramatic revisions to the penal code, including ones mandating life imprisonment for pushers, because they held that such measures would make the task of investigating (e.g., securing evidence) and prosecuting (e.g., securing jury convictions) more difficult. Even though officials at the Narcotics Bureau occasionally managed to find sponsors for longer sentences in the legislature, local reformers managed to scuttle such proposals in committee or convince the governor to veto the bills.

While the period between the 1946 and 1957 represented a time of relative stability in New York State's antidrug policy, the period between 1958 and 1962 represented a period of sudden change. A random event—a riot at a women's prison and Anna Kross's subsequent move to end rehabilitation services—dramatized the scarcity of hospital facilities for drug addicts and sparked the formation of a locally generated statewide coalition for the rehabilitation model. White reformers in New York City and their allies across the state, including in the media, pushed drugs onto the political agenda and forced legislators outside New York City to take action. Rising drug addiction rates then placed politicians and bureaucrats between an administrative rock (a capacity shortage) and a political hard place (public awareness and highly mobilized civic associations). Led by Senator Metcalf, they negotiated a policy that in the abstract met the goals of the rehabilitative ideal but did not provide adequate resources to support it. Furthermore, to spare the costs of a new department and to gain the support of agency heads worried that a new department would compete with their organizations for scarce state resources, the issue network charged the Department of Mental Hygiene with the execution of the program. This compromise meant that the responsibility for implementation fell on bureaucrats whose primary interests and expertise were not in the area of narcotics control.

While the state's issue network kept African American drug users in mind when enacting Metcalf-Volker, the group was not representative of the people coping daily with addiction and its consequences. Driven by their values and informed by social statistics, a dense network of predominantly white local civic leaders, medical professionals, and public officials spent the 1950s fighting to rescue addicts in Harlem. Early on, they fashioned a causal story that stressed the structural origins of addiction, and, encouraged by moral certainty and scientific skepticism, they maintained with abiding vehemence that "criminal prosecution neither spares the community nor cures the addict." However, white reformers studied and confronted these social tragedies from a distance, sheltered by the privileges of their social and professional positions. Reverend Eddy lived in upper Manhattan, but the Yale-educated minister from Connecticut did not have to. His presence in upper Manhattan was a choice: a testament to the strength of his moral code and the benefits of his racial position.

Working- and middle-class African Americans were not afforded such luxuries. The racial order not did allow them to witness these tragedies at a remove. They had spent the 1940s and 1950s fighting for and securing some of the rights and trinkets of American citizenship. Now, because of persistent residential segregation, they were trapped in a "junkyard by the sea" with people they believed were determined to steal their hard-fought security and destroy their consumers' republic. Consequently, while white reformers were scoring a win for the old penology, working- and middle-class Harlemites, stuck outside the corridors of power, were fashioning a defense for the new penology. Their isolation did not last. When drug addiction became a serious threat to the life chances and lifestyles of working- and middle-class African Americans, they infiltrated this policy arena, and the politics of punishment in New York State were never the same again.

Reverend Dempsey's Crusade and the Rise of Involuntary Commitment in 1966

"REV. DEMPSEY IS GOING TO WASHINGTON," read a headline in the *Amsterdam News* in 1962. The black newspaper's homage to Frank Capra's classic film about the earnest and indefatigable Mr. Smith and his eventful sojourn in the nation's capital was revealing commentary on Rev. Oberia D. Dempsey and his antidrug crusade. Although much more confrontational and boisterous than the prim Mr. Smith, Reverend Dempsey was no less beloved by his community. Before becoming the youth minister at the Abyssinian Baptist Church and an aide to Adam Clayton Powell Jr., he had served as assistant pastor at Mt. Lebanon Baptist Church, one of Brooklyn's largest congregations. There he worked under Rev. Dr. C. L. Franklin, an influential local black pastor who, as chairman of the National Baptist Convention's Social Action Commission, was well integrated in a national network of civil rights leaders and deeply involved in the national movement. While in Brooklyn, Dempsey worked tirelessly as vice president of the borough's NAACP chapter and became a popular youth leader. In 1952 he was ranked fifth in the *Amsterdam News*'s "10 Leading Brooklynites." A few years later, he accepted his position at the "Mighty

Abyssinian," taking his civic skills, resources, and acclaim to Harlem. In 1957 "A Dempsey Fan," sent the *Amsterdam News* a letter praising the minister: "I am proud that Rev. Dempsey is in Harlem, for he is desperately needed, young daring, fearless, liberal-minded, willing and ready to listen to the problems of one and all. I sincerely believe he is destined to be one of the great leaders of our generation." In 1959 he was elected "Mayor of Harlem," a ceremonial position bestowed by the residents of the community, receiving 24,702 out of the 71,202 ballots cast. By 1962 Dempsey had assumed leadership of the new crusade, and now under its auspices this "daring" and "fearless" grassroots leader was going to Washington, D.C., to give voice to the discontent brewing on the streets of Harlem.[1]

By the early 1960s, many Harlemites had begun to lament the community's decline. In 1962 Rev. Richard A. Hildebrand remarked with deep regret, "Many of us join . . . in remembering when Harlem was world famous as a center of Negro culture, instead of a worsening symbol of a racial ghetto, infested with crime and slum dwellings." Harlem's councilman Earl Brown, coauthor of the landmark 1957 Sharkey-Brown-Isaacs law outlawing racial discrimination in apartment rentals and chair of the City Council's six-person Special Narcotics Committee, observed, "Riverside Drive, formerly a street of grandeur, has become an avenue of muck, muggers, and roomers. It is worth your purse plus your life to venture forth on it after sunset." But disgruntled residents did not sit idly by as violence and vice laid waste to their neighborhood. In late 1959, the *Amsterdam News* announced that church and club leaders had begun a "crusade to end violence and crime on the streets of Harlem, and also eliminate the loud-mouthed hoodlums who desecrate the word mother with the most vile language ever uttered." "I'M ANGRY with myself for waiting all this time," Mrs. Mary Smith confessed in late 1962. Smith, the owner of a beauty salon on West 145th Street, founded the Committee for

Neighborhood Improvement to clean up the streets of Harlem because she was tired "of listening to filth and profanity every time I walk into the street. I am sick of blaming the police and our churches for the countless neighborhood wrongs." She vowed, "[From now on] I'm going to tell it like it is." In the summer of 1962, the Harlem Evangelical Association launched the Harlem Crusade, open-air rallies held throughout the community because "the rise of dope addiction and alcoholism along with the ever increasing immorality must be met head-on in our Harlem community." "This is a crusade against the evils of our day," proclaimed Thomas Skinner, one of the main speakers at these rallies. Thus, unlike the initially aimless Mr. Smith, Reverend Dempsey went to Washington with a purpose. He was part of a larger grassroots movement against insecurity and disorder.[2]

In Washington, Dempsey was among like minds. For years, federal officials had implored New York officials to adopt harsh sentences and embark on aggressive policing strategies. In 1957, during his testimony before the Joint Legislative Committee on Narcotic Study, Paul Williams, the U.S. attorney for the Southern District of New York, inveighed against supporters of "soft approaches" to drug addiction and trafficking, saying, "They have hoped to foist upon the people of this country an unwarranted pity for the downtrodden drug user." He lambasted liberals for trying to "engender a popular prejudice in the addict's favor." In 1958, at a meeting in the West Village, Samuel Levine, from the Bureau of Narcotics, maintained that "dope addicts are characterized by mental instability and immaturity, and usually have a criminal record" and that "the addict is equally as vicious as the seller, who is not addicted." When pushed on whether addiction was a medical or criminal problem, Levine responded, "Yes, it's a medical problem, but it's contagious. . . . [T]hese people have to be removed from the community for treatment." Few were more uncompromising in their devotion to punitive approaches than Harry J. Anslinger, the U.S.

commissioner of narcotics. From the late 1940s until his retirement in 1962, Anslinger, "a bald-headed, bull-necked man who devoted his life to stemming the international traffic in narcotics," extolled the virtues of aggressive policing and long criminal sentences and repeatedly impugned antinarcotics approaches adopted by the New York State narcotics control network. In 1959 he testified before a congressional committee, "One thing about New Jersey is this. It is not one of our trouble spots. Northern New Jersey could very likely be, but what we have often told people in New York City, with all this terrific problem, they wonder why they have it, take a ferryboat rise across to Jersey City where you do not see the addiction." Anslinger explained that New Jersey had fewer drug users because of "the attitude of the courts and the good law you have there. The police are vigilant, excellent police in New Jersey." When asked whether "good law" and "vigilant police" drove traffickers to New York, Anslinger responded, "That is just where they land. New York City gets the garbage of New Jersey because these fellows go over to New York where they can operate without too much risk."[3]

Members of New York's narcotics control network loathed the hard-nosed commissioner. In 1959 Dr. Herbert M. Berger, chairman of the State Medical Society's committee on narcotics, complained that Anslinger was "a despot, interested only in maintaining the status quo." Chief Magistrate John M. Murtagh called for Anslinger's retirement, charging that the "Commissioner regards the addict as an immoral vicious social leper." Despite the punitive views of Anslinger and other federal narcotics control officials, the rehabilitative approach reigned in New York State during the 1950s. The Metcalf-Volker Act of 1962 was a complete repudiation of the ideas and strategies Anslinger and other federal officials attempted to impose on New York during the 1950s. Perhaps fittingly, Anslinger retired in 1962. With his departure, the federal government lost a powerful proponent of punishment. As the *Milwaukee Journal* put it, "Now that Harry J. Anslinger has retired as head of the narcotics bureau, prospects are brighter that narcotics addiction may be handled as a socio-medical [problem] rather than just a police problem."[4]

Enter Reverend Dempsey. By the early 1960s, the Harlem pastor had emerged as the leader of the community's crusade against drug addiction and crime. Unaffected by the machinations of Anslinger and other federal officials, Dempsey's crusade, drawing on indigenous class-based values and the unique experiences of Harlemites, also considered drug users risks to the community and argued that they should be removed from the community for treatment. In 1966 Dempsey got his wish. On April 8 Governor Rockefeller signed a bill permitting the involuntary commitment to a mental health facility, for up to five years, of prostitutes addicted to drugs and drug addicts found guilty of a crime. It also authorized the involuntary commitment of addicts even when no crime had been committed. Specifically, the legislation allowed a relative or "anyone who believes that a person is a narcotic addict" to share with a state supreme court justice or county judge "knowledge, information or belief" that an individual was a drug addict, and it permitted the judge to order the "alleged narcotic addict" to submit to medical examination. If the individual was found to be an addict, the law permitted the judge to remand him or her to the custody of a five-person commission for treatment for up to three years. Rockefeller also signed a second bill that revised the penal code, increasing the minimum sentence for anyone selling to a person under twenty-one from seven to ten years and the maximum from fifteen to twenty years, and increasing the minimum for anyone selling to a person over twenty-one from five to seven years. It also raised the minimum sentence for any person found guilty of possession with the intent to sell narcotics from five to seven years.[5]

White liberals were incensed. Assemblyman Albert Blumenthal from Manhattan said, "We're deluding the public if we say we're going to cure addicts by locking them up for three years. Perhaps we should tell the public that we're faced with a threat as great as the bubonic plague, and until we find a cure we're going to set up a concentration camp in every community." Senator Manfred Ohrenstein and Assemblyman Jerome Kretchmer lambasted the measures, complaining, "Those who persist in pushing for a compulsory program have no concept of its futility." The senator added, "The compulsory program isolates the addict like a leper. What we need is a medical program for the ambulatory treatment of addicts so they can function as productive members of society while being treated for their illness." Rockefeller's new narcotics control program—involuntary commitment and increased criminal penalties—represented a seismic shift in the politics of punishment: a disavowal of the principles that had defined Metcalf-Volker and the rebuffing of white liberals that had dominated drug policymaking in New York State during the 1950s. They had successfully resisted federal demands for more punishment. They had successfully beat back attempts to increase sentences for drug offenses. They had successfully defended criminologies of the welfare state. But not this time.[6]

METCALF-VOLKER NEVER LIVED UP TO EXPECTATIONS. A YEAR after the *Journal-American*'s full-page advertisement praising the new law, the newspaper labeled it a "tragic failure." In 1963 Rev. Lynn Hageman, executive director of the EHPP, which was instrumental in the bill's passage, complained that "[p]resent facilities seem to be far too meager for an adequate testing of the basic philosophy set forth operationally in the Metcalf-Volker Act." Because of the scarcity of hospital beds, the Department of Mental Hygiene rejected 43 percent of arrested addicts from New York County who requested and were eligible for commitment. Additionally, the authors of the legislation never considered how users would react to the program. The New York State Commission of Investigation found that voluntary commitment did not work because "the vast majority of addicts, afforded such an opportunity [to elect treatment for periods ranging from one to three years in lieu of criminal prosecution], simply chose a short stay in prison and return to [a] life of addiction and crime on the streets." In 1963, the year the law went into effect, only 880 out the 3,075 individuals eligible for civil commitment under the law requested commitment. By October 30, 1964, only 88 out of the 615 addicts accepted for commitment were still receiving treatment—whether in a hospital or aftercare—and only 28 had remained in the program long enough to have their charges dropped.[7]

Although the negative consequences of Metcalf-Volker's inadequacies redounded mostly to the people of Harlem and other minority neighborhoods, the state's narcotics control network remained dominated by white middle-class reformers. In 1962 Rockefeller appointed Reverend Hildebrand to the newly created New York State Council on Drug Addiction, but white reformers, medical professionals, and law enforcement officials, who espoused the old penology and helped design Metcalf-Volker, dominated the advisory group. Dr. Henry I. Feinberg, president of the New York State Medical Society, chaired the group; the vice chairman was Phillip B. Thurston, a family court judge. The other members included Mrs. Raymond W. Wilkes, a civic leader; Rabbi Jacobi M. Sable; Dr. Harold R. Graser, a psychiatrist; and Irving Lang, who served as a Legal Aid Society defense lawyer and a prosecutor under Manhattan DA Frank Hogan. That same year, the New York City Department of Health sponsored the Conference for Clergy on Narcotics Addiction. Attendees enjoyed sessions on "Pastoral Services for the Addict" and "The Role of the Clergy in a Total Program." Reverend Dempsey, despite being widely recognized as a pastor involved in this issue, was not on the program. In 1963 Mayor Wagner held a reception for the President's Advisory Commission on Narcotics, which was holding two days of closed meetings at City Hall to study New York's narcotics problem. Invitees to the reception included all major actors within the state's narcotics issue network, including those from civic associations like the Community Council of Greater New York and the Citizens' Committee for Children and religious groups like the East Harlem Protestant Parish and Catholic Charities. Despite the concentration of the city's narcotics problem within Harlem, African Americans were in the minority. Kenneth Clark, C. Raymond Jones, Mark Southall, Reverend Dempsey, Dr. M. Moran Weston of Harlem's St. Philip's Episcopal Church, and Harlem Assemblyman Lloyd E. Dickens received invitations to the event. But none of them was invited to speak. Instead, familiar faces, including Police Commissioner Michael J. Murphy, Frank Hogan, and Anna Kross, testified at the meeting.[8]

Shut out of the state's narcotics control network, Harlemites nevertheless marshaled the resources of black civil society to publicize their problems and persuade white public officials to do something about drug addiction and trafficking in their community. James Booker regularly used his column in the *Amsterdam News* to decry Harlem's dope problem and shame white political leaders into action. Months after the passage of Metcalf-Volker, Booker complained, "Narcotics conditions [are] getting worse with summer coming. You can help by writing the Mayor and the President, demanding a local narcotics hospital now and less conferences and press releases." A few weeks later, he wrote, "Leading officials inform us they are about to crack down on one of Harlem's biggest dope and numbers rings. . . . Which reminds us that still not enough is being done to curb the narcotics menace uptown." After the 1962 election, Booker wrote, "What happened to all that campaign talk about people doing something about the growing narcotics problem. It's getting worse, and after-care and rehabilitation are badly needed. What about it Mr. Attorney General, Mr. Governor, and Mr. Mayor?"[9]

As they had during the early civil rights campaigns, working- and middle-class African Americans organized to rid their community of drugs and crime. In June 1962, the People's Civic and Welfare Association, following a conference at the Harlem YWCA, urged the mayor to push President John F. Kennedy to finance work camps for the rehabilitation of drug users and asked the mayor to "call monthly meetings of all law enforcement agencies (Federal, state and city) to discuss, coordinate and execute collective actions to rid New York State of all hoodlums." In the fall of 1962, Dempsey led a seven-week "anti-dope drive." Toward the end of the drive, thirty civic leaders signed a four-point plan:

1. Urge President Kennedy to push Congress to provide funds for the construction of a hospital in the New York area to treat, cure, and rehabilitate addicts.

2. Also urge the President to mobilize all law-enforcement agencies to unleash their collective fangs on dope pushers and smugglers.

3. Urge Gov. Rockefeller to also push a similar crackdown.

4. Spur Mayor Wagner and Police Commissioner Michael Murphy to turn loose the city's police, including the transit and housing lawmen, on criminals and narcotics dealers.

As the proposals of the People's Civic and Welfare Association and Reverend Dempsey show, working- and middle-class African Americans constructed a unique conception of their drug problem. Unlike white reformers and liberal politicians, Harlemites considered drug addiction and trafficking public safety issues. For them, drug abuse and crime were inextricably connected. Although they were willing to support more hospitals for drug users, they believed that aggressive policing must accompany a rehabilitative strategy.

Rev. Oberia Dempsey presents the 1965 Achievement Award of the Anti-Crime,
Anti-Narcotic Committee of the Upper Park Avenue Baptist Church to William Reid,
chairman of the New York City Housing Authority. Mrs. Julia Rivera of the committee
observes. (Courtesy of the La Guardia and Wagner Archives, La Guardia Community
College/The City University of New York.)

Moreover, pleas for white officials to "unleash" the "collective
fangs" of law enforcement were not limited to pushers and smugglers but included "all hoodlums."[10]

Reverend Dempsey and other activists found ways to build coalitions and bring the issue network to Harlem. As mayor of Harlem
and pastor of the Upper Park Avenue Baptist Church, Dempsey
shrewdly cultivated relationships with public officials, like Mayor
John Lindsay, by dispensing rewards, such as the Anti-Crime, Anti-
Drug Committee's Achievement Award. In July 1962, Dempsey and
Gladys Coleman of the 119th Street Block Association, held a mass
rally to warn about the dangers drugs posed to the community's

children. Members of a variety of block associations, church groups, and fraternal organizations along with 250 children marched for two hours and held a rally to protest Harlem's drug and crime problems. Accompanied by two drum-and-bugle corps, the marchers carried banners and placards inscribed with foreboding messages: "Children, Narcotics Mean Death"; "Why Should Harlem Be Destroyed by Narcotics Peddlers?"; and "Narcotics: Parents, Warn Your Children." Speakers included Mark Southall, New York State Attorney General Louis Lefkowitz, and Edward F. Carey, deputy chief inspector of the city's narcotics bureau. Both Lefkowitz and Carey captured the mood of the crowd. The attorney general asserted that while poor economic conditions create "fertile ground" for lawlessness, "slums do not in and of themselves create the delinquent and the criminal." Carey declared that it was "the narcotics addict rather than the peddler that we are chiefly interested in" because drug users spread narcotics more than drug dealers. "Apparently, misery loves company," he scoffed. In September 1963 Dempsey organized a rally and four simultaneous antidrug marches throughout Harlem. In early 1964 he held a "monster rally" at the Abyssinian Baptist Church. Speakers included a broad array of law enforcement officials, local politicians, and Harlem's religious leaders. At the event, Dempsey presented a resolution that called for "an immediate investigation of the narcotics racket in New York City right now, the removal of all known drug addicts from the streets now, and for tougher laws covering the smuggling of illicit drugs into this country, and more cooperation by the individual citizens."[11]

This harsh demand for the "removal of all known drug addicts" was becoming a consensus proposal in Harlem. To accomplish it, several Harlem activists resurrected an old idea: turning Ellis Island into a rehabilitation facility for drug addicts. In 1958 members of the state's narcotics control network briefly agreed that Ellis Island provided them with additional capacity. They believed that the state's narcotics problem was essentially an addiction problem. As such, tackling it required rehabilitation resources rather than physical removal. Some experts reasoned that successful treatment required removal because drug users needed to be protected from the community—the environmental conditions that caused and sustained their habit. After learning the actual costs of refurbishing the island, however, public officials and policy experts dropped the Ellis Island plan. In the early 1960s, Harlem activists revisited the idea but for very different reasons. To them, the state's narcotics problem was primarily a crime problem. While they were unwilling to treat drug users as criminals, Harlem residents and activists felt that the community needed to be protected from them. In August 1963 three elected officials from Harlem, Assemblyman Southall, City Councilman J. Raymond Jones, and State Senator James L. Watson, went to Washington to encourage Attorney General Robert F. Kennedy to endorse the Ellis Island proposal. A few weeks later, they sent a telegram to Senator Edmund S. Muskie, chair of the subcommittee determining the fate of the island, asking him to convert it into a rehabilitation center. Attributing the community's decline to drug users, the telegram stated, "The problem of addiction is a major source of New York's crime, as these sick persons need money to support their habits. Establishment of a center in the New York region on the now vacant Ellis Island would go a long way to helping curb one of the great social problems of the city." In 1964, as Governor Rockefeller developed his legislative agenda, Assemblyman Southall sent him a telegram asking him to "introduce bills to strengthen the state's narcotics program and for [a] takeover of Ellis Island to house narcotics addicts to aid in their rehabilitation."[12]

As Harlem's narcotics crisis deepened, Dempsey also began to embrace involuntary commitment. In 1965 he circulated petitions urging the newly elected mayor of New York City to take the following steps: "1. Declare all habitual narcotics users to be sick people in need of medical assistance. 2. Empower the city and state to construct a huge facility to house and treat them. 3. Set up rehabilitative centers to train cured addicts in employable skills and help re-integrate them into society. 4. Call for a voters referendum in 1966 to possibl[y] enable the city to do the last two above." Dempsey's 1965 petition differs from the 1962 version in one very significant way: while the earlier petition evinced some compassion for addicts while urging political leaders to use all of the powers of the state against "dope pushers and smugglers," the later petition beseeched political leaders to marshal the powers of the state against the addict. The 1965 petition certainly proposed rehabilitation and job training, but Dempsey made the provision of these services contingent upon addicts' removal from the community.[13]

To understand the nature of this common threat and the push for involuntary commitment, it is important to explore how residents described their experiences with drug users. In late 1965 a resident of the Bronx's Mott Haven section captured the prevailing sentiment when he wrote Mayor-elect Lindsay about the city's "most prodigious [problem], dope addiction": "I have seen dope addicts watching people with looks that give their diabolical intentions away." Confirming this man's assessment, a 1966 Kraft survey of black and Puerto Rican Harlem residents showed that respondents listed drug addiction as the "worst," "next worst," and "third worst" problems facing the people of Harlem. Housing was a close second. Crime and juvenile delinquency constituted their next top concerns. Respondents also agonized over "family life" and economic issues, including high prices and jobs. Few focused on prejudice. In fact, similar proportions listed "too many people on welfare" and racial prejudice as the worst problems facing people in Harlem. Respondents were also asked to list the "biggest problems" on their block. Most listed "dope addiction," followed by "bad kids" and crime. Housing, including safety in buildings, remained a top issue.

Smaller proportions mentioned "winos and drunks," "noise," and "dirty streets."[14]

Working- and middle-class African Americans were not simply reacting to the prevalence of drug addicts, "bad kids," and "winos and drunks"; they were reacting to the insecurity these individuals brought to their community. One of those interviewed for Kenneth Clark's study of Harlem was asked if a lot of drug addicts hung around his block, to which the twenty-nine-year-old man responded, "A lot of them? We even have pushers in the block. That's why the junkies are hanging around the corners." When asked whether there was a lot of stealing, this man replied, "Plenty of it. They haven't broken in lately but still a whole lot of stealing and carrying on. Somebody has to be at home at all times. One person stays home and somebody else goes out [to] do everything. If not, when you come back you'll be emptied out head to toe." In the follow-up interviews to the Kraft survey, one sixty-six-year-old black woman complained, "Hoodlums in the Street and the people breaking into your apartment. I just bought a new radio in November, and they stole that. I am not a young lady, to go out and buy more. But the biggest problem is to go out for a walk. You don't know when your apartment is going to be robbed." She groused, "These damn niggers getting too much for their needs. They just ain't ready. . . . Everything is wrong up here. These niggers is crazy. Them damn dope addicts and muggers snatching your pocketbook. I seen the teen-agers selling dope on the street." She complained about "crawling over dope addicts trying to get in and out your house!" "Them dope addicts has just took over. The wino is just as bad. Teenage pushers in the block."[15]

Of course, some residents and activists offered alternative conceptions of Harlem's travails as well as different prescriptions. For example, in late August 1961 A. Philip Randolph, the legendary president of the Brotherhood of Sleeping Car Porters, formed the

Emergency Committee for Unity on Social and Economic Problems because "[c]onditions in Harlem have deteriorated to the point" that "religious, political, business and civic leaders must now take an intelligent and unselfish stand." He invited a diverse array of activists, including Percy Sutton, Anna Arnold Hedgeman, a community leader and former aid to Mayor Wagner, Malcolm X, and Bayard Rustin to join this endeavor and confront the "economic distress and moral decline that plague the black communities of New York." The group blamed Harlem's recent decline on racism in the labor market and the "job crisis confronting black workers"—the increasing demand for skilled labor and the decreasing demand for unskilled labor. Accordingly, the group considered drug users casualties of these structural challenges and expressed great sympathy for them: "[P]utting [drug users] behind bars is not the solution to curing drug addiction. Further, when the 'users' of drugs are released from prison, society fails to give them a chance to prove their sincerity to live a decent life." The committee stressed the necessity of a robust rehabilitative and educational program, "a crash program that is both preventive and corrective in character." At the same time, they called for an aggressive strategy against pushers, urging that "ample effort be made to apprehend the pusher and that a life time sentence without parole be made the punishment to meet the crime of pushing narcotics." While endorsing a ramping-up of police activities, the Emergency Committee was also very critical of the police. The group decried police brutality and demanded that police officers "be tested on their attitudes toward racial and ethnic minorities, and where indications of sadistic and hostile attitudes toward minority peoples exist, these officers be relieved of their responsibilities."[16]

Although the Emergency Committee enlisted some of the most influential figures in the black rights struggle, it is important not to overstate its significance. First, its positions on drugs and crime did not represent the views of working- and middle-class African

Americans. The committee considered drug users members of the community defined in racial terms. When the committee wrote that "[o]ur brothers and sisters and children are being poisoned and destroyed by increasing dope addiction" and that "[n]othing is being done to save our community," the term *community* encompassed both black drug users and nonusers. But surveys, interviews, petitions, and editorials show that working- and middle-class African Americans excluded junkies from the community, which they defined in class terms. While many working- and middle-class African Americans were not willing to criminalize addiction in the early 1960s, the risks junkies posed to person and property forced many blacks to promote their expulsion from the community. Second, the Emergency Committee did not last very long. Randolph lost interest, and he and others turned their attention to the national civil rights movement, specifically the famous March on Washington for Jobs and Freedom. Malcolm X's tension and subsequent break with the Nation of Islam in early 1964, his hajj, and his assassination in 1965 muted, then silenced his voice.[17]

Instead, this policy arena was dominated by different voices. During the 1950s, only two coteries of actors constantly wrangled over drug policy in New York State: white federal narcotics control officials and the white-dominated issue network. Of course, the legislature and the governor's office got involved at particular moments in the legislative process, but the universe of people and groups consistently involved in the drug policy formation process— problem definition, agenda setting, the formulation of policy proposals and drafting of legislation, and the implementation or monitoring thereof—were limited to members of the state's issue network and federal officials. In the 1960s the state's reformist issue network remained engaged, but significant changes occurred at the federal level. Not only did Anslinger retire in 1962, but after the White House Conference on Narcotics and Drug Abuse the federal approach to addiction also shifted in a progressive direction.

Describing this change, David F. Musto writes, "Under an on-slaught of increased drug abuse and addiction, rising crime against property, and a renewed faith in medicine and psychological treatment, federal drug-abuse statutes retreated from death penalties and mandatory minimum sentences to more reliance on treatment, flexible sentences, and even addiction maintenance." After years of federal officials trying to impose a punitive paradigm on New York, national policy had begun to resemble local initiatives. Then a new movement entered the policy arena: Reverend Dempsey's antidrug, anticrime crusade. After being left out of the drug policy debates during the 1950s, Dempsey and his allies had mobilized a thick network of local churches, community groups, and civic associations on behalf of the concerns and ideas of working- and middle-class African Americans and had become a permanent fixture in this issue area. Consequently, beginning in the early 1960s, the opposing trenches of these policy battles were led by the white-dominated issue network and black community activists from Harlem.[18]

As Dempsey and his allies started to infiltrate this policy arena and reframe the state's narcotics problem, members of the issue network held on to the same causal story and policy responses they had fashioned during the 1950s. As Dempsey and others began to view the failures of Metcalf-Volker as indications of the moral weaknesses of junkies, members of the issue network viewed the persistence of addiction and crime as manifestations of deeper structural problems. In 1964 Dr. Paul H. Hoch, commissioner of the Department of Mental Hygiene and one of the architects of Metcalf-Volker, said:

There are a number of reasons for addiction and not all have the same causes. We know that the bulk of addiction lies with deprived minority groups. As long as poverty, slums, unem-ployment, and similar depressed conditions exist, addiction will flourish. By the same token crime will also flourish in the same areas and among the same group of people. The causative relationship between crime and addiction is, I believe, greatly overestimated. They are rather simultaneous results of the same generative factors.

Middle-class Harlemites once advanced this theory. In the 1940s African American activists, in response to the white gaze, stressed the structural origins of crime in public, but in private they bewailed the behaviors of the urban black poor for threatening their safety and endangering their claims of racial equality. As they experienced greater liberty in politics and the market economy, working- and middle-class African Americans began to publicly denounce junkies, muggers, and "hoodlums" for endangering their security and assaulting their consumers' republic. Ensconced within the safety of their racial position, middle-class white officials and experts did not suffer the same indignities, and, as a result, their values remained geared toward reform rather than removal.[19]

As drug addiction and crime increased, members of the state's issue network continued to push rehabilitation. In April 1965 the Community Council of Greater New York reaffirmed its belief in a medical approach, telling the Mayor's Temporary Commission on Narcotics Addiction, "The addict should be recognized as a sick person suffering from a treatable illness." A representative from the Jewish Board of Guardians suggested modifying all laws that "would interfere in the carrying out of a concept of narcotic addiction as an illness to be treated." That same year, the state senate's Committee on Mental Hygiene held a daylong hearing in the city. Witnesses included mostly medical professionals, law enforcement officials, and public health officials. Reverend Dempsey also testified. Earlier that month he had sent the committee a letter requesting that he be allowed to "testify on various aspects of narcotics addiction and treatment and proposals for state legislation." His appearance notwithstanding, the final report sounded nothing like him. Instead, it captured the prevailing views of the state's issue network. Senator Manfred Ohrenstein, a Democrat from Manhattan, the committee's chairman, attributed rising addiction to the inherent flaws of punitive approaches: "To date the primary attack on this problem has been to treat addiction as a crime and to jail the violators. The continued rise in addiction is the best proof that this method of containing addiction has been a failure." He added, "We have made a small start in this State toward treating the addict as a medical problem. I am convinced, however, that the inroads made by our present programs are miniscule [sic] when compared to the overall problem." Consequently, the report advocated supporting and expanding experimental projects and increasing the resources for existing rehabilitative services.[20]

In the immediate aftermath of Metcalf-Volker, drug policy development in New York State proceeded as it had during much of the 1950s. Committed to rehabilitation yet constrained by limited capacity, the issue network secured only modest policy victories. On the advice of the Department of Mental Hygiene, the Bar Association of New York City, and other members of this issue network, the governor established an experimental drug maintenance program. After witnesses testified about the growing use of barbiturate and amphetamine drugs among white teenagers to the senate's Committee on Mental Hygiene, Rockefeller signed a bill regulating the possession and sale of these drugs. Mounting public concern about drugs and crime, however, did not culminate in harsher sentences. Although the legislature passed several bills ratcheting up penalties for various offenses, members of the state's issue network, especially local law enforcement officials, continued to hold sway over revisions in the penal code. Civic groups like the Community Service Society opposed more punishment on principle, and the city's law enforcement community, including the

New York Police Department, prosecutors, and judges, opposed excessively punitive criminal sentences they deemed unworkable or burdensome on the operation of criminal justice agencies. In several instances, Rockefeller deferred to officials in New York City and civic associations and vetoed the bills.[21]

As in the 1950s, the legislature of the 1960s, constrained by capacity limitations, responded to popular demands for action by establishing an investigatory panel: the Joint Legislative Committee on Narcotic and Drug Addiction. Like commissions and committees before it, this panel held hearings across the state. But unlike previous fact-finding bodies, this committee heard from working- and middle-class African Americans. On December 6 the joint committee listened to thirteen witnesses at Harlem's Union Baptist Church, including Reverend Dempsey and Mark Southall. Activists elevated an alternative frame for the state's narcotics problem. Dempsey said that over the course of his twenty-year antidrug crusade state and city officials had failed to end "this monstrous evil, drug addiction." He testified, "Thousands of people in our community are afraid to go to work in the morning and they are afraid to return to their homes at night. They never know if they will return to their humble apartments and find the valuables they left behind still intact." In contrast, Dr. Donald B. Louria, chairman of the New York State Council on Drug Addiction, said that medical professionals, public officials, and law enforcement agencies "all agree that the addict is a sick person—there may be some disagreement as to the nature of the underlying illness but there is complete consensus that the addict is sick and deserves treatment." While Harlemites deployed a language of risk, members of the issue network continued to advance a discourse of clinical diagnosis. While Louria drew attention to the sickness of drug users, Dempsey drew attention to the plight of the community, injecting a new, indigenously constructed frame into this debate. Despite the consensus behind Louria's approach, Dempsey's frame created a crucial opportunity for elected officials in New York State who felt pressured to enact significant narcotics control legislation and confront crime.[22]

With the 1966 election approaching and the public clamoring for major action against drugs and crime, Rockefeller needed to act. After the passage of Metcalf-Volker and his reelection in 1962, the governor had shied away from enacting another major narcotics control program. Like governors before him, Rockefeller, faced with significant resource limitations, constantly stressed the need for federal intervention. In January 1965 he declared, "We must intensify our State efforts, while continuing to urge the President and Congress to assume the Federal Government's fair share of this responsibility." Finding an avenue for federal action, he added, "Certainly, addiction is both a cause and result of poverty and, as such, should be given major attention in the Federal Anti-Poverty programs." During an interview with Albany's WTEN-TV in September 1965, the governor was asked, "[A]re you going to recommend a bigger budget next year for the problem of narcotics?" Rockefeller immediately responded, "Well, I have recommended [that the] Federal government . . . do [its] job. . . . They haven't been able to stop it coming into the country." The politics of 1966, however, would require more from the governor than blame avoidance. The 1965 mayoral election in New York City served an agenda-setting role, as drug addiction was a central issue in the campaign. Additionally, Abraham Beame, the Democratic candidate, endorsed a medical approach. The talking points for the Democratic ticket of Beame, Frank O'Connor, and Mario Procaccino described the narcotics problem as first and foremost a medical problem: "Addicts are treated as criminals—they should be treated as SICK PEOPLE." The ticket's policy proposals followed this logic, including setting up treatment centers in every borough. Not to be outdone, John V. Lindsay, the Republican candidate, called for a comprehensive strategy: "While Abraham Beame . . . was calling for a hospital-based drug maintenance program, John Lindsay was calling for a broader attack, not only on pushers and addicts but on the social conditions which breed addiction."[23]

In search of a bold program to distinguish his campaign from any potential Democratic challenge and to show his commitment to solving the problem of drugs and crime, Rockefeller's aides reached into the "policy primeval soup" for a viable solution, and the governor searched for a causal story to justify his solution. In terms of the former, the governor's staff readied legislation modeled after the 1961 California antidrug measure, which had been garnering positive attention. The law permitted the involuntary confinement of addicts and allowed, after a period of six months, for addicts to be moved to outpatient status. As such, it removed drug users from streets and provided them with medical services. In terms of the causal story, working- and middle-class African Americans—in telegrams, petitions, and forums—supplied Governor Rockefeller a rationale for involuntary commitment. In 1965, at a public meeting with the governor at Harlem's Salem Methodist Church, members of the community "told him like it is." The audience included Rev. David Licorish of the Abyssinian Baptist Church and Dr. M. Moran Weston of St. Philip's Episcopal Church. Rockefeller asked Weston, "Would you feel people would accept the isolation of addicts together with training to prepare them to come back?" Moran replied that he could not speak for others, but he "personally felt hospitalization to withdraw addicts from drugs and training them in skills once they've been treated would be helpful." Weston, who, as head of the Health Committee of the Harlem Neighborhoods Association, supported bringing public health resources to the community to help addicts in 1961, now supported their "isolation" from the community and advised the governor to take this course of action. Thus involuntary commitment as a policy idea existed at the nexus of the experiences and values of working- and middle-class African Americans and the electoral interests of Governor Rockefeller.[24]

In his annual message to the legislature in January 1966, Rockefeller outlined a dramatic new approach that spoke to the experiences and desires of working- and middle-class African Americans: "We must remove narcotics pushers from the streets, the parks and the school yards of our cities and suburbs. I shall propose stiffer, mandatory prison sentences for these men without conscience who wreck the lives of innocent youngsters for profit. Society has no worse enemy. . . . Narcotics addicts are said to be responsible for one-half the crimes committed in New York City alone—and their evil contagion is spreading into the suburbs." Rockefeller also disclosed that he would recommend "legislation to act decisively in removing pushers from the streets and placing addicts in new and expanded state facilities for effective treatment, rehabilitation, and after care." In February 1966 he unveiled his proposals in a speech, entitled "War on Crime and Narcotics Addiction: A Campaign for Human Renewal." He began by saying that drug addiction "is at the heart of the crime problem in New York State. Narcotics addicts are responsible for one-half of the crimes committed in New York City alone—and their evil contagion is spreading into the suburbs." Although the speech acknowledged that drug addiction had invaded "the split-level homes as well as the coldwater tenements," the speech focused more on the drug problem in "the coldwater tenements." Rockefeller's address mostly voiced the anxieties of working- and middle-class Harlemites. Two key passages reveal as much. Toward the beginning of the speech, Rockefeller declared, "Our citizens should not have to live in uncertainty and fear. They should be able to count on the security of their persons and property. They are entitled to expect their communities, streets, parks, places of business, and homes to be safe from criminals." At the

beginning of the section entitled "The Challenge: Crime and Narcotics," the governor stated:

> Addiction spreads through a neighborhood like a virulent
> infection. Its unfortunate victims, prisoners of a relentless
> craving, lure the weak into the habit in order to help obtain
> drugs for themselves. With this infection comes crime—theft,
> burglary, mugging, prostitution, assault and murder. A des-
> perate addict will steal, attack, and even kill to get money for
> drugs or the drug itself. Thus many of our urban streets, parks,
> school yards, playgrounds and subways have become unsafe
> at night. Even in broad daylight, they are often the hunting
> grounds for pushers of narcotics.

Rockefeller took this message into the 1966 campaign. He claimed
that his Democratic opponent's election would mean that "narcotics addicts would continue to be free to roam the streets: to
mug, to purse snatch, to steal, and even to murder." In 1962 Rockefeller took his cues from the state's issue network and allied civic
associations and newspapers, but electoral pressures and public
sentiment forced him to search for a new solution.[25]

Many African Americans welcomed Rockefeller's strategy. The
Amsterdam News claimed that the new program was a direct response to the city's black community. It reported that the new proposals were stirred "by [Governor Rockefeller's] recent meeting
with Harlem officials and a follow-up closed session with an influential group of Negro leaders." Not surprisingly, the newspaper was
elated and filled an editorial with a variety of felicitations: "We congratulate Governor Rockefeller"; "We agree wholeheartedly with
the Governor"; and "We pledge our support!" The rest of the editorial betrayed the paper's real motivations and class-based biases. In
terms of the former, the paper proclaimed, "We are for any move
that will take addicts off of the streets and subject them to treatment

and aftercare supervision." Thus, while it endorsed a medical approach, removing drug users was an important, if not primary, concern. In terms of the latter, the newspaper, unlike Randolph's Emergency Committee, did not believe the "crippling" problem of drug addiction and the "misery" it precipitated yoked the fate of working- and middle-class African Americans to the fate of the urban black poor. Instead, it found common cause with others: "We believe New Yorkers from the split level homes to the cold water tenements will join the governor in his fight against narcotics addiction."[26]

The joint meeting of the members of the Abyssinian Baptist Church and St. Philip's Episcopal Church at which Reverend Weston counseled the governor to adopt compulsory commitment signified the class-based origins of the antidrug politics of Harlemites. These were no ordinary churches. "Throughout the nineteenth century," Gilbert Osofsky wrote in 1966, "St. Philip's was reputed to be the most exclusive Negro church in New York City. . . . Its members were considered 'the better element of colored people.' . . . This reputation as a fashionable institution made membership in St. Philip's a sign of social recognition. . . . St. Philip's was also recognized as the 'wealthiest Negro church in the country,' and this recognition has continued to the present day." Not only was the "Mighty Abyssinian" one of the largest Protestant congregations in the nation by the 1940s and the religious home for many prominent African Americans, but it also operated as an organizational center for civil rights activism in New York. Even though it served as one of the most significant institutions in Harlem, it did not cater to the black bourgeoisie. Instead, it welcomed migrants from the South as well as other elements of Harlem's working class. Thus this meeting signaled the emergence of a new status group that joined Harlem's working class and "better element" and that was formed in response to the common threat posed by junkies and pushers.[27]

By 1966 the number of minority members of the state legislature had reached an all-time high of twelve, and they made their positions known on this issue. Some were wary of Rockefeller's legislation, but even in their resistance they affirmed the indigenous African American causal story animating the new policy. Addressing his white colleagues, Senator William C. Thompson from Bedford-Stuyvesant said, "[F]or most of you gentlemen who do not know a drug addict, I have seen more of them than you will in your lifetime because part of the heart of drug addiction is in my community." He told them that he was not "taking the civil libertarian view." Instead, he criticized the legislation for not immediately appropriating funds to set up the program. Thompson voted for the bill. Harlem's state senator Basil Paterson, after discussing his concerns about the potential indiscriminate labeling of people as addicts, affirmed his support for a vigorous legislative response to the growing drug and crime problem: "I am seeking legislation because . . . I represent Harlem and East Harlem . . . and I venture to say, after a conference with the Borough commander this morning, that there is no doubt I represent the area of greatest addiction; and I might part with some people when I say I am not concerned about some of the compulsory elements of this bill. I am not." Representing his community, he told the senate about the indigenous mobilization against drug addiction and trafficking: "Ever since I knew this bill was coming out, I have been going throughout my district; and I would tell some of you men, if you have not had the experience, it is an interesting thing to go to a parent association meeting and find them getting reports from a narcotics patrol captain. This is throughout many of the areas I represent. They have a problem." Explaining how drug users had assaulted the consumers' republic, Paterson said, "You find barber shops where they have to take the equipment out every evening at eight o'clock so as to prevent it from being stolen by addicts; bars that you find bolted at ten thirty at night." Finally, describing the terror drug users fomented, he stated, "People are afraid to venture into the streets or even into their own corridors of their own building, their homes being their castles." During his critique of the legislation, Paterson gave voice to the grievances of working- and middle-class Harlemites and elevated the indigenously constructed frame that defined the rationale for Rockefeller's new strategy.[28]

Some African American leaders dissented. "The Governor calls this human renewal. . . . I call it human removal," Percy Sutton, Harlem assemblyman and former member of Randolph's Emergency Committee, remarked during the debate in the Assembly. Sutton, however, responded very differently at an emergency community meeting on a slate of recent burglaries of businesses along 135th and 145th Streets. The burglaries as well as everyday street crime had terrified and enraged the neighborhood. For example, George Ellis of Degeorge Ladies', Men's, and Children's Wear had been attacked twice near his store and had been robbed in January. Ellis sent letters to the police commissioner and the *New York Times* pleading, "Help! Help! Help! Day and night we are at the mercy of the hoodlums that infest our streets. The shops and offices have to operate with doors locked, and opened only to known customers." He explained, "The trouble here is the junkies and hoodlums think they are over and above the law." This was the dominant sentiment expressed at the meeting. Attended by ninety people, including residents, black politicians, police officers, and representatives of the mayor's office, the meeting began with Assemblyman Mark T. Southall reading a prepared statement that said in part, "This is an emergency situation. All the well-intentioned discussions of the deprivations and poverty existing in Harlem cannot condone the actions of these petty thieves, punks, and gangsters." Referencing black success and rejecting structural explanations for crime, he continued, "It is time we face reality that from these very same conditions of Harlem have come many [fine] leaders, lawyers, judges, doctors, teachers, performers, businessmen." Embracing punitive solutions, Southall declared, "We urge the maximum punishment for every criminal apprehended and convicted until this crime wave has been completely terminated." Reverend Dempsey attributed the burglaries to the community's narcotics problem and said that many shops had to go out of business because they had become prey for "thugs." Sutton espoused the punitive attitudes of many of the speakers and the assembled crowd: "There is no civil rights action involved. . . . Black criminals are preying on black merchants. We need effective law enforcement." It is quite plausible that Sutton, who harbored broader political ambitions that required the support of New York's white liberal elite, crafted his rhetoric during the Assembly debate on involuntary commitment in a manner that would benefit his particular interests. It is also possible that he genuinely distinguished between "black criminals" and drug users. Either way, his statements before the Assembly did not reflect the views of working- and middle-class black Harlemites. Neither many of his black peers in the legislature nor most of his constituents were civil libertarians on this issue.[29]

White liberals and many white reform-minded Democrats tried to defeat the bill. Richard Kuh, one of the drafters of Metcalf-Volker who had retired as an assistant district attorney, called the "unbridled discretion" given to judges one of the law's "major defects." He said that the governor's proposal scrapped "the Metcalf-Volker Law without real effort." Ephraim S. London, chairman of the New York Civil Liberties Union, said his organization would mount a legal challenge to the program because involuntary commitment "violates all of our concepts of civil liberties." The NYCLU also urged legislators to end criminal penalties for possession of "small" amounts of drugs because these laws violated the constitutional prohibition against cruel and unusual punishment. In the senate, critics of the program offered three amendments. Senator Ohrenstein, who said that "there is no evidence that compulsory treatment would work" and who had succeeded in getting the legislature to establish a methadone maintenance program, introduced an amendment that would have removed involuntary commitment. Senator Thompson proposed an amendment that would have appropriated $5 million for research on drug maintenance. Senator Whitney North Seymour Jr. proposed an amendment that would have made compulsory commitment conditional on the finding that the individual could have been cured. All of them were defeated by voice vote. The involuntary commitment passed the Republican-controlled senate overwhelmingly, fifty-nine to three. The bill followed the same trajectory in the Assembly, where liberal reform-minded Democrats tried to amend the legislation but were soundly defeated, and it passed the Democratic-controlled Assembly 151 to 7.[30]

In order to appreciate this staggering legislative success for such a controversial proposal, it is important to explore how the governor's aides, in consultation with vested interests, designed a bill that would maximize support. During the 1950s the state's narcotics issue network, based in New York City, drove state drug policy development. Because of the growing attentiveness of suburban and upstate publics to this issue and because of his abiding political ambitions, Rockefeller, unlike his predecessors, took a keen interest in this policy arena and his office assumed responsibility for formulating and implementing narcotics control policies. Consequently, the center of gravity for drug policymaking in New York State shifted from the issue network to the Rockefeller administration. This was not particularly unusual for the governor, whose office drove much policymaking during his tenure: "[o]nly after priorities were largely decided and announced in the governor's annual message were legislative leaders advised of his program and their comments sought."[31]

This venue shift meant that during critical elections the conceptual foundation of narcotics control policy was tied to Rockefeller's political interests and the specific structure the policy assumed was contingent upon the interests and ideas of other powerbrokers within the legislature, the issue network, and interest groups. While involuntary commitment was a product of an indigenous causal story and the political exigencies of the governor, the interests and ideas of members of the issue network and legislative leadership shaped the design of the actual program. Like Senator Metcalf during the drafting of Metcalf-Volker, aides in Rockefeller's office, attuned to policy constraints, shepherded the new program to final approval by designing it in a manner that would garner the most support while achieving the governor's political objectives. The law established the Narcotics Addiction Control Commission (NACC) in the Department of Mental Hygiene "with general powers to conduct the narcotic addiction program." At the end of 1965, the joint legislative committee proposed a dramatic reorganization of the state's narcotics control bureaucracy because current agencies "operated under divided authority." The idea was born out of the failures of Metcalf-Volker. In 1964 Kuh, one of its drafters, said that "no new statutes were needed. What was needed . . . was more imagination and more funds." And, according to him, bureaucrats charged with the law's execution lacked dedication: "When, in 1963, half a million dollars was lopped from its budget, representing one hundred to-be-added beds, Mental Hygiene made no effort to dramatize its plight in order to get public support for restoring those funds." Kuh also criticized the commissioner of the department for not formulating a comprehensive anti-addiction plan that integrated and focused programs spread across various state agencies, which the law empowered him to do. Kuh observed, "No such plan has, as yet, been unveiled. All agencies in the state continue to pursue their own separate paths, without any over all unified aim or design." Given the importance of this idea to several members of the issue network as well as to the leadership in the legislature, the governor's office wisely incorporated it into their final plan.[32]

The policy's design split the issue network, dividing law enforcement officials and reformist civic associations and creating fissures among civic groups. In its report on New York's narcotics problem, the state Commission of Investigation recommended that "[m]inimum and maximum sentences upon conviction for sale of narcotics drugs and possession of narcotics drugs with intent to sell be substantially increased." But the final legislation on drug sentences featured moderate increases, following the more judicious appraisals of the law enforcement community. Moreover, because of the rehabilitation element, district attorneys backed the proposal. Speaking at a meeting of the State District Attorneys Association, Frank S. Hogan said that the governor's proposal "is massive and . . . really addresses itself to this sickness." The involuntary commitment bill authorized the Narcotics Addiction Control Commission to "conduct research and aftercare programs in contrast with private and municipal narcotics addiction treatment facilities." Accordingly, under the new law voluntary agencies that operated rehabilitation and aftercare programs would be able to receive state funds for their services. While this provision was not enough to secure the support of the New York City chapter of the National Association of Social Workers, it managed to gain the support of groups like the Community Service Society of New York, which represented agencies that would have benefited from the law. Additionally, the city was able to benefit from funds controlled by the commission. This is not surprising given that the details of the program were finalized in a series of meetings with Mayor Lindsay's aides. With the passage of the program, the mayor now had the ability to implement his own antidrug strategy. Consequently, Lindsay, who had campaigned the previous year on a more progressive strategy, endorsed the program, and when Rockefeller signed the bill into law, Lindsay congratulated him on "this important piece of legislation" and pledged "full cooperation."[33]

As with Metcalf-Volker, capacity was also a constraint on the political viability of Rockefeller's new program, as the program required the construction of new facilities. Financing such an effort had always been a formidable political barrier, but the governor, who attributed the lack of a program to the lack of sufficient resources in 1965, found ways to pay for one in 1966. The legislation appropriated $6 million for the formation of the commission and $75 million for the construction of new facilities, but none of the money was provided for in the governor's budget. To fund this program, Rockefeller had planned to request $6 million in a supplemented budget near the end of the legislative session. The governor, who had been opposed to relying on uncertain federal support in 1962, said that he had spoken with President Lyndon B. Johnson and was "confident" that "we will get support for aspects of the program." Therefore very few resources would be immediately expended on the problem. Because of this, Senator Thompson called the legislation an "$81 million fraud." However, this "fraud" conditioned the successful passage of the governor's new program.[34]

"MY [PRINCIPAL] FEAR ABOUT THIS BILL," DR. HERBERT BERGER, a narcotics expert with the New York State Medical Society, wrote Governor Rockefeller about Metcalf-Volker in 1962, "is that when it has failed to solve the narcotic problem (and I sincerely believe that this is the inevitable result) then the advocates of ever more punitive action against these sick people will cry, 'We have tried humane methods and they do not work.'" In 1962 white reformers and liberal politicians scored a significant win for penal welfarism. Yet it was a pyrrhic victory, for it was a hollow policy. The lack of funding and insufficient leadership undermined the success of the celebrated new drug program outlined in Metcalf-Volker. The state did not make sufficient hospital space available to meet the need, and most of the drug addicts committed under the program left treatment because of the inadequacy of rehabilitation resources.[35]

The failure of this monumental liberal policy placed white middle-class reformers and liberal politicians on a collision course with working- and middle-class African Americans. Both groups provided contrasting theories for the state's heroin epidemic. The precipitous rise in drug addiction was not lost on the coterie of medical professionals, law enforcement officials, public health bureaucrats, and civic leaders who guided drug policy development and administration in the state during the 1950s. They faced this problem by retreating to the confines of their progressive ideology. They relied on scientific evidence and reformist ideals and tried to secure more resources for existing rehabilitative programs and new experimental treatments. While many white liberals viewed drug addiction in terms of the available scientific evidence, working- and middle-class African Americans understood the problem viscerally. They linked drug addiction and crime and resisted structural explanations for both.

Of course, there were alternative voices within the community. A. Philip Randolph's Emergency Committee stressed racism and joblessness and found common cause with drug users. However, this and similar efforts were short-lived and did not represent the prevailing attitudes of Harlem's working and middle classes. Drugs and crime had reconstructed class categories within black neighborhoods in New York. Shared insecurity precipitated the formation of a new class-based status group that did not, like Randolph's Emergency Committee, consider junkies part of their community and found common cause with working- and middle-class whites. Furthermore, while Randolph and others turned their attention to the national civil rights struggle, Reverend Dempsey and others pressed on with their antidrug, anticrime crusade. They met the astonishing rise in drug addiction and related crimes with adamant candor. Isolated from the state's narcotics control network during the 1950s, Dempsey and other activists and residents mobilized aggressively to tell elected leaders, law enforcement officials, and bureaucrats about Harlem's drug and crime problems and to effectuate change during the early 1960s. They insisted that their narcotics problem required the removal of drug addicts from the streets of Harlem. At private meetings and public hearings, they urged the mayor, the governor, and the president of the United States to take addicts from their community and place them in isolated camps. Many residents and activists tempered their proposals by suggesting that addicts deserved treatment, rehabilitation, and job training, but these proposals first demanded their removal.

During the 1950s white reformers and liberal politicians were able to withstand popular and societal pressures as they implemented and reworked narcotics control policy. They developed policies that were defined by their own middle-class morality, expertise, and institutional position. In fact, they ignored the advice of powerful federal officials like Harry J. Anslinger and successfully beat back attempts to impose the federal consensus on New York. But this time was different. Rising crime rates and rates of drug addiction created a more "attentive public" on these issues and, as a result, politicized drug policy more than it was politicized during the 1950s. In 1966 growing public concern emanating from both white and black neighborhoods meant that politicians could not afford to simply defer to experts, bureaucrats, and policy activists. Because of this attention, Rockefeller and his office joined the fight over narcotics control policy in this state, and they pursued a policy that would further the political interests of the governor. Because 1966 was an election year, Rockefeller could no longer rely on piecemeal solutions, symbolic actions, and empty calls for federal intervention. Enacting a program that included rehabilitation and took addicts off the streets threaded the needle. This approach also worked for many legislators. They too felt the need to pass bold anticrime legislation. And Democrats could point to the rehabilitative component as a win for their preferred approach to the narcotics problem. Many African American politicians who knew that the program constituted human removal appreciated the anger and electoral pressures in their districts. Like other Democrats, they pointed to the rehabilitative features to assuage their own ideological discomfort.

In many ways, this story is Capra-esque. The role that Dempsey and other working- and middle-class activists in Harlem played in the enactment of involuntary commitment in New York State is an exhilarating tale about the triumph of the everyman over entrenched interests—in this instance, the entrenched power of the predominantly white issue network that engineered drug policy for well over a decade. Yet this policy moment inspires none of the warm sentiment and feel-good reverberations that define Capra's classic yarns, as it is also a harrowing tale about an assault on the downtrodden and despised. Working- and middle-class African Americans fulfilled their democratic responsibilities and drug addicts lost their rights. But this narrative, marked by such perplexing duality, did not end here. It had only just begun.

4

Crime, Class, and Conflict in the Ghetto

IN 1970 DANIEL PATRICK MOYNIHAN PROCLAIMED, "There is a silent black majority as well as a white one." About this "silent black majority," Moynihan, in a memorandum to President Richard Nixon, wrote, "It is politically moderate (on issues other than racial equality) and shares most of the concerns of its white counterpart." The "stable elements"—the "silent black majority"—had been "generally ignored by the Government and the media." "The more recognition we can give it, the better off we shall all be," he insisted. This memorandum updated the analysis that appeared in Moynihan's controversial *The Negro Family: The Case for National Action* in 1965. At that time he warned, "The evidence—not final, but powerfully persuasive—is that the Negro family in the urban ghettos is crumbling. A middle-class group has managed to save itself, but for the vast numbers of the unskilled, poorly educated city working class the fabric of conventional social relationships has all but disintegrated." By 1970 the Nixon aide had found cause for optimism and apprehension. In terms of the former, he asserted, "In quantitative terms, which are reliable, the American Negro is making extraordinary progress." In terms of the latter, he reiterated the devastating force of the "tangle of pathologies" he discovered in 1965, writing, "The incidence of anti-social behavior among young black males continues to be extraordinarily high. Apart from white racial attitudes, this is the biggest problem black Americans face, and in part it helps shape white racial attitudes." Moynihan stumbled across another disconcerting trend: "Black Americans injure one another. Because blacks live in *de facto* segregated neighborhoods, and go to *de facto* segregated neighborhoods, the socially stable elements of the black population cannot escape the socially pathological ones. Routinely their children get caught up in the anti-social patterns of the others." Essentially, a "tangle" of social forces—including racial advances, racial segregation, black underemployment, and the breakdown of the family—placed the "silent black majority" into intense contact and conflict with the urban black poor. The instability fostered by the "anti-social" behavior of the urban black poor posed a serious threat to the children and life chances of working- and middle-class African Americans, the "stable element."[1]

Undeniably Moynihan's reflections should be treated with some skepticism. In fact, a cross-racial group of influential civil rights leaders, including Kenneth B. Clark, Dorothy Height, and Whitney M. Young Jr., derided the memorandum for minimizing persisting racism and for advocating a period of "benign neglect" on racial matters. They scolded Moynihan for claiming that "America's Negro population has achieved 'enormous gains' and made 'extraordinary progress' in the last two decades." Attempting to repair Moynihan's allegedly faulty history, they explained, "These gains have been significant, but they have not been monumental. Nor have they brought equality to black people." At the same time, the blistering missive never explicitly protested the questionable moniker Moynihan conferred upon the black middle class—a peculiar response given the inimical reactionary politics of the white "silent majority."[2]

Charles V. Hamilton, an African American political scientist, remained dubious, to say the least. He found the appellation wanting. In response to the controversy, Hamilton penned an essay that asked, "Is there a 'silent black majority'?" His answer pointedly contradicted Moynihan's assessment. After describing the racially conscious lifestyles and political views of "black people who drive buses, work in the post office, on an assembly line, in stores and factories, in gas stations, as shipping clerks," Hamilton averred, "If this a 'silent black majority,' it is not to be confused with the connotations of the 'silent white majority.'" The term "silent white majority" implied "conservatism on racial and economic matters," support for the Nixon administration's Vietnam policy, support for "our police," and "'being fed up to here' with the 'riots' and campus disturbances."[3]

Not satisfied with painting the differences between the silent majorities in broad strokes, Hamilton, an expert on black politics, refined his own portrait of the black variant. He deconstructed the "silent majority" concept and delineated the ways the "silent black majority," to the extent such a phenomenon even existed, varied from its white analogue. Hamilton claimed, "[Members of the silent black majority] believe it is better to work than to be on welfare, but they do not believe that most welfare recipients are freeloaders. Some came from a welfare background, and many still have friends and acquaintances who are recipients. They condemn fathers who desert their children, and, interestingly, are generally unsympathetic to the position that economic conditions forced the father out of the home." Articulating an early precursor to arguments about "linked fate," Hamilton argued that working- and middle-class African Americans did not reject social welfare policies because they appreciated the plight of the urban black poor. While acknowledging the moral regard the black silent majority held for work and the opprobrium they heaped on fatherless households, he argued that their personal experience with poverty—whether because it was in their recent past or in their family—sustained their support for liberalism.[4]

Hamilton's discussion of crime is particularly noteworthy. He also viewed African American attitudes toward policing through a "linked-fate" lens. To the black silent majority, "[t]he police are not pigs, but neither are they seen as dedicated protectors of the black community. [Members of the silent black majority] are as concerned about 'crime in the streets' as any middle-class person, and they want effective measures taken to combat it. But they want police protection, not police persecution, and because they believe the incidence of the latter is greater than [the] former, they believe the present law-enforcement systems must be viewed suspiciously, rather than optimistically." Hamilton does not deny the black middle-class embrace of law enforcement. That working- and middle-class African Americans were concerned about crime was neither controversial nor surprising. But he situated this concern within a broader history of police corruption and brutality and posited that working- and middle-class African Americans considered persecution a greater threat than crime in the streets. Consequently, these considerations fostered profound mistrust rather than unconditional support. The police were never "our police."

Not everyone shared Hamilton's perspective. In 1972 Bill Webster, an African American assistant superintendant of the Oakland Unified School District, published *One by One,* a novel that, according to Webster, depicted "the frustrating dilemma of the Black middle class and its confusion resulting from heightened militancy among Blacks." The story revolves about the trial of Vernoon Peel, a young black militant accused of murdering three white policemen and represented by a white liberal attorney. An African American assistant district attorney, Benjamin Waddell, the novel's protagonist, is selected to prosecute Peel. Waddell is unquestionably conflicted: he fears he is being used as a pawn in the highly publicized trial but also decries the tactics of black militants, and he understands Peel's rage but deplores Peel's moral code. Referencing this tension in an interview about the book, Webster said, "The Black middle class is caught between two diametrically opposed value systems. The militant is rejecting white middle class values while the silent majority of Black people are aspiring toward those same values. While they empathize and support the activists, they don't want to be sacrificial lambs."[5]

The story follows Waddell as he tries to navigate these racial, ideological, and moral tensions—as he tries to find his own voice. And, in the end, he does. Waddell tells the jury, "I can *understand* the *possible* events which created a Vernon Peel—a cop killer." Then he says, "This country has had enough madness, what with the riots of recent years, student turmoil and the Vietnam war. Men, unlike animals, must have some all-encompassing parameter by which [they] govern themselves, and such a yardstick must be enforced without compromise." Waddell and Peel, as the novel shows, have similar personal histories, similar reasons to be disenchanted and angry. But they make different choices, hold different values. Accordingly, Webster presents an alternative picture of the black silent majority wherein working- and middle-class blacks are more like their white counterparts than in Hamilton's analysis. While they share a similar history with black militants, they also share the value system and aspirations of the white silent majority.[6]

In his magnum opus, *The Crisis of the Negro Intellectual,* Harold Cruse offered yet another view of the black middle class. Writing in 1967, Cruse, who along with Amiri Baraka founded the Blacks Arts Theater in Harlem, viewed the community's black middle class with suspicion. "The middle classes of Harlem that furnish community leadership," the social critic wrote, "are neither sovereign nor solvent; neither independent nor autonomous. They thrive on the crumbs granted them by the power structure for keeping the unruly masses mollified." Cruse attributed this lack of independence to the reliance of black professionals on white patronage.

Because of this they competed among themselves "over which brand of community uplift is best for soothing the tortured ghetto soul 'twixt Hell on earth and Heavenly hereafter," and they could "be depended upon to rubber-stamp every design the power structure projects to 'redevelop Harlem.'" According to Cruse, the black middle class was, to steal a phrase, full of sound and fury, signifying nothing. With much less scorn, Hamilton formulated a similar explanation for the behavior of black political elites in New York City. Specifically, the political scientist spoke of the existence of a "patron-recipient relationship," wherein community leaders receive resources to operate programs and, as a condition of the receipt of these funds, are prohibited from engaging in partisan political activity. Hamilton argues that this system of exchange did more harm than good because it depoliticized poor black communities and maintained the political status quo.[7]

Given these conflicting conceptions and theories of the black silent majority, questions abound: Was there a black silent majority? If so, what were its origins? What were the core elements of its ideology? How did it relate to the urban black poor? How did it relate to black militants? How did it interpret the "tangle of pathologies" within black communities? How did it understand drug addiction and crime? Did it guard the old penology or endorse the new one? Were its politics authentic or products of power? What did the black silent majority actually signify?

IN ORDER TO DISCERN THE ORIGINS OF THE BLACK SILENT majority, it is important to hear the grievances working- and middle-class African Americans accumulated over the late 1960s and early 1970s. As drug addiction, crime, and urban blight grew unabated, black attitudes continued to exhibit great distress. New York City's black community rated drugs and crime as its top concerns. In November 1971 an aide to U.S. Senator Jacob Javits forwarded him a "progress report" that Representative Charles Rangel mailed to his constituents. In the newsletter, Rangel discussed the results of a recent questionnaire, noting, "There was almost unanimous consent that narcotics is our number one problem, followed by housing and lack of State and City services." In the memorandum that accompanied the document, the aide wrote, "Rangel's survey confirms what you and I already know: drugs and housing are the major issues." In 1973 the *Amsterdam News* and radio station WLIB conducted a poll that asked, "What is the single issue in New York today that Blacks should be more concerned about?" Consistent with the findings of Rangel's survey, about 60 percent listed drug abuse, 58.7 percent listed housing, and 58.3 percent listed education. The residents felt as if they were drowning in an awful confluence of social pathology, insecurity, and visible signs of urban decay. That same year, Louis Harris and Associates, based on their recent survey of Harlem residents, concluded, "The cumulative impact of the feeling of powerlessness, of the feeling that the neighborhood is declining, of the awareness that major problems of crime, drugs, housing and employment exist, and that community services and facilities are, for the most part, inadequate is that a majority of residents do, indeed, feel trapped."[8]

Churches and their parishioners felt trapped. In 1966 Rev. Edward T. Dugan of the Roman Catholic parish of the Resurrection, a mostly black parish of 1,800 people, disclosed that a survey of his parishioners indicated that "the average person had been held up at least once." After attributing the crime problem to "poor junkies," Father Dugan described the situation "as a tragedy for the little people." Many churches reduced the number of nighttime services and activities because "many residents refuse to leave their homes at night." Rev. E. G. Clark, pastor of Harlem's Second Friendship Baptist Church, stated, "Because of the circumstances, 90 per cent of the people refuse to come out at night . . . even on Sunday." Moreover, black churches, despite their sacred place in the community, were not spared. These sanctuaries were frequently compromised and looted: "Burglars broke into Salem Methodist Church . . . and stole 15 typewriters used in a job training program sponsored by the church and Eastern Airlines. They came back two weeks later and stole a tape recorder and a record player. A block away burglars stripped Williams Institutional Methodist Episcopal Church . . . of its public-address system and microphone. . . . Although the church had hired a night watchman, they broke in again and made off with the chancel carpet." Given the centrality of the church to African American social life, this criminal activity affected a large segment of the community, particularly the elderly. In 1966 a small survey of senior citizens in Bedford-Stuyvesant indicated that only 13.3 percent never attended church. Around 40 percent attended regularly, and another 25.2 percent occasionally.[9]

Local businesses found themselves in similar dire circumstances. Crime closed off access to and degraded the quality of the consumers' republic that black entrepreneurs had built. Mrs. Cleo Weber, owner of a beauty parlor, reported that her "shop had been burglarized twice in less than three months." Expressing her own consternation with Harlem's drug and crime problem, Weber said, "You have a little business and you struggle so hard, and you can't even carry your money home at night. . . . And you can't say anything to these people. You're afraid to. They're dangerous." Lou Borders, whose clothing store had been burglarized twelve times in twenty years, said, "That soul brother stuff—you can forget about it." Borders, owner of one of the oldest black stores in Harlem, asked, "How much can a man take?" A small 1972 survey of mostly minority firms in Bedford-Stuyvesant suggests that experiences were quite common. Of the nineteen business owners interviewed, fifteen reported being negatively affected by crime and twelve indicated they had installed security devices to protect their business.

When asked to identify the "main cause" of their troubles, more named addicts than any other factor. A representative from the black-owned Carver Bank interviewed for a different study of Bedford-Stuyvesant conducted in 1970 and 1971 echoed these concerns: "We've noticed the reluctance of many of our customers— especially the older ones—to come in and make deposits in their savings accounts. I've had more than one tell me things like 'It may be only ten dollars, but one of these guys is really hard up, he'd mug you for ten cents.'" The female owner of a small candy and cigarette store in Bedford-Stuyvesant was more blunt: "Whether they're still on a high, or just coming down from one, they're the most dangerous. Why don't I leave? Lady, how old do you think I am? Where would I go?"[10]

All in all, drug addiction and related crimes posed an existential threat to churches, businesses, and civic organizations. Because of racial segregation, these firms and organizations had developed a niche in black communities, but crime had threatened their viability. Not only were they victims of drug addicts, but their members and customers were so afraid of being mugged by junkies that they no longer attended meetings or patronized businesses. In 1965 Philip A. Smith, chairman of East Harlem's Upper Madison Avenue Community Association, wrote Senator Robert F. Kennedy, "We have made repeated complaints to the police and other authorities regarding the rapid increase of addicts coming into and roaming through our neighborhood. . . . People are desperately afraid to walk the streets. As a consequence, houses of worship, community organizations, and adult education centers have noted a sharp decrease in attendance, and our merchants are adversely affected. Crime, indeed, murder, is now a part of daily life." Six years later, the *Amsterdam News* reported that "some sections of the so-called Harlem business section after nightfall [look] like a ghost town. People continue to be afraid to walk the streets at night. Churches, lodges and other fraternal organizations curtail or even discontinue services and meetings." The editorial added, "The Silent Majority of Harlemites who sit by and watch their community be taken over by the criminal elements without taking any kind of stand are simply surrendering to these elements."[11]

Yet "the Silent Majority of Harlemites" did not sit by and watch. They fought. Many advocated for drastic measures. Reverend Clark declared, "We need constant patrolling, but we've begged for patrolmen but we can't get them." "Oh, they come over, but they always leave," he added. James Lawson, head of the United African Nationalist Movement, complained, "They have 360 plainclothes men . . . and 320 of them are on from 8 until 4 and they are out chasing numbers writers, numbers control and small black number bankers. They should be working on narcotics and protecting the individual citizen." He also criticized the courts, saying, "The judge will give a numbers writer six months but someone who robs some poor innocent person gets off with 60 days." Reverend Dempsey, who declared that "[i]t's gotten out of hand," rehashed old complaints and refurbished old proposals: "Take the junkies off the streets and put 'em in camps. . . . Sure, the Civil Liberties Union and the N.A.A.C.P. would howl about violation of constitutional rights. But we've got to end this terror and restore New York to decent people. Instead of fighting all the time for civil rights we should be fighting civil wrongs."[12]

Not everyone embraced this punitive impulse—at least not completely. Andrew Gainer, whose Harlem hardware store had been burglarized fourteen times in two years, advocated a mix of law enforcement and structural solutions. He shouted, "To hell with civil liberties! . . . People are being destroyed by dope and crime every day. Yes, let's bring back the Tactical Police Force. I'd even bring mounted police." At the same time, Gainer stated that he and a group of local business leaders, Harlem Citizens for Safer Streets, would lobby Governor Rockefeller for a program of free narcotics for addicts, a three-year rehabilitation program, and job training.

However, a 1971 survey of Harlem business owners indicates that this was the minority view. The top four proposed solutions for the community's crime problem were punitive: "stricter law enforcement and an improved court system" (21 percent), "more policemen" (16 percent), "take junkies off the street" (9 percent), and "more severe punishment for criminals" (6 percent). In contrast, only 4 percent listed "curb unemployment," and only 2 percent listed "rehabilitation of addicts and criminals." Capturing the smoldering resentment among Harlem's business leaders, the *New York Times* reported, "Harlem's Negro merchants and clergymen, alarmed by what they regard as a rising tide of criminal violence by blacks against blacks, are demanding harsh punitive action. These middle-class Negroes say they want the Tactical Force, a symbol of police brutality to many Harlem residents, assigned to all Harlem precincts." Thus most businesses in Harlem sanctioned only part of Gainer's program. They rejected structural solutions and said, "To hell with civil liberties!"[13]

Caught in the throes of urban decline and social disorganization, working- and middle-class African Americans were under siege and overwrought. Their "respectable" lives, which they had worked so hard to create, were now being jeopardized by ne'er-do-wells stealing their property and accosting their person. These offenses and frequent affronts on houses of worship and businesses nurtured the punitive impulses of working- and middle-class Harlemites. Given the threats that drug addiction and crime posed to working- and middle-class African Americans, many in Harlem and other black neighborhoods in New York City felt they constituted a "silent majority" of decent, law-abiding citizens victimized by the recklessness and immorality of a dangerous minority. They felt imprisoned by drug addicts. And they responded in kind. They now believed policing and prisons—the systematic removal of junkies—represented their own path to salvation. Lou Borders, Mrs. Weber, and others spoke to these complex emotions and evaluations: the sinking feeling that junkies were beyond repair and that society had refused to notice; the firm belief that political institutions had abnegated their responsibilities and that "decent citizens" had become liberalism's sacrificial lamb and criminals had become its cause célèbre; and the ever-present and throbbing sense that enough was enough.

Daily indignities ignited a grassroots movement against crime, a fierce backlash against junkies, pushers, "thugs," and "vagrants." Tired and angry, working- and middle-class African Americans were not afraid to give the governor a piece of their mind. After one visit to Harlem did not go well for the governor, Wyatt Tee Walker, a former aide to Dr. Marin Luther King Jr., informed the governor, "The black community is in a very ugly mood and have some very legitimate reasons for being so. Most of it is despair, and any candidate who comes into their midst will feel the brunt of their venom and hostility." This event was not unique. Rockefeller "was repeatedly confronted with the drug problem by angry residents at his 'town meetings' in black communities." African American ministers frequently charged that "drugs were being openly sold on the streets of Harlem without police interference and demanded action." Before an address at a meeting of the 100 Black Men, Joe Persico warned him, "Questions are expected to deal with drugs[,] crime, black business opportunity . . . government opportunity for blacks." Of course, "government opportunity for blacks" did not encompass the needs and aspirations of the community's poor. Like "black business opportunity," it was a call for more opportunities for mostly middle-class African Americans.[14]

The community's anger was on full display during a town hall meeting Governor Rockefeller held in Harlem in 1967. Attendees mentioned most of the community's pressing problems, including housing, sanitation, and jobs. Crime, however, was clearly the top concern. As Rev. Ivan Moore, pastor of Walker Memorial Baptist Church, put it, "The members of my congregation are afraid. Fear is the worst thing that confronts us." He told the governor, "Twelve years ago I had . . . evening services. This [had to be] curtailed because [of] the snatching [of] pocketbooks and crimes against the parishioners." Moore called for a meeting with city officials, including representatives from the local precinct, because he wanted "to get down to brass tacks" and because the "people of our community, the respectable people, should hear a voice or the voices of our city and our state, stating to them that there is some possibility of handing out some hope for some protection." Comptroller Mario A. Procaccino, a symbol of white backlash in New York City, also attended the meeting and spoke to the community's anxieties. He declared, "The upswing in crime, and particularly crimes of violence, has reached a point where the number one preoccupation of our citizens—yes, even before jobs, housing and education—is the fear for their safety and the safety of their families. Our City has become a city of fear." Then the comptroller proceeded to outline his anticrime strategy. In addition to proposing several innocuous items, such as improving street lighting and creating a system of "police-alarm boxes" similar to fire-alarm boxes, he advocated a very punitive approach. He criticized lenient sentences doled out to juvenile offenders, saying, "Consideration ought not to be given to the young hoodlums who commit crimes of such violence and viciousness as to demonstrate a total disregard for the lives of others." Then he proposed that "the State legislature designate as crimes such acts as the mugging and knifing of victims and assaults with a dangerous weapon, when such acts are perpetrated by anyone over the age of thirteen years of age." Despite the harshness of his views, his comments were "interrupted by applause several times." Others questioned his strategy. Rev. Moran Weston, rector of St. Philip's Church, remarked, "There is no doubt that the pastors who have spoken are correct in what they say—that there is great fear on the part of many people." But, Weston contended, the "basic cause of crime is [pervasive poverty], reaching every area of our life and our community." He maintained that

Procaccino's approach constituted "revenge on young people and adults who are victims of experience." But the available survey evidence indicates that most Harlem residents and businesses sided with Procaccino's approach.[15]

In 1969 a hearing of the State Joint Committee on Crime provided working- and middle-class African Americans another opportunity to voice their frustrations; their testimony exposed the tensions in black anticrime attitudes. Everyone described the challenges in similar terms: "citizens" were being victimized by "junkies." The speakers supplied a variety of theories for the problem: some blamed organized crime, some blamed structural conditions, and some blamed lax law enforcement. Some articulated a mix of behavioral and structural explanations. Senator Paterson "declared that the root causes of crime must be attacked meaningfully. In addition to a poor educational system, unsatisfactory housing and health conditions, and inadequate or no-advancement type jobs (all of which are the status quo in Harlem), a very important root cause of increasing crime is disrespect for the law, its enforcement and its administration. Addicts are everywhere visible and easily identified, but nothing appears to be done." Paterson's remarks underscore the ideological contradictions permeating black opinions: the same people who believed that broader social forces were partly responsible for Harlem's crime problem drew on their class-based morality to hold individuals responsible for Harlem's condition. The first position calls for jobs, social services, and rehabilitation; the second calls for punishment.[16]

Ultimately the immediacy of Harlem's crime problem caused the black silent majority to abjure their progressive sympathies and indulge their conservative instincts. Constant insecurity prompted them to seek, before all else, the removal of the threat—primarily junkies. Assemblyman Hulan Jack's testimony is very illuminating. During the Harlem "crime wave" episode in the early 1940s, Jack downplayed in public and private the neighborhood's crime rates and emphasized the structural roots of juvenile delinquency, saying things like "[S]ociety has denied the youth of Harlem a chance to live as a normal citizen." At the 1969 hearing of the State Joint Committee on Crime, Jack struck a markedly different tone. Similar to his previous statements, he acknowledged that Harlem had become a "breeding ground for crime because of the lack of proper education facilities, the social and economic effects of discrimination, and the pervasive frustration felt by the people." But this time Jack "recommended that the penalty for mugging be raised to life imprisonment because of the mortal danger it poses for victims. Without their drug, narcotics addicts become . . . maniacs." Jack also denounced the leniency of the criminal justice system: "Statistics from the State Department of Correction reveal that [the] prison population has been declining since 1957 while arrests for major crimes have doubled. This, together with the present judicial trend toward granting probation, has resulted in the present problem of approximately 76,000 people, arrested but released, who are roaming the streets repeatedly molesting people." The assemblyman's priority was clear: dislodging the criminal threat. Because of this, Jack castigated officials for allowing individuals to plead to lesser sentences and continued to connect this leniency to petty crimes: "District Attorneys, judges, defense counsel and the Probation Department are all responsible for the increase in guilty pleas to lesser crimes than those charged. This permits defendants to get by with a very light sentence and to very shortly be back on the streets again molesting innocent citizens." Jack also articulated one of the core claims of the black silent majority: the idea that the criminal justice system was aiding guilty criminals instead of protecting "innocent citizens" and, as a result, was partly responsible for the insecurity and chaos—the daily molestations—endured by "decent citizens."[17]

Rev. Oberia Dempsey outside Upper Park Avenue Baptist Church in 1970. (Reprinted with permission from "Blacks Declare War on Dope," Ebony *25, no. 8, June 1970, p. 31. Copyright © 1970 by Johnson Pulishing Co., Inc.)*

For his part, Reverend Dempsey pleaded for the total—though perhaps temporary—expulsion of drug addicts. In order to accomplish this, he proposed a new system that "would permit the state to 'draft' hard core narcotics addicts into health or rehabilitation camps, semi-military in form. Draftees could be housed in barracks or tents and paid $15 per month." The reverend also challenged the collective wisdom of social workers and the medical profession: "[He] rejected the view of many social workers, doctors and psychiatrists that community treatment is preferable. He found that method to be ineffective and wasteful of time and money. With the establishment of camps, addicts (who account for 70 to 90 per cent of Harlem's crime) would be taken out of the environment which has poisoned them, out of contact with the organized crime market." Anticipating opposition from the ACLU and claims about the unconstitutionality of such a plan, Dempsey "insisted that it is a . . . grave unconstitutional situation that allows the addicts to harass innocent citizens and force churches to close at night." Connecting civil rights and aggressive policing, he said, "New York State, having been the first to enact anti-discrimination in housing laws, must now act to prevent organized crime and local hoodlums from destroying society." Like other members of the black silent majority, Dempsey doubted expert knowledge, divided the social world into "criminals" and "innocent citizens," and likened the fight for greater public safety to the fight for civil rights. According to the black silent majority, junkies were putting hard-earned material gains at risk, so dealing aggressively with them would help fulfill the promise of earlier civil rights victories.[18]

Many working- and middle-class African Americans also resented the ways black militants glamorized violence and used racial ties to validate criminal tactics. They found one particular event extremely appalling. In 1972 the Black Liberation Army, in retaliation for the killing of inmates during the prison riot at Attica, assassinated two police officers, one black and one white. Incensed by the tragic event, an anonymous letter to the *Amsterdam News* urged readers to "cast out" those "who call themselves our brothers" and kill police officers. "A liberation army they call themselves. If that were so, why don't they liberate you from the only thing you have to fear, rather than ooze from beneath rocks like low slime and assassinate the only men who have sworn to protect you against all harm." In early 1973 the *Amsterdam News* published "an open letter to the average cop on his beat in our communities." "In a nutshell," the letter stated, "we want you to know that you are not alone when you walk your lonely post in the dark, and we would further like you to know that when it comes to the enforcement of the law, the overwhelming majority of the Black community is standing solidly behind you." The letter's description of the black community, particularly criminals, is telling. The letter asked rhetorically, "Then who are these people who are shooting at me?" The answer: "The poorest player on the team is always the one who is first to shout 'Let's kill the umpire.'"

> And the poorest player on the team in the Black ghetto is the criminal element which refuses to go to work and make a decent living, but instead, chooses to make his living by stealing and robbing others of the fruits of their labor. . . . You thus become the target of the criminal—the hunter—as you go about protecting the rights of the hunted. . . . [We] can tell you that the situation has reached a point where many decent fathers and mothers will applaud you for locking up a member of their own family when they refuse to stay within the bounds of decent society. We restate once again that black people have suffered too long and overcome too much to now allow themselves to be misled by a small group of cold blooded killers seeking to legitimize and romanticize their actions under the banner of "Black Revolutionary Liberation." Be assured the loud mouthed vocal minority on the corners who boo and jeer when you lock up a criminal, are not representative of the hard working people watching from their apartment windows—people who are afraid to come down on the corner for fear of being mugged or robbed. Your support, your backup are the people behind those closed doors who stay off the streets because the streets have too often become the property of hoods. The vast majority of communities want to come back to the streets of Harlem. They want to stroll down the avenues unmolested. They want to attend prayer meetings at night. In short they want to liberate themselves from the jails of their homes.

The *Amsterdam News* subtly appropriated the trope of the silent majority. It claimed to speak on behalf of Harlem's hardworking, moral majority who heretofore had been unknown to the cop as it had been silenced by fear and eclipsed by a lawless minority. Drawing on a class-based morality, the paper described this minority of criminals and militants as people who refuse "to go to work and make a decent living" and who have decided instead to abscond with the "fruits of [the] labor" of the silent majority. Rather than perceiving Harlem's decline as the consequence of larger structural forces and policy failures, the paper viewed the community's problems in terms of class conflict. According to the open letter, life in Harlem had been defined by a contest between the "poorest player on the team" and "decent," "hardworking people"—a war between the "hunter" and "the hunted." The paper also maintained that "the hunter" and "the hood" were not victims of chronic joblessness or racial segregation. Instead, the famed black newspaper argued that "the hunter" and "the hood" simply "refuse to stay within the bounds of decent society." Furthermore, this apologia reconfigures familial lines. Rather than linking the fates of the silent majority and the urban black poor, the *Amsterdam News* cast its lot with the cop. It linked the future of working- and middle-class African Americans not with those seeking "Black Revolutionary Liberation" but with working- and middle-class whites in "split level homes."[19]

What the open letter insinuates with metaphors and symbols the black writer Orde Coombs makes plain in an essay about the "three faces of Harlem" published the following year. These "three faces" included "a growing, but relatively insecure middle class," "a poor, frustrated working class," and "an underclass." "With the advent of [civil rights] laws and a semblance of equal opportunity," he wrote, "the heavy glue of a united front has come up watery." Reflecting on the tensions between middle-class African Americans and the urban black poor, Coombs opined, "The black middle class [has been under attack] for its inability to 'do something' about the marauding bands of black underclass men who, for whatever societal reasons, make life in the cities of this country one of unbearable apprehension. The black middle class can do very little, however, about this group, since its language of exchange is different, its values are different, its priorities are different." The Yale-educated author claimed that progress diversified the interests of the black community. In fact, he argued that racial advances created a material and moral chasm between middle-class African Americans and the urban black poor. Not only were their fates not linked, but, because of their values, they interpreted the world in dramatically different ways. They spoke different languages.[20]

According to Coombs, the black working and middle classes were not just wary of their poorer brethren. They feared them. "These black men and women of achievement stand in terror of an underclass that cannot see methodical achievement on its horizon and despises it in others," he wrote. Coombs depicted Harlem's middle class as the prey of the nihilistic and wicked black poor who fed off their hard work and ransacked their consumers' republic. He argued, "The underclass, released from hoping about a future, lives by its wits and for today only. Everything is to be ripped off. Every person is a potential mark." Adding insult to injury, working- and middle-class African Americans not only had to withstand the insecurity and violence engendered by an audacious minority, but they also had to witness people behaving recklessly and with impunity. All of this, he maintained, tapped the conservative impulses of working-class African Americans:

> [Working-class blacks] are, after all, the ones who must live in the ghetto. They are the ones who, through lack of education and opportunity, cannot take advantage of the [civil rights] gains of the past decade. They are the ones who take the morning train to Scarsdale, who drive taxis, who work as elevator operators or countermen, who see their meager earnings torn apart by inflation, who return home at the end of each wearying day to find their television sets gone or some

new calamity visited upon them. At the core of this black man's festering resentment is his knowledge that some people in his building do not work, yet more than manage to make ends meet. He sees the drug pushers and he knows that the police know who they are. He touches the hustler's "ride," and he understands that he can never call such an expensive piece of steel his own.

While Coombs's strident, cynical perspective speaks more to his own prejudices than the worldviews, experiences, and aspirations of Harlem's poor, it nonetheless voices the anxieties and anger of the black silent majority and lays bare the origins of the working- and middle-class "backlash." The black middle class renounced racial ties and denounced previously held progressive beliefs because they felt under assault by the urban black poor, who, they maintained, rejected the middle-class values of individual responsibility and re- spectability. This threat and its concomitant fear and anger caused the black silent majority to seek out technologies of control.[21]

But this is just New York. If Coombs was right, then working- and middle-class African Americans in cities throughout the country should have expressed similar frustrations. They should have been as angry, as Harlem's experience with drugs and crime was not altogether unique. Black urban neighborhoods across the United States endured greater insecurity during the late 1960s and early 1970s. Based on his analysis of homicide data, Charles Murray concludes, "[I]t was much more dangerous to be black in 1972 than it was in 1965, whereas it was not much more dangerous to be white." Criminal victimization surveys of residents in Chicago, Detroit, Los Angeles, New York City, and Philadelphia reveal rela- tively high rates of victimization for both whites and blacks. Whites in these five cities reported being victims of personal larceny (without contact) at similar or higher rates compared to blacks, but blacks reported also being victims of aggravated assault and robbery (without contact). Moreover, African Americans were primarily victimized by other African Americans.[22]

Survey evidence from cities across the country reveals the intensity of black fears. In a 1969 survey of whites and blacks conducted in Baltimore, over 50 percent of black respondents feared being beaten up, raped, or having their home broken into, while only a little over 30 percent of whites feared they would experience these crimes. Almost 50 percent of black respondents feared being robbed on the street, compared to only 29 percent of whites. Most startling, 37 percent of black respondents feared being murdered, while less than 25 percent of whites expressed this fear. Unsurprisingly, these threats caused both blacks and whites in Baltimore to alter their behavior—blacks more so than whites. Sixty percent of black respondents reported looking over their shoulder when hearing footsteps, and over 50 percent reported "staying home in evening" and "talking to callers through the door."[23]

Survey evidence also exposes the contradictory ideological impulses animating their preferred prescriptions. During the late 1960s and the early 1970s, African Americans in Washington, D.C., were extremely concerned about crime and drug addiction. A 1972 survey of residents, including a sample of inner-city residents living in the Shaw, Stanton Park, Trinidad, and Ivy City neighborhoods, indicated the inner-city residents were more likely than residents in other parts of the capital and suburban residents to list crime as the "most serious" issue facing the nation. Nearly 40 percent of inner-city residents reported that the police were "not tough enough," compared to 29.4 percent of respondents in the rest of the "Beltway" and 33.7 percent of suburban respondents. In this survey, 65 percent of respondents from the suburbs believed that courts were not severe enough, compared to 52 percent of inner-city respondents. In a 1973 poll of Washington residents, 90 percent of respondents described drug addiction as a serious problem, but black respondents expressed a positive view of rehabilitation. The poll also revealed that "blacks were more likely to identify drugs as the most serious problem, to be knowledgeable about existing drug rehabilitation programs, to rate those programs as 'good,' but were less likely to accept addicts as neighbors or coworkers." Responses to the 1970 Black Buyers Survey of 2,000 urban black households further exemplify the contradictions within African American attitudes toward crime. Sizable proportions of respondents approved of both punitive policies and structural solutions. Over 90 percent of respondents said that "better educational opportunities" and "better job opportunities" would be "very helpful" or "somewhat helpful" in curbing the crime problem. At the same time, over 80 percent indicated that "[keeping] offenders off the Street and in jail" would be "very helpful" or "somewhat helpful." A near majority of respondents also endorsed "tougher police policies." How could African Americans hold such inconsistent thoughts? How could they support both punishment and reform?[24]

In order to understand how working- and middle-class African Americans navigated these conflicting ideological impulses, it is important to excavate the indigenous construction of crime. A series of fourteen cartoons depicting "black-on-black crime" published in the *Chicago Defender* in 1974 powerfully illuminates how working- and middle-class African Americans throughout the United States framed the crime problem in their communities. In one, the phrase " 'Brother'HOOD in BLACK COMMUNITIES" and the image of a large menacing figure holding a gun and towering over a group of modest houses reinforces the idea that black communities were being terrorized by black criminals. " 'Brother'HOOD" also mocks the notion of racial solidarity promoted by some leaders at that time and suggests that "hoods" were testing the limits of racial ties. The horror and panic on the face of the black woman in another cartoon portrays the dread that crime fostered in African American neighborhoods. The depiction of the offenders in this second cartoon is also telling: they are drawn like monsters and

Chicago Defender *anticrime editorial cartoons by Chester Commodore, 1974. (Courtesy of the* Chicago Defender.)

they are small, implying the young age of the "hoods" committing "thefts," "rapes," and "murders." The article that accompanied the cartoons profiled the "War on Crime," an initiative sponsored by the Coalition of Concerned Women, and it spoke to the sense of crisis observed in the cartoons: "In recent days, we have all been shocked by crimes of violence that have taken the lives of innocent people. Neither our streets nor our homes are safe any longer. Citizens are attacked in broad daylight. Our children are preyed upon by persons of evil intent. . . . We have become more and more restricted in our coming and going. We are forced to live behind barricades, in constant fear of attack." While acknowledging the problems of police brutality and corruption, the article also emphasized that "[i]t is the duty of the police to give protection and to apprehend offenders" and that "citizens can do much to assist the police, as well as save lives and property by simply reporting suspicious activities to them."[25]

The editorial cartoons and the accompanying article begin to resolve the contradictions found in the Washington polls and the Black Buyers Survey, pointing to three significant factors. First, they reinforce the urgency of the crime threat. Second, they suggest that, despite prior ideological commitments and previous distrust of the police, "risk aversion" caused the black silent majority to select short-term punitive action over long-term structural solutions. Of course, this calculation depends on the framing of losses and gains. For example, if "linked fate" is operative, then the consequences of punitive policies—the mass incarceration of other African Americans—would be understood as losses rather than gains. This leads to the third significant factor: working- and middle-class African Americans conceived of the "black criminal" as the other and, drawing on class-based notions, attributed the actions of the "black criminal" to individual values—"evil intent" and the like. Despite the progressive tradition in African American politics, experiential assessments of crime threats and moral judgments of individual character ultimately determined when black middle-class values were deployed on behalf of punishment or reform.[26]

Editorials published in African American newspapers throughout the United States during this period reveal the ideological repercussions of the severe and daily risks working- and middle-class African Americans endured during the late 1960s and early 1970s. In 1970 the *Atlanta Daily World* published an editorial entitled "Crime Must Be Stopped" after the shooting death of a bank attendant at the Citizen's Trust Company's Hunter Street branch. After describing the incident, the editorial asserted, "It goes hard for the Christian heart to say this, but stiffer measures, all the way up to capital punishment, seem to be the only tangible way to protect that portion of society, which has not fallen under the heels of hardship and become animals. Animals!" It noted, "This bank, which has apparently become a target of hoodlums, and has young female tellers scared out of their wits, has employed numerous black people for years, and is making a major contribution to the cause of advancement in Atlanta." The editorial outlined and defended extreme policy measures: "The only immediate remedy seems to be to crack down hard (forcing an end to police 'slow down'), and withholding soft feeling until all who rob, loot and kill, are removed from society, be it by electric chair or life in prison; be it retaliation at the hands of guards, posted to protect the public." The editorial ended, "This is harsh, but when good citizens must bite the dust repeatedly while in the progressive peace and dignity of law and order, it's time for stronger measures." The *Atlanta Daily World* believed "harsh" solutions, including the death penalty, would prevent "good citizens" from enduring further losses. It clearly did not believe that "good citizens" would suffer from these punitive policies. Rather, "immediate" remedies would cost only individuals who deserved those costs: "Animals!"[27]

The evolving opinions of Renault Robinson, a decorated black police officer and civil rights leader in Chicago, speak to the causal significance of risks. Robinson was no go-along-to-get-along African American activist. He was a fierce opponent of racism within Chicago's police department. In 1968 he founded the Afro-American Patrolmen's League, "an organization aimed at improving police service to the black community and at getting more blacks into policy-making positions in the department." In 1969 Robinson forcefully declared, "We were hired as the white man's assistant in dealing with blacks. . . . But we are a new breed of police and we refuse to be oppressing armies for the Establishment." Not surprisingly, he became "public enemy number one for the [Chicago Police Department]" in the 1970s. Given this résumé, Robinson's extremely conservative essay on crime is quite stunning. No stranger to weighty oratory himself, he mocked sober, scholarly reflections on crime: "One of the faults of the black community is that we have developed a rhetoric which is overly profound. We have learned to be so damned fundamental that we are unable to deal with anything that meets the eye." Questioning the practical relevance of this "fundamental" rhetoric, he stated, "The latest series of meetings held in relation to the killing and injuring of black people by each other is an example of this [phenomenon]. Profuse and detailed commentaries on the socio-economic conditions that lead to crime have been [provided]. Psychological insights into anti-social behavior have been disclosed. . . . But nobody has told us how blacks can, here and now, do something about every black [man, woman, and child] having to be fearful in every black neighborhood in Chicago." Interestingly, Robinson did not reject sociological explanations for crime: "We recognize that poverty, overcrowding and poor education are elements of the bad situation that exists." But this sociology did not offer any immediate solutions for the "wholesale fear by good citizens and [the] tyranny [of] blacks against blacks." Ridiculing liberals, he wrote, "It should be certainly clear to the so-called fundamental thinkers their liberal tolerance of criminal behavior may ease their intellectual middle class consciousness.

However, this foolishness has sentenced the peaceable hard working blacks of the ghetto to a horrible brand of tyranny of hustlers, murderers and extortionists." This urgency and risk aversion caused Robinson to endorse the deployment of brute force: "Some of the things we plan to do shall involve the use of legal, but naked force. We are reluctant to do this but the security crisis in the black community forced this upon us." Robinson's hypocrisy is difficult to digest but easily understood. This staunch opponent of police brutality, corruption, and racism was able to sanction methods he once abhorred because the recipients of this force were in the community but were not of it. For Robinson, class-based morality defined the boundaries of community. His community included "good citizens" and "hard working" people. They were black, for sure, but they were not "hoodlums," "hustlers," "murderers," and "extortionists."[28]

Two editorials in Washington newspapers offer additional insight into these interpretative processes. In December 1972 the *Washington Afro American* published a scorching editorial on crime. It read, "This is the season to be jolly, but to hundreds of District residents it has become a period of fear and apprehension, and in some instances, grave sorrow. Crime is the cause of the dilemma, and it is time responsible citizens began to look at their own city and criminal growth in proper perspective." Placing the crime threat "in proper perspective" meant dismissing structural explanations for crime and emphasizing individual character: "The exceedingly high incidence of housebreakings, pocketbook snatchings, robberies, shoplifting cases and shootings are not simply the outgrowth of bad social conditions. It is time to recognize that basic honesty has a lot to do with it. Honesty begins at home and makes little difference whether or not you are poor, unemployed and whatsoever." "Proper perspective" also meant rebuffing arguments about racism: "It is also time that we stop blaming everybody else for the criminal acts which occur in our neighborhoods. The victims of most of these criminal acts are black, and the instances are by no means racially motivated. . . . [T]he vast majority of these acts are caused by black people, and in the end the whole city, which prides itself on being a Black City . . . suffers." Again, the intensity of the threat and the recasting of the victim sustained and validated black punitive attitudes.[29]

In order to understand why African Americans in Washington and throughout the nation supported rehabilitation while exhibiting little sympathy for drug addicts, one only has to examine the columns of William Raspberry, an African American writer for the *Washington Post*. In 1973 he composed a provocative piece excoriating drug addicts. It began, "There is one piece of the drug-abuse puzzle that hardly anybody wants to handle. It's almost as though we forget that it's there. That is the question: What is wrong with drug addicts?" Raspberry insisted, "All it would take is for the poor schnook on the street to say: No thanks. And *unless* he says no thanks, it is extremely doubtful that any antidrug program will work." Then he stated, "I know it's not nice to call him an idiot, and I do understand that frustration, alienation and pain of various sorts can make you do foolish things. But somehow it has never sounded convincing to me—even when I've said it—that 'conditions' make people turn to dope." After a cursory discussion of scientific evidence, he wrote, "I am fully aware of peculiarly degrading effects of black urban poverty. But I'm also aware that nobody chases anybody else down and jabs a needle into his arm." As expected, this editorial garnered much attention, so much so that he was forced to respond. In a follow-up editorial, he wrote, "It strikes me as potentially very harmful to suggest to people that they are not responsible for their bad choices, and that applies whether the bad choice is dropping out of school, robbing a store or shooting up dope." He also said, "[I]t is important that all of us understand our culpability in social problems in a general sort of way and do what we can to set things right. . . . But it is more important for those who consider ourselves 'victims' of one sort or another to recognize the extent to which we are our own victimizers—and our own hope of salvation." Thus, in the abstract, rehabilitation was consistent with the progressive sensibilities of working- and middle-class African Americans. Yet working- and middle-class African Americans also believed that addiction and the criminal activity it cultivated—these "bad choices"—were choices freely made by bad people.[30]

Black punitive attitudes and the evaluations that produced them were not simply knee-jerk reactions to crime. Rather, they were products of the material and moral context of black class identities and class conflict. Postwar political and economic advances and urban decline produced both full citizens and criminals. These citizens drew on the moral content of indigenous black middle-class status—the politics of respectability maintained and nurtured in churches and civic organizations—to understand the criminal threats and the individuals that perpetrated them. A 1974 "photo editorial" on "black-on-black crime" in *Ebony* clarifies this context. The magazine began by narrating scenes that, the editors believed, had become commonplace in African American communities: "On the South Side of Chicago, a middle-class black man parked his car about half a block from a busy intersection, walked to a mailbox on the corner and was halfway back to his car when he was assaulted by two young men who knocked him down, took his wallet, kicked him and tried to stab him with a knife." Each vignette was described in the same way and betrayed the magazine's class bias by portraying the crimes as a conflict between the middle class and "assassins." Then, after discussing the "misuse of black brotherhood," the magazine ruminated on the "the causes of crime among blacks": "Crimes has always been greater in areas of poverty, and the causes are legion. The poor man struggling to keep his family fed and clothed will sometimes, in desperation, rob a store. But the bulk of crimes are committed by those who are psychologically, outside of society." Next the magazine outlined "what can be done." Implicitly embracing the trope of the silent majority and expressing sentiments shared by the *Amsterdam News'* "open letter to the average cop," it stated, "Within every black ghetto, the good law-abiding and hard working people greatly outnumber those who live outside the law. The law-abiding people must, therefore, demand the right to live in peace and in safety, and that demand must be made, and enforced, by whatever means are necessary. The black criminal must be told in no uncertain terms that his assaults and his thievery and his dope-pushing and his murders will no longer be suffered in silence." The "black criminal" "must be made to know that decent black people are going to use their ballots and their marching feet to demand that the politicians they have elected now provide them with adequate, truly effective police protection as well as amelioration of all the horrid social conditions in which criminality breeds." Like Robinson and the editorial boards of African American newspapers across the country, the editors of *Ebony* understood the sociological roots of crime but were far more concerned with the everyday terror working- and middle-class African Americans confronted in their neighborhoods, and they sanctioned retributive measures because such action would hurt only those who knowingly operated "outside of society."

The black silent majority's concerns included not only perceived threats to their welfare but also the actions of black militants whom they blamed for taking attention away from their daily problems. In 1967 William Raspberry reported receiving a phone call from a woman who identified herself as "an ordinary Negro." She asked, "Why it is that people never pay any attention to what we ordinary Negroes think? . . . Let Stokely Carmichael or somebody come into town to raise hell, and you can't see him for reporters. People get the impression that he's speaking for us. He's not, but we don't have any way to make our voices heard." Interpreting these complaints,

Raspberry wrote, "There is justice in [these] complaints, but not much surprise. The extremists on both ends are considered news because of the sheer shock value of their utterances and actions. By this system of news judgment the man who gets up in the morning, kisses his wife, goes to work, comes home and gets a good night's sleep isn't news." He added, "The opinions of the silent middle—which is the overwhelming bulk of the population—simply isn't news in the conventional sense. The eccentric view or action is." In 1970, at the seventh annual "fight for freedom" dinner sponsored by the local NAACP branch in Gary, Indiana, Roy Wilkins chastised this "silent middle" for permitting militants to monopolize the public stage. He proclaimed, "We have a black silent majority in this country that is too quiet." The civil rights leader said that for every extremist that "shouts down with the mayor, down with the governor, down with the president, down with universities, there are 100,000 good Negroes who stay at home, do their jobs, pay their taxes and raise families. When the time comes for violence, these middle [class] blacks will rise up and put this down."[31]

While the consternation expressed in Raspberry's column might be interpreted as fear of the white gaze, it was not. The black silent majority was not afraid that militants like Stokely Carmichael would draw the ire of whites and scar the entire race. Instead, the black silent majority, as the *Amsterdam News'* encomium to the "cop on the beat" expressed, was angry that black militants consumed all the media attention and defined the political agenda for working- and middle-class African Americans, placing racial issues above the more pressing problem of crime. In 1970, after two white cops were shot, Audrey Weaver wrote a column in the *Chicago Defender* criticizing Jesse Jackson's racial activism and his inattention to urban crime. The piece began, "The 'silent' black majority here is seemingly doing a slow burn over the Rev. Jesse Jackson's role in the Windy City's latest police killings. . . . Many . . . are angrily asking—where was Jesse before those white cops were shot and what was he doing to actively help stamp out the kid violence that has been haunting us every day for over three years." A tenant in a Southside housing project told Weaver, "We're the prisoners and the gangs are our guards." One person from the Northside confided, "I was born in Chicago—grew up in a rough neighborhood and we had gangs . . . but we didn't have or use weapons like these kids do today. . . . Jackson doesn't seem to realize that these kids are a tremendous threat—he yaps about riot action and tension because a white victim is felled—well, these gangs have black citizens suffering the same amount of tension." Another Chicago resident expressed similar concerns in a separate letter to the editor, writing, "While Jesse Jackson talks about war on poverty, while Ralph Metcalfe talks about police reform and police brutality, while Lu Palmer talks about white racism, while Russ Meeks talks about prison reforms, while Renault Robinson talks about racism in the Chicago police department, while the black media preaches . . . 'hate whitey': the [day-to-day] slaughter of blacks by blacks goes unabated."[32]

Although many contemporary historical accounts situate urban riots and black militancy within the mainstream of African American politics, they were not. Throughout the 1960s, polls consistently showed that only a minority embraced black nationalists and militants. In 1964, 22 percent of African Americans in New York City believed that Roy Wilkins was "doing the best for Negroes," while only 6 percent named Malcolm X, and 55 percent said that the NAACP was the organization "doing the best for Negroes," while only 3 percent named Black Muslims. In a 1966 national Harris Poll, 62 percent of African Americans said Roy Wilkins was "helping" the "Negro cause of Civil Rights," while only 18 percent said black power advocate Stokely Carmichael was helping. In fact, 34 percent said Carmichael was hurting the cause. That same year, a *Newsweek* poll revealed similar attitudes: 64 percent approved of Wilkins, while just 19 percent approved of Carmichael. Two years later, a CBS News poll found that only 6 percent of African Americans agreed with Carmichael. A 1970 ABC News poll of African Americans in Baltimore, Birmingham, Detroit, New York, and San Francisco revealed that 83 percent of African Americans viewed the NAACP favorably, while just 37 percent viewed the Black Panthers favorably. About 30 percent held an unfavorable view of the Black Panthers. Despite this minority status, black radicals captured the imagination of white liberals and drew the attention of white conservatives. While conservative white elites condemned the violent tactics of black militants and liberal white elites justified them, the black silent majority felt invisible—unheard and unanswered.[33]

To discern the authenticity of the black silent majority that emerged in New York and throughout the country, it is useful to examine the National Black Silent Majority Committee (NBSMC). In July 1970 Clay J. Claiborne, publisher of a weekly African American newspaper, announced the creation of the NBSMC by stating, "We have organized to raise the voice of patriotism and responsibility for the black silent majority and to demand the rightful share of national attention due us as the majority within the black minority." Echoing concerns expressed by Raspberry, Wilkins, and working- and middle-class blacks throughout the country, Claiborne, the director of the new group, said, "There are millions of black Americans who work every day, keep their kids in schools, have never been to jail, pay their taxes, shop for bargains, have never participated in a riot—but are being shouted down by a handful of black militants." Two years later, the NBSMC published " 'Right On' . . . to What?," a "handbook for blacks on being a patriotic American." The pamphlet linked militancy to communism and crime and provided a detailed overview of the "subversive," "barbarous," "guerilla" tactics of "black extremist groups," including the Black Panthers, the Student Nonviolent Coordinating Committee, and the Republic of New Afrika. The "anti-communist" and "pro-America" NBSMC warned "law-abiding black citizens" against believing racial justifications for violent actions and reminded readers that "crime and violence carried out by militants and ordinary black criminals is aimed primarily at the black community itself, not at the 'white establishment.'" Finally, the document implored "law-abiding black citizens" to remain vigilant and work with police in order to prevent "revolutionary-guerilla fanatics" from turning "America's cities into battlefields."[34]

While the black silent majority was indigenous and organic, NBSMC was alien and contrived. Put simply, it was a front for the Republican Party. Claiborne was not simply a member of the GOP; he was an operative. In 1962 he became the assistant to the chairman of the Republican National Committee (RNC). Before that he had served as associate press secretary for the New Jersey Republican State Committee. In 1964 he became director of minorities at the RNC, a post that got him into some trouble. During the presidential election, he took pictures of African Americans, mostly Democrats, working in the mailroom of GOP headquarters and used the images in campaign literature with the caption "Top Negroes working for Barry." The following year Claiborne was charged with violating New Jersey election laws. While employed by the RNC, he ordered 1.4 million leaflets to promote a write-in campaign for Martin Luther King Jr. but did not affix his name to the leaflets, which was illegal. Instead, the signature on the handbills, which showed up in cities across the country, read, "Committee for Negroes in Government, Louisville, KY." New Jersey's attorney general called it "an attempt to split the colored vote." Dr. King called it a "cruel and vicious attempt to confuse my people." Despite Claiborne's being acquitted, conservative columnists Rowland Evans and Robert Novak reported that "blacks of all political persuasion were convinced that Sen. Barry Goldwater's high political command ordered and financed the leaflets." Although much more transparent and legitimate than the 1964 ploy, the NBSMC was no less a creature of the GOP. The National Republican Congressional Committee (NRCC) funded Claiborne's nationwide road trip to recruit members for the new organization. Neither party officials nor Claiborne denied a connection between the group and the party. Claiborne hoped it would be "helpful to the Republican Party." John T. Calkins, executive director of the NRCC, had a more specific goal: he wanted to increase the number of blacks voting Republican from 10 to 12 percent. In 1972 Claiborne called Camp David to request funds to distribute "Partners in Progress," a leaflet that pictured all the African Americans working in the Nixon administration and highlighted the administration's efforts on civil rights. He also informed the White House that he had organized a Black Youth National Tour "supporting the re-election of the President and the election of a Republican Congress."[35]

Unlike the black silent majority, the NBSMC was not broad-based. In 1970 thirty individuals sat on the executive committee and the membership numbered 3,000. Claiborne predicted on national TV that the committee's membership would grow to a half million. In 1971, Claiborne claimed a membership of 9,000; in 1972 a spokesperson for the group said that the membership numbered 31,000. It is unclear who the members actually were and whether they were in the mainstream of black communities. Contemporaneous reports suggest otherwise. William Raspberry, who eloquently and forcefully used his column to articulate the grievances and values of the black silent majority, viewed the NBSMC with a jaundiced eye. Right after the group's launch in 1970, Raspberry interviewed Claiborne in his "nicely furnished Capital Hill office." "[Surrounded by plaques to himself and photographs of [President Nixon]," the NBSMC director admitted to Raspberry that he "is having his greatest response from white people, although he says that, proportionately, he's getting almost as many inquiries from blacks." Claiborne also shared a request he received from white leaders in Cairo, Illinois, a city with a long and tragic history of lynchings and racial unrest, asking him "to come in and make peace in that warring community." In 1971 the *Sacramento Observer*, an African American weekly, reported, "Since its inception, the National Black Silent Majority Committee has been met with silence from most of the nation's black leadership, but it has been commended by conservative newspapers and columnists and at least one U.S. Senator, Strom Thurmond."[36]

DANIEL PATRICK MOYNIHAN'S REFLECTIONS ON THE BLACK community have been the subject of much scrutiny, debate, and criticism. But Moynihan was right about one thing: there was a black silent majority. Broad postwar political, social, and economic forces improved the life chances of some African Americans and harmed those of others. These forces also relegated many of the black winners and all of the losers of postwar political and economic shifts to the same impoverished environments. The "tangle of pathologies" cultivated by persistent segregation and economic change ensnared both the urban black poor and working- and middle-class African Americans. From the late 1960s until the early 1970s, working- and middle-class African Americans in New York City endured exceedingly high crime rates and high rates of drug addiction. They also worried about vagrancy, vandalism, alcoholism, and dirty streets. These conditions gave rise to a group of working- and middle-class African Americans who felt themselves under assault by a criminal minority and felt ignored by societal institutions they believed paid more attention to individuals who rejected traditional norms and American values. This black silent majority did not blame their problems on white racism or capitalism. In fact, they were much less concerned about racism and civil rights than they were about urban social problems.

As Orde Coombs surmised, working- and middle-class African Americans stood "in terror" of the black underclass. The near

dystopic state of many urban neighborhoods created conflict between working- and middle-class blacks and their underemployed
brethren. To be clear, urban decline did not create a Hobbesian condition "where every man is enemy to every man." Certainly, life
was disproportionally "poor, nasty, brutish, and short." But it was
not solitary. Working- and middle-class African Americans did not
trade an atavistic past for an atomistic future. They continued to
perceive themselves and their interests in terms of a broader community. They just reconfigured the boundaries of that community.
They no longer understood their community in strictly racial terms;
crime threats prompted them to view themselves as members of a
broader class-based community of "decent citizens," "hard-working
people," and Bible-believing churchgoers. When they thought
about the black underclass, they did not see brothers. They saw
hoods. They saw monsters.

This conflict beget strange bedfellows. Contrary to Charles V.
Hamilton's assertions, many working- and middle-class African
Americans did not consider police brutality a greater concern than
crime. "The cop"—a white individual who was the source of brutality, a guardian of the racial status quo, or someone who was just
plain mean—was resuscitated by the black silent majority. They
found common cause with him, and, to the extent that they were
critical of law enforcement, they complained about inaction and
corruption. Additionally, as the black silent majority turned to the
police, they increasingly turned their backs on black militants and
liberalism. Webster's *One on One* makes it quite clear: working- and
middle-class African Americans felt overshadowed by black militants and neglected by liberalism. To the black silent majority, black
militants flouted the norms they had so faithfully abided by, values
they considered crucial to their achievement of civil rights and their
pursuit of the American dream. Moreover, the garishness of black
militancy had taken attention away from daily indignities hardworking people endured in America's ghettos. The black silent

majority found liberalism equally wanting in the late 1960s and early 1970s. They believed it abetted the amoral individuals responsible for the chaos in urban black communities. They resented liberal middle-class whites for indulging black militants and criminals. They derided the structural solutions liberalism proposed and mocked the sociology that validated those solutions. To them, those were ideas without relevance or remedy. Certainly the black silent majority still possessed liberal sympathies, but exigent circumstances and class-based morality limited who the black silent majority believed deserved the benefits of progressive policies and reduced the urgency they attached to those interventions.

Probably few things would have convinced Harold Cruse of the autonomy of the black silent majority, but comparing it to the NBSMC helps to verify its independence. In public transcripts, Clay Claiborne echoed the concerns of many black citizens—tax-paying, hardworking people who kept their noses clean, attended church, and remained faithful to middle-class values as they pursued the American dream. He spoke to the alienation felt by working- and middle-class African Americans who were unnerved by black-on-black crime and disturbed by the violent tactics of black militants. The hidden transcripts of the NBSMC, however, tell another story. They expose artifice, subterfuge, and partisan intrigue. Claiborne, a Republican functionary, used the NBSMC to promote and validate the ascendant conservative political regime and undercut black criticism of the Nixon administration. The black silent majority that emerged in New York and throughout the country represented a fundamentally different political phenomenon. Its members appropriated the Nixionian trope of the silent majority to draw attention to their tribulations rather than to legitimize Republican politics. The NBSMC was a man. The black silent majority was a movement. Despite its ever-growing membership rolls, the NBSMC never achieved a broad base of support within urban African American communities. Accordingly, the organization relied on the support of the Nixon administration, Republican campaign committees, and white donors. In contrast, the black silent majority grew from within urban neighborhoods.

It would be a mistake to reduce the activism of the black silent majority to white patrons or the reproductive power of the American racial order or neoliberalism. It is certainly the case that some leaders of anticrime campaigns in New York and elsewhere benefited from the financial support of government agencies and white charities, including support from the Rockefeller family. But Rockefeller did not twist the arms of leaders in Harlem. To the contrary, local leaders had been bending his ear for over a decade and elevating the new penology. These activists were not quiescent or conciliatory; they were confrontational. They were not sentinels of the status quo; they were agents of change. Moreover, Reverend Dempsey and others were parts of broader grassroots efforts fueled by the time and energy of everyday black folk. The patron-client relationship cannot explain the petitions signed by thousands, the marches and rallies, the letters to editors, appearances at hearings, town halls, and emergency meetings. Ultimately, the black silent majority was full of sound and fury. The sound was indigenous, the fury real. And it signified a great deal.

King Heroin and the Development of the Drug Laws in 1973

HIS NAME WAS WALTER VANDERMEER. He was twelve years old. He was light-skinned and sported an Afro. He was four feet, eleven inches and weighed eighty pounds. On a Saturday night in 1969, Walt, as he was called, left his Harlem apartment, telling his mother he was going to pick up the newspaper. He never returned. His small body was found Sunday at 4:00 P.M. in a locked bathroom in a building around the corner from his home. The child had overdosed on heroin. Along with his corpse, the police found two glassine envelopes, a syringe, and a bottle cap used to cook heroin. Walt was wearing a Snoopy sweatshirt with an ominous inscription on the back: "Watch out for me. I want to bite somebody to relieve my inner tensions!"[1]

Both the black and the white press blamed the alienation and anger that contributed to Walter's addiction and demise on his environment and his family, particularly his mother. John Schoonbeck, a child care counselor, met Walt at Manhattan's Floyd Patterson House, a residential treatment center for troubled youth. Following the child's overdose, Schoonbeck wrote, "Why Did Walter Die?," a sad account of the child's life. Born into a poor, broken family,

Walter "often subsisted on potato chips, baloney and sodas." When Walter was five, the government deported his father back to Suriname for violating immigration laws. The fifth of ten children from his mother's several marriages, only he and four others still lived with her as she struggled on a $412 monthly welfare check. Schoonbeck also reported that two months before Walter's death, the landlord had evicted the family for nonpayment of rent, and they had been forced to move into a "single dingy room" in the home of friend, where there "was only one bed for all six of them." Schoonbeck witnessed firsthand the scars of Walt's background:

> At the Floyd Patterson House, Walt was the youngest of ten children in my group, but by far the toughest and most severely disturbed. Nobody knew quite what to do for Walt. He needed enough to eat, clothes to wear, adults to model himself after, toys to play with, a place to live. He needed and asked for lots of love, support and dependability. He got none of these—and it enraged him. He had learned to suspect everyone, and if he thought he was being crossed or cheated, his anger was uncontrolled. At first, he would kick a door, his eyes lowered; then he would smash things and curse. Eventually he would work himself up to a fight. Once I tried to get him in a shower to cool him off; after half an hour he succeeded in putting me in the shower. We knew that his emotional problems were beyond our capacity to treat. In October 1968, Family Court ordered Walt remanded to the custody of his mother, Mrs. Lilly Price. Neither the boy nor his mother was present at the court hearing.

Mrs. Barbara Banks of West 117th Street, Walt's godmother, confirmed the boy's challenges, saying, "He had been having trouble. [His mother] was supposed to take him to a psychiatric clinic, but she never followed through. . . . The boy was starved for attention and affection. It just got to the place where he just roamed the streets." Walter found his adult role models on the street. The street taught him and, in a way, loved him. Mrs. Banks remarked, "The crowd he was with—men on the avenue let him hang on the streets . . . just like a little hustler." Schoonbeck writes, "The child spent the rest of his short life looking for a father surrogate. His search was limited to the area around Harlem's West 116th Street, where—like many children who grow up there—he learned about hustling, dope and sex before he was ten."[2]

Walter's funeral took place at the First Corinthian Baptist Church at 116th Street and Seventh Avenue. His family was there, but one of his brothers had to be escorted from Rikers Island to the church in the morning so he could view the body. Before services began, the brother was returned to prison, where he was serving three years for robbery. Hundreds of people went to the funeral parlor on St. Nicholas Avenue to pay their respects. Many people walked in asking for "the little fellow who died." At the funeral, Walt was eulogized as a child whose "search for love and affection" cemented his demise. The minister said, "There are many brokenhearted mothers here in Harlem tonight. . . . It isn't because you haven't tried. It's because there's someone just around the corner . . . who'd rather give [your child] a drink of liquor than a drink of water."[3]

Walt's death very quickly influenced policy and the debate over drug addiction in New York. His story ended up in a draft antidrug curriculum for students in intermediate and junior high school produced by the New York City Board of Education. After reprinting the initial *New York Times* article about the incident, the draft document offered the following discussion questions: "How did Walter get money to support his drug habit?"; "Why is there always a danger that the heroin user will overdose?"; and "Who is responsible for the tragic death of this young boy?" The curriculum also proposed activities to accompany the discussion. The instructions for the first activity stated, "Walter's mother had many problems. Dramatize a scene that could have taken place in his home the week before his death." The instructions for the second suggested, "Role-play what you think Walter would have told us about his drug habit, if we had gained his trust."[4]

This tragic event inspired *King Heroin*, Al Fann's play about the dangers of drug addiction that ran for a month at Harlem's St. Philip's Community Theater in 1971. As Fann remembered, "I was absolutely stunned. . . . I had some idea of the drug problem from working with my drama students (in Harlem's Haryou-Act Anti-Poverty Program). But the thought of that 12-year-old kid dying from an overdose really shook me. My first reaction was, what a goddamn waste of human life." Fann continued, "One thing that really struck me was how the community had learned as far as is possible to ignore the junkies on the streets. Young addicts would be swaying and bowing on the sidewalks while little kids played ball, other citizens walked by and cops drove by. Nobody even looked at them. It was amazing." As with Maryat Lee's *Dope, King Heroin* drew attention to the harsh realities of narcotics addiction. As *Jet* described it, the play was "intended to depict the bleak, alienated existence of the drug 'underworld.'" "No scene is painless," *New York Magazine* declared. "[O]ne must watch the withdrawal agonies of a high-school girl, the misery of three addicts writhing in a hospital waiting room and unable to see a doctor, a junkie describing how he saw a pal sniff pure lye, and more." The story and characters resonated with the people of Harlem. One mother of four young children praised the play: "It was just great. . . . If only these younger ones would take heed." The play also allowed residents to vent. Audience members frequently told an actor who played a dealer that they hated him. At the end of one scene, an eighteen-year-old girl shakes uncontrollably and cries out, "I'm a junkie, mama, I'm hooked. I need a fix. Now do you understand?" "Keep me warm, mama," the girl sobs as she falls into her mother's arms. The mother shouts, "What are we gonna do, Jesus? Oh, God, look down here and help me to save my child." After the lights dimmed one night, the audience responded to the scene by shouting, "Right on" and "Let it all hang out."[5]

Less than two years later, Governor Rockefeller unveiled his infamous drug program mandating life sentences for individuals convicted of selling *any* amount of "hard" drugs, including heroin, cocaine, and hashish, and life sentences for those convicted of violent crimes while under the influence of such drugs. Traditional explanations for the laws have correctly drawn attention to the governor's conservative makeover and the role his perennial quest for the presidency played in his ideological conversion. Though useful, this account offers little insight into the final design of Rockefeller's controversial plan and the structure of the drug control regime that had been developing since 1966. Despite the perceived harshness of the drug laws, they were much less draconian than their original incarnation, and they were just one component of a broader complex of policies that blended the old and new penology. Examining this broader policy history requires tracing narcotics control policy over this period, paying particular attention to the ideas and mobilization of the state's issue network and the black silent majority, and probing how working- and middle-class African Americans confronted "King Heroin" and how children like Walter Vandermeer shaped indigenous frames, activist strategies, and policy preferences.[6]

THE 1966 PASSAGE OF INVOLUNTARY COMMITMENT AND THE creation of the Narcotics Addiction Control Committee did little to affect the state's drug problem. Implementation was harder than enactment. A year after passage, Lawrence W. Pierce, the African American chairman of the New York State Narcotics Addiction Control Commission, appeared on WCS-TV's *Newsmakers* and offered a status report on the state's new drug policy. The chairman tried to put a positive spin on it, but the news was not good. The state slashed the appropriation for the program; there were no full-time doctors and no adequate hospitals. Pierce also acknowledged that the state was ready to accept only 8,400 addicts—not even 10 percent of the state's addict population. By July 1967 only 1,009 individuals were under the care of the Commission. Delays in legal proceedings also limited the number certified as addicts. Making matters even worse, only 1,841 beds were available. There were incremental bureaucratic shifts to help administrators execute the policy. In 1968 the State Narcotics Commission established the Bureau of Professional Education to provide technical assistance to staff administering educational and rehabilitation programs. The Commission spent much of the early years on this type of bureaucratic and technical activity, but in their defense, implementing the policy required this drudgery. Identifying sites for rehabilitation and education programs was one thing, but officials also needed to evaluate public and private agencies and individuals for accreditation.[7]

The careful process of implementing a safe and comprehensive rehabilitation regime required more time than the people of Harlem were willing to give. Events continued to galvanize black communities. Walter died in December 1969, but his was just one of many tragic stories. Addiction among youths was on the rise. In 1940 no teenagers (age fifteen to nineteen) died because of drug abuse. That number climbed to 79 in 1967. Then, after dropping slightly in 1968, it rose to 248 in 1969. In early March 1970, a fifteen-year-old girl died of a drug overdose in the apartment of Edward Hamm, the thirty-six-year-old owner of Teen City, a popular teen hangout spot and suspected drug den at 162 West 116th Street. For six weeks, members of Harlem's Canaan Baptist Church picketed Teen City. One Sunday the pastor, Rev. Wyatt Tee Walker, a former assistant to Dr. Martin Luther King and an aide to Governor Rockefeller on urban issues, stood on the trunk of a white Mustang parked in front of Teen City and, with the help of a bullhorn, shouted, "We are trying to save our children." He urged his 300 parishioners and other onlookers, "Let us know the minute you find out the name of a pusher." He added, "We've been living dangerously for a long time and we're not afraid to name names. . . . I am convinced God is concerned about the narcotics peddlers on 116th Street." Walker ended this sidewalk service by leading his church and onlookers in the Lord's Prayer.[8]

These overdoses inspired many working- and middle-class African American women to act. Black women had always been deeply involved in grassroots antidrug movements in the city. They were central to each of Reverend Dempsey's campaigns, providing much of the legwork and passion. By 1970 black women had become so frustrated that they formed their own organization, Mothers Against Drugs (MAD). Describing the impetus for this grassroots mobilization, *Ebony* reported:

> The women are angry. And they are representative of a new mood in New York's black communities. In Harlem, Bedford-Stuyvesant, Brownsville, and South Bronx, a backlash is surfacing—a backlash against the heavy drug traffic in their communities and against all who benefit from it. A black silent majority that long has suffered from the influx of community-destroying killers such as heroin is preparing to confront those distributors—they call them "murderers of our children"—of the deadly poisons that are so readily available to youths on street corners and in innocent-looking candy stores and teen hangouts.

One mother of an eighteen-year-old girl who died of an overdose kept repeating "Kill the pushers" when asked what should be done. MAD's main tactic was recording the names, addresses, and license plates of known drug dealers and supplying that information to the district attorney's office. The organization also engaged in direct action to expand rehabilitative services for addicts. About a dozen members of MAD and the Academy for Black and Latino Education engaged in a sit-in at St. Luke's Hospital, requesting that "more than 40 of the hospital's 715 beds be set aside for addicts and that the hospital cooperate with community organizations in developing programs for addicts." The four-day sit-in ended after the hospital announced that it would "establish a 28-bed center for the detoxification of adolescent drug addicts." In March 1970 MAD and a group of 200 young people tied up traffic from 59th Street to 125th Street as they marched to Roosevelt Hospital to press for more hospital beds for the detoxification of juvenile drug addicts.[9]

MAD was just one node in the growing grassroots network of community groups fighting addiction and drug dealing. As the *Amsterdam News* put it, "Harlem's silent majority has declared war on narcotics." In 1970 Dempsey tapped this civic energy to organize a march on Washington and draw attention to the nation's drug crisis. The reverend secured the participation of a dense and diverse collection of civic, religious, and political organizations, MAD, two Democratic clubs, the New York Branch of the NAACP, the Epsilon Sigma chapter of the Phi Beta Sigma Fraternity, and the National Afro-American Labor Council. The organizers hoped the march would pressure national political leaders to fight the international drug trade and make the penalties for pushers more severe. Before the rally, Dempsey and other organizers met with Robert J. Brown, special assistant to President Nixon, at the White House to discuss their proposals. "Where will it end?" Dempsey asked. "First marijuana then speed balls, heroin, coke and in no time we will be back in the lawless days. We must stop now. It's our moral obligation. . . . This is the beginning of a national movement."[10]

Harlem leaders and residents lobbied political officials, advocating a two-pronged approach that combined the old and new penology. To confront the public safety threats posed by pushers and adult junkies, the black silent majority asked for more aggressive policing and harsher sentences; to confront the problem of ju-

Governor Rockefeller with prominent Harlem politicians Percy Sutton (left) *Manhattan borough president, and Charles Rangel* (right) *U.S. Representative, in 1970. (New York State Archives. Governor. Public information photographs, 1910–1992, 2006–2008. 13703-83, Box 15, Number 1499.)*

venile addiction, they pushed for more rehabilitative resources. As crime and urban decline worsened, working- and middle-class African Americans continued to lose sympathy for adult addicts, who they saw as increasingly less deserving. Adult users were victims of their own choices. Juvenile addicts, however, were victims of the immorality of others, most especially unscrupulous and malevolent pushers, wayward and willful older junkies, and occasionally the mother whose life of sin (e.g., promiscuity, out-of-wedlock births, and "shacking up") interfered with good parenting. These children were innocent; they deserved second chances. These dual frames shaped the content of narcotics control policy development from 1966 to 1973.

In the run-up to another election in 1970, Rockefeller accelerated his antidrug efforts. After years of African Americans urging the governor to call in the state troopers, he announced a dramatic policy shift in February 1968: he would move large numbers of state troopers into large urban areas to combat drug trafficking. In an interview about the new policy, Rockefeller explained, "Well, the state has been spending a good deal of money, as you know, in trying to rehabilitate addicts. This is a slow, expensive process. We now come to the conclusion that the State will supplement local police and Federal agents in rooting out the agents—the people who are the big boys who are importing the narcotics and distributing them, and try to go after the sources of the narcotics themselves." He also stated, "While one person is being corrupted with drugs and is mugging and murdering in New York—or in any part of our State—I, as Governor, have the responsibility to leave no stones unturned to protect the public which will be victimized, and protect young people who are being sucked into this." These comments attest to the growing influence of black activists in Harlem: the policy responded directly to their pleas and was defined by the portrayal of adult drug users that emerged from African American communities. For working- and middle-class African Americans the drug problem was not simply about addiction; it was also about crime: "mugging and murdering." As such, it required policing as much as, if not more than, a medical cure.[11]

Facing reelection, Rockefeller attended to the rehabilitative desires of New York's black silent majority. On February 24, 1970, he stood in the Red Room with Republican leaders and state officials to announce a "declaration of total war" against juvenile drug abuse. He described the "more widespread abuse of drugs, down in elementary schools as well as the high schools." Rockefeller said, "we can and we must make it plain to the corrupters of our youth that this is a war." The governor stated, "It is up to our entire citizenry to back the police, to expose all known corruption and weaknesses of enforcement, and above all, to dry up the market for the drug peddler through education and treatment of his victims and potential victims." Rockefeller then outlined a new plan to combat juvenile drug addiction. As MAD and other grassroots organizations had called for, Rockefeller's anti-juvenile-addiction strategy emphasized education and rehabilitation for "youthful addicts and drug abusers." The plan appropriated over $500 million for the development of a special antidrug curriculum and the training of 10,000 teachers to use this curriculum. It appropriated $65 million in aid for local government agencies operating drug treatment programs, authorized local agencies to provide these services or contract out to voluntary groups, and authorized the State Housing Finance Agency to issue an additional $200 million in bonds to finance the construction, acquisition, or refurbishing of rehabilitation facilities for the use of local agencies or voluntary groups. It also authorized the Division for Youth to create and operate "residential youth development programs to which any youthful addict or drug abuser under the age of eleven may be admitted." As Rockefeller explained, the "underlying concept" of the new program was that "the youthful drug abuser can be reached and rehabilitated best through those programs, agencies, and persons with which he is already in contact."[12]

While drug policy certainly turned to the right after 1966, the reform-minded issue network managed to leave its imprint on the state's narcotics control strategy. As they had before, members of the issue network convinced the governor to veto legislation that increased criminal penalties for drug crimes. In 1968, on the advice of the Committee on Criminal Courts, Law, and Procedure of the New York City Bar Association, the governor vetoed a bill that would have made it manslaughter in the second degree for an individual to inject another person with an illegal drug when that injection produced the death of the person. The committee argued that the legislation contradicted definitions of intent and culpability enshrined within the penal code. That same year, Rockefeller vetoed a bill increasing the penalties for the sale and possession of "dangerous drugs" because it was opposed by several members of the issue network, including the Narcotics Addiction Control Commission, District Attorneys Association of New York, the Federation of Protestant Welfare Agencies, the New York State Council of Churches, the Community Service Society of New York, and the New York Civil Liberties Union. In 1969, on the recommendation of the Narcotics Control Addiction Committee and Committee on Criminal Courts, Law, and Procedure of the New York City Bar Association, the governor increased penalties for the possession of and intent to sell a certain amount of stimulants or depressants. That same year, on the advice of the Narcotics Addiction Control Committee and the State Administrator of the Judicial Conference, Rockefeller vetoed legislation that would have expanded the population of individuals susceptible to the state's involuntary commitment law. In 1970 the issue network exploited the urgency created by the black silent majority and the electoral imperative facing the governor to achieve modest victories for their rehabilitative strategies. That year, the administration approved $433,000 in grants to finance methadone maintenance programs in New York City and nearly $4 million in grants for drug abuse programs in New York City. For youngsters sixteen or younger, over $2 million was allocated to establish and operate twenty methadone maintenance clinics and over $1.5 million to support twenty treatment centers.[13]

While many working- and middle-class African Americans believed children deserved rehabilitation and educational programs, they still considered older junkies threats and described them as members of a broader criminal element jeopardizing the safety and welfare of citizens. So they decided to take matters in their own hands. In 1965 Dempsey began carrying a pistol and wearing it in the pulpit. He also organized armed militias, including Operation Confiscation and Operation Interruption, campaigns in which he and 200 armed volunteers would track pushers and report them to the police. In addition to confronting addicts and pushers, armed volunteers would escort women to church and to the market. Defending these actions, he said, "We don't advocate taking the law in our own hands . . . but the emphasis of the law is placed on protecting the rights of the criminal, not the decent citizen. I think every addict who is on the streets must be removed from Harlem." Although the reverend certainly wore the weapon with some flair, the gun was more than political theater. By the mid-1960s, Dempsey had begun to fear for his life—and for good reason. On a Thursday night in September 1964, an associate of Dempsey answered the phone and heard a gruff, raspy voice say, "Just tell the Rev. Mr. Dempsey that if he keeps up his expose of the Harlem dope racket, then we'll take steps to shut his mouth for good." In 1971 Dempsey became a crime victim. The official police report of the incident read, "[Dempsey] while responding to a knock at his [apartment] door was confronted by 2 unknown [Puerto Rican males], one of whom slashed [Dempsey] with a knife attempting to rob him. Dempsey also told the police that he recognized one of the assailants as a drug addict from the community."[14]

Like Dempsey, many Harlemites found the police presence wanting, so they responded in a similar way. In October 1967, 700 Harlemites attended a rally at the St. Charles Roman Catholic Church to implore officials for more police protection. The organizer, James B. Brodie, director of the Drew Hamilton Community Center, indicated that he would not go as far as Reverend Dempsey, but he asserted, "The muggings and rapes and robberies here have reached a point that the people must do something." He suggested "forming an auxiliary civilian police" where civilians "could ride in the prowl cars," "freeing the police to patrol on foot, where they are needed." Others did go as far as Dempsey. That same year, Charles Davis, who claimed that he got 2,000 people to sign a letter to the mayor requesting more protection, recruited five men from

Lenox Terrace House, the middle-class black development, for his "citizens patrol." During an interview with the *New York Times,* Davis even brandished the .30-30 Winchester rifle he used to escort women to the subway in the morning. In 1969 the *New York Times* reported, "In Harlem, at least three groups advocate dealing very firmly with the addict. Some members of all groups admitted they were armed when they went into the street to search for addicts. Others said they dealt with addicts and pushers only with their fists. The intention among members of all three groups was simply to drive addicts and pushers from their neighborhoods— there was little talk of rehabilitation or hospitalization."[15]

Black militants also considered vigilantism a necessary response to junkies and pushers. In 1967 James Lawson, leader of the United African Nationalist Movement, warned that the community would be "moved toward a vigilante state unless action was taken soon." In 1969 the Harlem Youth Federation also advocated a "militant approach" to junkies. Hannibal Ahmed, the group's president, who was under indictment for conspiring against white police officers, warned children about pushers and junkies. The federation would have children sing:

Eee-I, Eee-o, Drugs must go,
Dah-dah-dah-dah-dah.
The pushers must be off-off-off,
Dah-dah-dah-dah-dah.
The people must work both day and night,
Time for us to put up a fight.
Eee-I Eee-o drugs must go,
Dah-dah-dah-dah-dah.

The sixty-member federation also polled Harlem residents between 110th and 155th Streets on the best approach to addicts. Two comments summed up the "consensus": "They are killing our people" and "They should be killed." In 1968 John Shabazz, a former bodyguard for Malcolm X, created the Black Citizens Patrol. Armed with machetes, the group handed out leaflets warning "all drug pushers" to "find another job or get out of Harlem by Jan. 1." The Black Citizens Patrol also made citizens' arrests of young people they caught breaking into cars. When Shabazz spoke to a group of teenagers in a church in Harlem the "spirit of meeting was almost evangelical." He involved the teenagers in a call-and-response. When he shouted "Only a first-class jackass would stick a needle in his arm and shoot up. What kind of fool would do that?," the teenagers responded, "Somebody who don't have nothing else to do." "What kind of dope is here in Harlem?" Shabazz asked. The teenagers yelled, "Cocaine! Heroin! Weight pills! Reefers!" "What's the youngest age of an addict that you've heard of?" "Eight!" Then Shabazz told the group how to respond if anyone offered them drugs: "You know what to do—knock the hell out of them." The teenagers applauded. Thus, while some militant activists were inclined to use armed self-defense to protect the racial community from the tyranny of white police officers, many of them were also willing to use violence against addicts to protect workers, citizens, and children.[16]

This grassroots vigilante movement continued into the next decade. In 1970 black assemblyman Waldaba Stewart said, "If [the crime problem] is bigger than police then we must organize vigilante operations and arm ourselves in defense of our home, our families, and our children. . . . I have reached the place where I am on the verge of being the leader of the proposed vigilante group. . . . I don't want to—but something has to be done." At the 1972 community hearing on crime, several people advocated taking up arms or reported that they had already done so. Rev. Paul F. Thurston testified that his church on 229 Lenox Avenue had hired a guard to protect parishioners attending services. Mrs. Louise Garcia of the 111th Street Block Association told the crowd, "Arm yourselves, and arm yourselves good!"[17]

Vigilantism increased so much that even the staunchest proponents of punitive action began to speak out against it. Dempsey in particular drew much criticism, even from erstwhile supporters. In 1965 the *Amsterdam News* told the pastor, "Lay that pistol down! . . . Harlem USA is not Dodge City, the Rev. Oberia Dempsey is not Matt Dillon and the junkies and dope pushers in Harlem are not playing in some TV drama called Gunsmoke—On the contrary they are real live characters who complicate our day to day living in Harlem." The paper pleaded with Dempsey, "You've been right—but you're wrong now Reverend! Please [put] that pistol down!" Vincent Baker, author of the 1969 NAACP crime report that embraced the death penalty and stop-and-frisk, among other punitive strategies, regretted that there "is an embryonic vigilante movement in this community. It's cropping up all over. Tenant groups are arming themselves." While he recognized a feeling of "anarchy and complete helplessness against marauding hoodlums," Baker considered such efforts anathema to his "law and order" campaign: "In towns of the Old West, where there was no law, people paid gunslingers to protect them from the depredations of marauding outlaws. . . . We don't need gunslingers, paid or unpaid, in our community. We want law enforcement by and through the law." "Vigilantism," he stressed, "is inherently undemocratic, antisocial and unsound."[18]

Of course, armed resistance was not the only or the dominant tactic employed by Harlemites. Many took to public forums to agitate for greater pubic safety. In late 1972, 500 people crammed into a room in the annex of Harlem's Salem Methodist Church for a public hearing on the community's crime problem, sponsored by Harlem Youth Opportunities Unlimited and Associated Community Teams (HARYOU-ACT), an anti-poverty agency. For four hours, community members listened to fifty people decry the neighborhood's drug and crime problem, lambast police inattention, and propose aggressive solutions. Attorney Fred Samuel, the chairmen of HARYOU-ACT's board, opened the hearing by stating:

> I charge the Mayor and the Police Commissioner with gross
> neglect of our community in failing and refusing to provide
> adequate police protection to Harlem as they do to White
> areas. This neglect is criminal. Perhaps 200,000 angry black
> residents will have to march on City Hall and Police Head-
> quarters to protest this criminal neglect, and to say to the
> Mayor and the Police Commissioner just how angry we are,
> to demand equal protection for our law-abiding citizens who
> are daily being mugged, raped, assaulted, molested and killed
> by a small but effective band of criminals who have made us
> prisoners in our own homes.

Samuel's exasperation was unmistakable and not at all unusual.
His words echoed the anxious spirit in the room and the rage per-
vading Harlem and illustrated the core beliefs of the black silent
majority. He reinforced the idea that a dangerous "band of criminals" was threatening the lives, life chances, and lifestyles of
Harlem's "law-abiding citizens" and the sense that the dominant
institutions of society favored the undeserving (i.e., junkies,
pushers, and "thugs") and neglected the deserving. To the extent
that Samuel and Harlem's black silent majority felt that racism
shaped policing strategies, they believed it caused police inaction,
not police brutality.[19]

As the narcotics problem in Harlem worsened, African Americans continued to "tell it like it is." In an op-ed piece published in
the *New York Law Journal*, Harlem's U.S. representative Charles
Rangel complained that "king heroin reigns supreme" in his community and pressed the Nixon administration to wage an all-out
war on the international drug trade. For Rangel, the situation in
Harlem had grown dire: "The effect of this epidemic is truly hor-
rifying. An atmosphere of fear and hate abounds as a derelict army
of addicts prey upon neighbors and friends." He depicted Harlem
as a wasteland ravaged by addicts: "Whole neighborhoods have

declined; others have become abandoned. Addicts have taken up scarce space in the community's hospitals, destroyed the functioning of our school system and forced desperately needed stores and hospitals to relocate outside Harlem. Those who dare to drive or walk through Harlem streets must experience the agonizing sight of seeing our children, the hope of the black nation, staring vacantly from door-ways and street corners, oblivious to reality around them." Suffused with epidemiological, militaristic, and Darwinian metaphors, Rangel's rhetoric did not flow down from the elite; it bubbled up from below. These were the rhetorical devices everyday folk employed to interpret their experiences and formulate appropriate responses. For example, one young "heroin fighter" warned addicts to seek help "because they are not going to be allowed too much longer [to] stand around the streets setting bad examples for our young brothers. To me their disease is contagious and a person with a contagious disease has no choice as to whether he should seek help. No. Society insists that he does."[20]

As African American politicians like Rangel and Stewart and everyday people like the women of MAD continued to "tell it like it is," Rockefeller continued to listen, and his own rhetoric adopted the black silent majority's framing of the state's drug problem. Months after Rangel's piece appeared in the *New York Law Journal,* Rockefeller published his own thoughts in the same periodical:

How can we defeat drug abuse before it destroys America? I believe the answer lies in summoning the total commitment America has always demonstrated in times of national crisis. . . . Drug addiction represents a threat akin to a war in its capacity to kill, enslave, and imperil the nation's future: akin to cancer in spreading a deadly disease among us and equal to any other challenge we face in deserving all the brain power, man power, and resources necessary to overcome it.

Some have described this and other Rockefeller statements about the "alleged army of addicts" as "hype" created by the governor's "public-relations men" to instill fear in whites for his own political purposes. Such assessments entirely ignore the role that African Americans played in shaping this discourse. For years the black silent majority had been pleading for white officials to wage a war on drugs. For years they described addiction as enslavement and a spreading disease. Rockefeller's rhetoric simply followed rather than led the indigenous African American construction of the state's narcotics problem.[21]

In early 1973, when Rockefeller announced his controversial drug program, he spoke directly to the fears and grievances of New York City's black silent majority: "This is a time for brutal honesty regarding narcotics addiction. . . . In this State, we have tried every possible approach to stop addiction and save the addict through education and treatment—that we could rid society of this disease and dramatically reduce mugging on the streets and robbing in the homes." Then, employing the black vernacular, the governor said, "Let's be frank—let's 'tell it like it is.'" Speaking truth to the legislature and the public, he confessed, "We have achieved very little rehabilitation—and found no cure." Sounding like the NAACP's 1969 anticrime report, he noted, "The crime, the muggings, the robberies, the murders associated with addiction continue to spread a reign of terror. Whole neighborhoods have been as effectively destroyed by addicts as by an invading army." The policy proposals the governor derived from this causal story were harsh and extreme. The plan included mandatory life sentences for all drug dealers, life sentences for drug addicts who committed violent crimes while under the influence of illegal narcotics, and the removal of protections for youthful pushers, so teenagers caught selling illegal narcotics would receive the same penalty as adult offenders. Drug pushers deserved the maximum punishment. Because addicts were incorrigible and jeopardized the welfare of the state's citizens, they also deserved extreme punishment. These policies were not meant to curb drug abuse. They were meant to curtail crime, insecurity, and disorder. Moreover, Rockefeller's testimony before a legislative committee on his proposal betrayed African American influences. For one, the governor frequently referenced Harlem and the views of its leaders. At one point, he even quoted at length a large proportion of Dempsey's testimony the week before, remarks in which Dempsey stated, "In Harlem, the non-addict has become the prisoner of the addict. . . . It is time to start thinking about the people who are the victims of these crimes by addicts." While it was certainly shrewd politics to draw attention to African American supporters, this was more than just symbolism or tokenism. The governor appropriated the indigenous framing of Harlem's drug problem and drug addicts. In response to one question, Rockefeller, channeling Dempsey and many other working- and middle-class Harlemites, stated, "I agree with you, we have got to protect the innocent. The innocent, though, are the ones who are beaten and killed in our society."[22]

The governor's controversial proposal instigated a fierce political battle that pitted the black silent majority against the state's narcotics control network. White liberals balked. Apoplectic, Manhattan assemblyman Albert Blumenthal accused the governor of throwing a "public temper tantrum." He charged, "Because his outlandishly expensive narcotics solutions have been disastrous failures, he has told us he will solve a narcotics [problem] of his own making with an unworkable and Draconian program pandering to public fears and insecurities." He added, "In his State of the State message, the Governor asked us to 'tell it like it is.' So I will do just that. I do not think the problem of crime can be solved with hysterical legislative proposals like those the Governor suggests." Representative Bella Abzug remarked, "Contrary to Rockefeller's claim . . . a comprehensive drug program that has been adequately funded and administered has yet to be tried." A report of the Committee on Criminal Courts, Law and Procedure of the Bar Association of the City of New York issued a stinging rebuke of the measures, describing them as a "concentration-camp approach." Sounding like their do-gooder predecessors, the committee argued that this approach "cannot be justified until programs of methadone treatment or heroin maintenance and more efficient administration of the system of justice have been tried and proved ineffective."[23]

Experts and law enforcement officials were adamantly against the governor's drug laws. While understanding the governor's frustration with the state's drug problem, Frank Hogan called the program "illogical in parts." The New York State District Attorneys Association opposed the elimination of plea bargaining, which they considered a key tactic for getting low-level dealers to inform on large-scale traffickers. They also believed "that the law should recognize a difference between the seller of a $5 bag of heroin and the seller of $5,000 worth of the same drug." Judges complained that the new law would overburden the state's judicial system. "I don't see how the courts could function at all," complained Harold A. Stevens. Mayor John Lindsay and the New York City police commissioner opposed the plan, believing it would make investigating and successfully prosecuting drug traffickers "infinitely more difficult." As the proposal neared passage, Lindsay urged Rockefeller to veto his own signature plan, saying, "In times of social crisis, every citizen and every public official is tempted by rage or frustration to turn to law enforcement and penal sanctions as a simple, final solution. The loathing we all share for drugs and their purveyors is now the subject of this temptation." He added, "These bills reflect this frustration but instead of meeting the challenge [these measures] would turn back the clock and negate all of the advances of the past few years."[24]

Working- and middle-class African Americans viewed the city's drug problem very differently. Rev. George McMurray testified, "The Mother AME Zion Church has two morticians. Each one has told me they bury thirty to forty young people a year who are victims of overdoses of drugs." Conveying how drug addicts had wrecked the social and economic vitality of the community, he said, "Even the neighborhood drugstore must close at sundown. And those who are sick cannot receive medical care from the doctors or fill their prescriptions at night because of the crime and mugging inflicted upon the citizenry. . . . The business leaders, both white and black in Harlem, who depend upon the citizens of Harlem for their livelihood, must pay high insurance premiums and also sell their merchandise beyond the price of the regular competitive market, because of the robberies they have." Finally, he pressed, "The drug traffic is destroying the vitality and influence of the black church in Harlem, which is our stabilizing institution. It is destroying it economically, because members cannot attend the religious services and various social and [fundraising] functions." So, while white liberals focused on the barbarity of excessive sentences, Reverend McMurray and other members of the black silent majority highlighted the barbarism of urban crime.[25]

Given this, it is hardly surprising that the black silent majority enthusiastically embraced the punitive measures. Several prominent African Americans publicly expressed support for the governor's proposals, including Eulace Peacock, the track star and rival of Jesse Owens, and Robert Royal, director of the Civil Service Division of the Local 144 of the AFL-CIO. On CBS, Vincent Baker, author of the 1969 NAACP crime report and founder of Citizens Mobilization against Crime, gave an eloquent rebuttal to the station's editorial on the program. Simeon Booker, an African American journalist who received plaudits for his coverage of Emmett Till's murder, penned an editorial in which he described Rockefeller's proposal as the work of a "great humanitarian." Les Matthews, columnist for the *Amsterdam News*, reacted by saying, "I'm in favor of burning them alive." The "Mayor of Harlem," Dr. Benjamin Watkins, reported that he had been robbed "at least six times" and did not use his car because his hubcaps would be stolen and "sold back to me." Given these experiences, Watkins favored the "harshest" methods possible to "remove this contagion from our community." Enunciating a key element of the black silent majority's politics, many African American supporters of the governor's plan acknowledged their abandonment of previously held views. Beny Primm, director of Bedford-Stuyvesant's Addiction Research Treatment Corporation, conceded, "I'm not a civil libertarian anymore when it comes to the destruction of lives. I hate to sound so conservative, man, but this is from five years in the field. I see it every day. People say, 'Lock pushers up, even if they're my son or daughter.' " A civil servant and a recent grandmother said, "I'm very much a liberal and a militant most of the time, but in terms of [the governor's proposal] I'd like to see it happen."[26]

Of course, not all African Americans supported the drug laws. In an illuminating exchange with Rockefeller during the governor's testimony, Arthur O. Eve, an African American assemblyman from Buffalo, articulated some black concerns and many of the complaints of actors in this issue network. Referencing the previous findings of the Joint Legislative Committee on Crime and presaging arguments offered by contemporary prison reform advocates, he discussed the flaws of incarceration: "We found that in the City of New York that if you were poor, if you were black and Puerto Rican, your likelihood for going to jail was considerably higher. The Committee also found that . . . our prisons today are a great contributor of crime and are not really a deterrent." Eve articulated a different causal story for the state's drug problem, saying, "We realize the gaps in education, housing, job opportunities are all very serious problems contributing to the development of crime and people moving into crime." The Buffalo politician derived from this structural account a searing critique of Rockefeller's proposed program. He argued that the legislation would "create chaos in the ghetto communities" and have "us ultimately leaving the community without hope of really correcting the serious problems that crime and many other things are the outburst of."[27]

Some Harlemites also opposed Rockefeller's plan. But, unlike Eve, these opponents did not necessarily offer a different causal story. Rev. Dr. James E. Gunther, pastor of the Lutheran Church of the Transfiguration, remarked, "I [would be] particularly impressed if [they go] after the real culprit. . . . I'm afraid that only the poor people will get caught." Mrs. Barbara Jackson suspected the government of trying to "round up young black kids, young black boys and put them in concentration camps." She complained, "Even itty bitty ones are on dope, so he just wants to throw them away for life." Like Mrs. Jackson, many Harlemites fixated on the proposed life sentences, which went too far for some. Mrs. Lillie Cain lamented, "To catch these young boys around here and give them life. . . . Life is a long time." Whether led by history or taken with conspiracy theories, some opponents, exhibiting great prescience, were adamant that Rockefeller's drug laws would claim the lives of "innocent victims"—young people, particularly young black males, already imprisoned by addiction and poverty.[28]

Even so, it is very easy to overestimate African American opposition to Rockefeller's drug program and miss the implicit ways they endorsed the policy. In early February a headline in the *New York Times* read, "New Drug Laws Scored in Harlem: Residents Voice Opposition to Governor's Proposals." The paper reported that "[s]ome 75 Harlem residents last night told two legislators of their opposition to Governor's Rockefeller's package of new laws on addiction." The reporter, however, missed important nuances in his own story, particularly crucial history. First, seventy-five people paled in comparison to the hundreds and sometimes thousands of people who marched, signed petitions, and packed town hall meetings to call for extreme sentences for pushers—sometimes life,

Poster announcing an anticrime meeting, 1973. (Courtesy of Rockefeller Archive Center.)

sometimes death—and to advocate for the removal of junkies, whether that be in the form of involuntary commitment to rehabilitation centers or in the form of incarceration. Second, the reporter unknowingly caught a glimpse of this grassroots activism: "Though some of the residents, *many representing community organizations*, said they supported the Governor's approach, most did not."[29]

The reporter did not fully appreciate the indigenous construction of this problem and its policy implications, though he did not miss it altogether. He ends the article by stating, "Despite the consensus of opposition to the Governor's specific proposals, there were also indications of widespread concern about the underlying problem of drug-related crime, which Fred Samuel, the chairman of Haryou-Act and the meeting's moderator, called a 'crisis that is holding us prisoner in our homes.' " The flyer for this event—"The Public Forum Gov. Nelson Rockefeller's Proposal to Impose Mandatory Life Sentences on Convicted Drug Pushers"—drives home this point. In bold black letters atop an emergency-orange surface, it invited residents to "fight crime," specifically "street violence," "muggers," "dope," "murder." It asked residents to "join the campaign for a safe Harlem" and to help "people," "the community," and "yourself." The flyer never asked residents to help drug users. Instead, it linked drug addicts and pushers to Harlem's crime problem and asked residents to defend "the community." The "innocent victims" were not young black males imprisoned by addiction and poverty; they were the "people" imprisoned by crime.[30]

African American opponents, regardless of the implications of their causal story, were in the minority. An aide told the governor that Clarence Jones, editor of the *Amsterdam News* and confidant of Martin Luther King Jr., who helped write the "I Have a Dream" speech, reported, "A poll of about 200 Harlem residents, conducted by the *Amsterdam News* staff, brought a dominant reaction in favor of your narcotics program." He added, "Jones personally is 100% for you." Only a few weeks after the passage of the law, the *Amsterdam News* called it "a powerful weapon against the wholesale use of drugs." The paper supported mandatory life sentences for nonaddict pushers because it considered drug dealing "an act of cold calculated, pre-mediated, indiscriminate murder in our community." This was not just an elite opinion; this punitive sentiment was popular. A *New York Times* poll taken in late 1973 (after the passage of the controversial proposals and after the virtues of the laws would have been adjudicated in the white and black press) confirms Jones's assertion: 71 percent of black respondents favored life sentences without parole for pushers.[31]

Just like during the debate over involuntary commitment, members of the state's narcotics control network found themselves on the opposite side of this issue from the black silent majority. This conflict was unmistakable during a live broadcast on WCBS-TV in which Reverend Dempsey and Gordon Chase, the health services administrator of New York City, debated the merits of mandatory life sentences for drug dealers. Similar to other health officials and experts, Chase derided Rockefeller's approach, labeling it "excessively tough," "cruel," and "unjust." He criticized the governor for giving up too soon on rehabilitation, saying, "I think the Governor's proposal in essence is throwing in the towel and acting hysterically. He's simply saying, my gosh, we can't do anything despite a lot of indicators that indicate we are making some progress. Let's throw everybody in prison." Of course, Dempsey had "a different point of view." Alluding to the effects of drug addiction and trafficking on the community, he remarked, "[T]he emphasis is just being placed upon the addicted person but I've got to think of the eighteen million people in New York State who are unaddicted." To the Harlem pastor, the governor's approach was neither "cruel" nor "unjust" because users and dealers had a simple and fair choice: "[I]f the law is complied with, the drug addict has nothing to worry about, not even the drug pusher. Just comply with the law."[32]

Dempsey and Chase also offered radically divergent characterizations of the city's drug problem. Chase saw progress: "[T]reatment is starting to work. . . . Overdose deaths are beginning to go down, drug related crime is beginning to go down." Dempsey quickly dismissed these positive signs, claiming that Chase's statistics did not sufficiently take into account "undetected" and "unreported" crimes. He added, "We've got to . . . [pass the governor's program] in a hurry because of the fact that if we were able to treat successfully the fifty-two thousand people that Mr. Chase has in his treatment program . . . , it would have no effect on the five hundred thousand, approximately a million drug addicts in New York City right this moment." Chase disputed Dempsey's numbers, saying, "I would like to see some substantiation for that. That just is not true." The reverend never substantiated his numbers, probably because he could not. Statistics bolstered Chase's position. After reaching an all-time high in 1971, the number of drug-related deaths in New York City had begun to decline in 1972 and, despite a momentary uptick in 1974, continued to fall. Nevertheless, the real issue here was not numbers; it was focus. Chase focused on the plight of addicts, while Dempsey emphasized the fate of the community. Public policies might have begun to reduce the rate of addiction, but they had yet to change the trajectory of black communities. Despite the real decline in addiction, working- and middle-class Harlemites still felt insecure. They remained afraid and continued to feel trapped by violence and vice. Dempsey was voicing these concerns rather than accurate statistics.[33]

The black silent majority was not just at odds with expertise, statistics, and sociology. It was also at war with liberalism. For instance, the "Mayor of Harlem" also defended Rockefeller's proposals against "neo-socialists" who called the plan "genocidal": "I think that those who propose leniency for the pusher, who have caused [the death] of junkies as well as [the death] of the victims of muggings, [are] certainly more genocidal than the author of a bill directed at saving lives, property and the freedom to function in Lawful Society." For Watkins and other members of the black silent majority, the privilege of white liberals afforded them the ability to empathize with pushers, junkies, and other individuals who flouted the law and disobeyed social norms and blinded them to the plight of "hardworking," "decent" citizens. Speaking to these grievances, Watkins wrote, "The proponents of a perpetuation of lawlessness, including Judges, Policemen, Legislators and Sociologist[s,] must answer the question—If you saw a pusher addicting your Son and Daughter would you jail him? I think they would want to kill him."[34]

Harlemites chided liberals for discounting their pain and dramatizing the potential suffering of junkies. Glester Hinds excoriated the "bleeding hearts" at a hearing at the Union Baptist Church in Harlem. With vituperation and without any guile, he testified, "These bleeding hearts will continue to shed crocodile tears [on] behalf of the distributors and pushers of narcotics but they never seem to say one word [on] behalf of the victims, that [suffer] from the evil perpetrators, who are determined to ruin our state and nation and the youth of America." He charged that the "bleeding hearts" sought to shield the crimes of "craven" drug addicts and refused to inform the public about "the invasion of homes by the criminal element, making them prisoners in their own homes." Then he said, "Ladies and gentlemen, the reason I have stressed the 'bleeding hearts' is that I do not believe that they themselves who supposedly stand up for the rights of the persecuted have been touched by this cancerous and deadly growth of addiction close to home or family."[35]

Nowhere was this tension between white liberals and the black silent majority more apparent than in the pages of the *Amsterdam News*. That same month, the newspaper reprinted an editorial from the *Wall Street Journal* entitled "Getting Serious about Drugs." The editorial highlighted the tension the governor's proposal engendered between white liberals and working- and middle-class African Americans: "The black's traditional political ally, the upper-middle-class reformer, opposes him on [this] issue." It explained, "The loudest screams about Governor Rockefeller's proposal came from the American Civil Liberties Union and so on, for example, while the strongest cheers came from the slums." This editorial made liberals the enemy of the dreams and aspirations of the city's black working and middle classes. It also impugned the motivations of white liberals, characterizing them as out-of-touch do-gooders, infatuated with their own ideas and oblivious to the grievances and desires of "hardworking" people in urban ghettos. Addressing the racial and class power dynamics in urban public policymaking, the *Wall Street Journal* stated, "Legislation to cure slum problems has tended to be written not by politicians with black constituencies but by politicians with upper-middle-class reformer constituencies"; as a result, urban policy appropriated "money to hire upper-middle-class social workers and lawyers to implement upper-middle-class 'solutions.'" Echoing sentiments expressed by Roy Wilkins, Reverend Dempsey, and others, it added, "No one has bothered to ask the folks in Harlem whether they would rather have Uncle Sam buy them a poverty war or lock up the drug addicts." By reprinting this editorial, the *Amsterdam News*, as it had when it published "an open letter to the average cop on his beat in our communities" less than two years before, turned on their erstwhile allies and the brand of liberalism that the ACLU, upper-middle-class reformers, and the *New York Times* had come to represent.[36]

Even though Rockefeller's drug laws managed to unite groups as ideologically opposed as the *Amsterdam News* and the *Wall Street Journal,* they faced an uncertain future in the legislature. Because the governor's proposals were not going to get many Democratic votes, Rockefeller needed the overwhelming support of Republicans in the legislature. This, however, was easier said than done. Several members of Rockefeller's own party, including those supported by the state's Conservative Party, considered the measures harsh and unworkable. Senator John R. Dunne, a Republican from Nassau County and chairman of the committee overseeing the legislation, said, "There has been near unanimous support for modification of the Governor's proposals . . . and a desire for less-rigid and severe penalties." Assemblyman Milton Jonas, a Republican from Nassau County, even said that there were "some major defects" in the program. This reticence, especially from Republicans, was born out of the legislature's own investigations of the state's crime problem.

In 1966 the legislature had created the Joint Legislative Committee on Crime, Its Causes, Control, and Effect on Society. Throughout the late 1960s, the committee consulted law enforcement officials, held hearings, and studied the available data, and they were not enthusiastic about heavy penalties. In its first report, the committee found that "the failure of past legislation to achieve its [objective] did not lie within the legislation itself but rather its failure was with the implementation of the legislation. . . . Each year we increased the number of crimes, each year we tried to make law enforcement more efficient and each year the number arrested increased. [But we] failed, time and again, to increase the ability of courts to cope with the increased loads." Consequently, the first and subsequent reports recommended reforms to the plea-bargaining system in order to increase the effectiveness and efficiency of the judicial process.[37]

Furthermore, the Joint Legislative Committee on Crime never blamed the city's crime problem on junkies or low-level pushers. The committee and the state's law enforcement community were much more focused on organized crime and much more concerned about developing legal strategies, such as wiretapping, aimed at effectively investigating and successfully prosecuting members of the mafia. It is not as if the committee did not hear the voices of Harlem. It actually held a three-day public hearing in Harlem in 1969, where everyone described the problem in similar terms: citizens were being victimized by junkies. In fact, it was there that the NAACP's Vincent Baker declared that "the silent majority in Harlem would welcome a police order to get tough." Nevertheless, the committee, led by Republican state senator John H. Hughes, rejected this causal story and its policy implications and concluded that Harlem and other minority communities were being victimized by organized crime. It contended that mafia enterprises in Central Harlem, South Bronx, and Bedford-Stuyvesant had "virtually nullified massive state, federal, and city spending to improve the economic situation of nearly one million residents." Instead of arguing that junkies and pushers in these areas were threatening the rest of the state, Hughes maintained that the activities of organized crime in minority communities "affected the pocketbook of every tax payer in the state."[38]

Given Republicans' alternative framing of the state's crime problem, Rockefeller's plan was in trouble by mid-March. In early April it suffered a near fatal blow—from friendly fire—when a conservative Republican assemblyman, Dominick L. DiCarlo from Brooklyn, chairman of the committee of jurisdiction on this issue, introduced an alternative bill. DiCarlo, a former prosecutor who once served as the vice chairman of Joint Committee on Crime, worried, as his son later recounted, "that with broad-stroke mandatory sentences, people who were not drug dealers would find themselves in the prison system." Consequently, his alternative package tried to retain for prosecutors and the police the tools necessary for apprehending large-scale drug traffickers and to put in place sentencing structures that would spare low-level dealers and addicts from unnecessarily long prison terms. The assemblyman's legislation did not eliminate plea bargaining; instead, it limited pleas for second-time offenders so they could not plead to misdemeanors. DiCarlo's plan also instituted maximum sentences of six to fifteen years for first-time felony offenders convicted of selling dangerous drugs (i.e., heroin, morphine, cocaine, and opium).[39]

DiCarlo's alternative plan was gaining steam among Republicans, particularly among conservatives. So on April 12 Rockefeller unveiled a revised program. From the beginning, his drug program had been criticized for ending plea bargaining, overloading the judicial system to process the expected rise in criminal cases, and imposing heavy penalties on low-level dealers and addict-sellers. Rockefeller solved the first two problems. In terms of the capacity concern, the legislature approved the governor's request to authorize up to 100 additional judges and appropriated over $20 million for additional district attorneys, legal aid services, court officers, and correctional personnel. The state also provided $13 million to expand courtroom facilities. And, similar to DiCarlo's legislation, the revised plan also permitted a limited form of plea bargaining in all the felony classes.[40]

These revisions, along with some strong-arming, were enough to woo vacillating Republicans who wanted to support the governor but also feared, given the complaints of the law enforcement community, that his original plan would hamper the investigation and prosecution of drug crimes. Ultimately, the idea of ending plea bargaining did not, as Senator Ohrenstein noted, "hold up for long" because "some voices of reason were raised—and these voices of reason were not so much raised this time by the Civil Liberties Union or-called soft-hearted liberals, they were raised by the prosecutors in this state and by highly respected police officials." In fact, Senator Vander Beatty was even annoyed that district attorneys and "the high police brass from New York City" came to Albany to fight for plea bargaining. He complained, "They could have been using their time more wisely, catching . . . addicts."[41]

While members of the state's issue network were able to reduce the harshness of the governor's original plan, the final legislation still imposed high sentences for crimes likely to be committed by racial minorities. Although Rockefeller claimed that his new plan imposed mandatory life sentences because anyone released after serving a mandatory minimum sentence would be on parole for the rest of his life, it borrowed much from DiCarlo's less punitive bill. It dropped hashish from the list of dangerous drugs and created three types of Class A felonies, all of which carried mandatory minimum sentences for individuals convicted of selling or possessing narcotics—heroin, morphine, cocaine, and opium. These revisions offered some relief for white middle-class teenagers experimenting with LSD and white middle-class housewives abusing diet pills but retained harsh sentences for users and dealers in minority neighborhoods. These racial disparities were not lost on activists and legislators. During the debate in the Assembly, DiCarlo pointed out that these amendments favored "white suburbs over the Black ghetto": "While Junior in College gets off if he passes an LSD pill, the kid in the ghetto who passes a 'nickel bag of heroin' will get life."

While the revisions to the final legislation appeased few of the program's opponents, they were enough to secure its passage in the legislature and the praise of the black silent majority. The New York State District Attorneys Association circulated a letter around the capital announcing its opposition to the amended plan. They complained that under the plea bargain rules they would "be permitted to take reduced pleas from heavy drug pushers but not from petty sellers of drugs" and warned that the "proscription against pleas could have significant negative impact on the enforcement of the drug laws" and that "the impact on the administration of criminal justice in general and on drug law enforcement in particular would be catastrophic." Nevertheless, the drug laws passed the Assembly, eighty to sixty-five. Only one Republican, Assemblyman DiCarlo, voted no. Four days later, the senate passed the bill, forty-six to seven.[42]

Senator Vander Beatty, the one African American to vote in favor of the legislation, commended "the Governor for his intestinal fortitude." He indicated that he "was 'totally committed' to the Governor's bill, although he considered it a 'compromise' that regretfully stopped short of capital punishment." Beatty also suggested that "making a distinction for addict-pushers—whom he described as 'vegetables' preying on the community—would only see big traffickers feigning addiction with false 'track marks' on their arms." Before the final vote in the Assembly, Beatty said, "If Blacks in my district are pushing drugs, I want them to have life in imprisonment. . . . They're poisoning our youth." At the bill-signing ceremony, Dempsey lauded the governor and the legislation, saying, "I'll say 'Long live Governor Rockefeller; long live our great legislature.' We congratulate you and, on behalf of many, many, many poor people in the slums of New York City and throughout New York State, I want to thank you for passing this law." Articulating the black silent majority's position, the Harlem pastor remarked, "We say this, that the addict is a sick person but we want the addict to get into treatment programs. Now we are not going to stand any longer and see decent citizens brutalized or subjected to punishment because someone is out there sick. That won't happen again." Expressing the black silent majority's resentment toward white liberals, Dempsey sarcastically exclaimed, "And I'm sorry for the bleeding hearts, I'm sorry for all of the people who are over-sympathetic with criminals and under-sympathetic with decent citizens who work and carry the burden of this state."[43]

Given the support among working- and middle-class African Americans, the no votes by black legislators are surprising but not unusual. Minority politicians, like all elected officials, have their own goals, ideas, and interests. Black legislators were Democrats, and Democrats did not want to give Rockefeller a win on this issue. Additionally, from 1966 until 1973, African American elected officials had become more liberal than their constituents because of a generational shift in black politics. In 1973 a large portion of the Black and Puerto Rican Caucus were relatively new members of the legislature and were anchored more in the radical politics of the 1960s than in traditional black civil society. For example, unlike his constituents, Senator Joseph Galiber of the South Bronx supported methadone maintenance and the legalization of certain drugs. In fact, the first line of his obituary in the *New York Times* read, "State Senator Joseph L. Galiber, a Bronx Democrat who took unpopular stands on crime and drug addiction." Furthermore, many minority officials viewed the conditions of their communities slightly more optimistically than the residents of these communities. In 1973 Louis Harris and Associates, who conducted a large survey of Harlem residents, also interviewed a small sample of Harlem leaders, elected and nonelected, to discern whether elites shared the views of everyday folk in the community. Among other things, the polling firm found that "despite their intense awareness of the problems, the leaders do not seem fully cognizant of the extent to which the residents feel trapped in Harlem. By 76%–18% (with 6% not sure) the leaders *disagreed* that 'things are so unsafe and unclean in Harlem, the only people who live here are those who can't afford to live in some better neighborhood.' But Harlem residents agreed with the same statement by 52–39% (with 9% not sure)." Based on their findings, Harris and Associates concluded, "The leaders of the Harlem community do not need to be educated to the seriousness of problems facing the area, but they nevertheless appear to understate the negative impact of these problems on the residents' acceptance of their life in Harlem."[44]

Their optimism notwithstanding, many minority legislators conceptualized the drug problem in a manner that was more consistent with the new penology rather than the old. Some, however, still embraced the old penology. Frequently near tears during the debate on the bill, Assemblyman Woodrow Lewis of Brooklyn disputed the governor's claims, arguing that "efforts in matters of treatment had not been exhausted." He also declared that "addicts are already imprisoned by the ills of our society." Others portrayed drug users as threats. While black Buffalo assemblyman Arthur Eve called the proposed legislation the "ghetto genocide bill," Harlem's assemblyman George Miller said, "We almost have genocide now with all the drug traffic." He added, "There are colonies of addicts all over my community." Queens assemblyman Guy R. Brewer's evolution on this issue is illuminating. In 1950, during an antidope meeting sponsored by the Pontier Democratic Club, Brewer, then a real estate agent, expressed outrage at the *Long Island Press*'s coverage of the drug problem in his community, which he called "a smear campaign against South Jamaica." Echoing the politics of responsibility, Brewer, after asserting his commitment to stamping "out the evils of the narcotics trade and its destruction of the souls and bodies of its victims," complained about the "manner in which a problem and condition which is citywide, had been played up by the press in such a sensational and vicious manner as to give the impression that South Jamaica and its environs is one whole, horrible area of narcotics peddlers, depraved crazed youth, and that the citizenry is unable to cope with the clutches of this octopus." James Williams, the club's president, pointedly challenged Brewer, saying, "Damn the real estate values. Our concern is the health and welfare of our young people. . . . It is time that the people of South Jamaica stopped burying themselves in the sand, and woke up to the dire situation which confronts us." By 1973 Brewer had awakened to the drug problem in his community. He had personal experience: drug addicts invaded his home and "walked off with various appliances and a considerable liquor stock that they packed off in my brand new suitcase." Thereafter the Queens Democrat took a "hard line" on this issue. Although not enamored with the governor's proposal, he supported mandatory life sentences for drug dealers except for young "experimenters who give drugs to friends." "You must understand," Brewer explained, "I cannot stand by and watch my community go down the drain." Thus even some of the black legislators who voted against the bill had undergone the same transformation on this issue as most middle- and working-class African Americans: they had come to consider junkies as threats to the persons and property of black citizens.[45]

The depiction of drug addicts as threats to the community also surfaced during a brief colloquy between Senator Beatty and Senator Robert Garcia, a Puerto Rican legislator representing the South Bronx and an opponent of the legislation. When asked by Beatty how someone distinguishes between an addict and a nonaddict, Garcia replied, "I think you and I both know who is an addict. We have enough experience knowing who is addicted and who is not addicted. . . . Look, I said last week, Senator, that as far as I am concerned, there are some junkies whom we will never be able to help, and they are no damn good, but the key is that we have to go after those people and try to help those people who have a chance, and that is all I'm doing." To be exact, he actually said that while "there [are] some junkies walking the streets of New York who I do not care to salvage, there are some junkies that [I] know personally or ex-junkies that have been able to rid themselves of the habit and walk a straight line." Garcia did not do his addict and ex-addict friends any favors, ceding ground to the causal story at the heart of the new drug: the new penology. *Junkie* is not a neutral term; it marks the drug user as the "other" and implicates individual behavior rather than social structure. By labeling both "good" and "bad" users "junkies," the senator from the South Bronx implicitly reinforced the "outsider" status of those who abused illegal narcotics and implicitly validated a policy approach aimed at controlling drug users instead of rehabilitating them.[46]

In the end, the black silent majority's significance was not in the number of votes it was able to garner for Rockefeller's program but the alternative frame it introduced into the policy arena, which denigrated junkies and dismissed structural remedies. Reflecting on this policy moment, Joseph Persico, Rockefeller's speechwriter, wrote, "I never fully understood the psychological milieu in which the chain of errors in Vietnam was forged until I became involved in the Rockefeller drug proposal. . . . This experience brought to life with stunning palpability psychologist Irving Janis's description of groupthink: 'the concurrence-seeking tendency which fosters [over-optimism], lack of vigilance and sloganistic thinking about the weakness and immorality of outgroups.'" The causal story that undergirded the drug laws defined black addicts and pushers as outgroups and maintained that the threat they posed to themselves

If you're caught with drugs after September 1st, you can go to jail for life. Don't get caught, get help.

Call
New York City
246-9300
Elsewhere in New York State
(800) 522-2193
Toll free.
Or write: Drugs, Box 8200, Albany, N.Y. 12203.
Don't get caught holding the bag.
The New York State Drug Abuse Program.

Poster for the New York State Drug Abuse Program, 1973. (Courtesy of Rockefeller Archive Center.)

and society was the result of individual choices rather than structural conditions. As a result, black addicts and pushers deserved harsh punishment. This framing did not emanate from the racial resentment of conservative legislators or their constituents. Working- and middle-class African Americans, including some of the legislators who voted against the bill, played a crucial role in the definition of the "weakness and immorality" of low-level pushers and drug addicts. In one instructive example, an aide sent the governor a memo that read, "We are delivering . . . posters to Reverend Oberia Dempsey on Wednesday for distribution throughout Harlem in store fronts. This distribution will be expanded to Bedford-Stuyvesant and other high addiction neighborhoods—for as Dr. Baird, Reverend Dempsey and others have pointed out, addicts in the streets don't read papers and just steal television sets and radios."[47]

A LITTLE MORE THAN TWENTY YEARS AFTER THE *NEW YORKER* profiled Charlie Reed, another black juvenile drug user, Walter Vandermeer, once again grabbed the attention of the city. But times had changed. Chronic joblessness, family dissolution, and racial segregation intensified the social disorder that had begun to engulf Harlem and its working- and middle-class residents in the early 1950s. The disappearance of work for young black males and the postwar reappearance of drug trafficking produced a social environment in which young people relied on illegitimate sources of income for survival, turned to dangerous recreations for amusement and comfort, and found belonging and meaning in cohorts of similarly disenfranchised individuals engaged in self-destructive behavior. Within this treacherous milieu heroin became king and ruled unjustly over both users and nonusers alike. According to the members of the black silent majority, King Heroin inaugurated a reign of terror that made them prisoners in their homes, impoverished their religious and civic life, and razed their budding consumers' republic.

Empowered by their newly won civil rights, members of the black silent majority vigorously battled King Heroin and reconfigured the politics of drug policymaking in New York State. Working- and middle-class African Americans exploited old organizational forms and founded a multitude of new committees and groups. They met, protested, and lobbied to combat the problems of drug addiction, drug trafficking, and crime in their neighborhoods. Reverend Dempsey and many other civic leaders took to the streets to agitate and entreat. With banners and bands, picket signs and bullhorns, leaders of block associations, church groups, women's groups, fraternal organizations, and Democratic clubs took to the streets to demand more police, shame addicts, call out pushers, and upbraid white and black political leaders for their perceived unresponsiveness to the problems of drugs and crimes in minority neighborhoods. Some even took up arms and formed marauding militias to protect women and children, expel pushers and bully junkies, and restore order to their communities.

Members of the state's issue network had a very different reaction to the reign of King Heroin. Because their racial and class position shielded them from subjugation to King Heroin, white reformers and law enforcement officials continued to embrace penal welfarism. Nevertheless, because of black activism and the political interests of Governor Rockefeller, drug policy shifted to the right. As they had done during the 1950s and early 1960s, members of the state issue network successfully leveraged their influence to scuttle efforts to impose gratuitously harsh sentences for possession and selling of drugs. As before, they had a difficult time getting the state to enact a robust rehabilitative approach. In 1970 they secured more resources for methadone maintenance and other medical strategies. Yet, because of the black silent majority's emphasis on children, a disproportionate share of new antidrug resources went to education and rehabilitation programs for individuals sixteen and under, who, despite a significant rise in teenage overdoses, still represented a relatively small proportion of the overall addict population.

After enduring the monopoly the white issue network held over this policy arena during the 1950s and early 1960s, working- and middle-class African American residents and activists assumed a leadership position in the late 1960s and early 1970s, and the indigenous antidrug, anticrime social movement that erupted in Harlem made the Rockefeller drug laws possible. While all available survey evidence indicates widespread black support for the Rockefeller drug laws, it was the mobilization of the black silent majority in addition to the attitudes of everyday black folk that created a political opportunity for the governor's contentious program. At community meetings and legislative hearings, working- and middle-class African Americans decided to "tell it like is," detailing the victimization of African American citizens at the hands of drug users as well as publicizing users' incursion on religious life and the consumers' republic in the ghetto. In plays like *King Heroin* and in songs taught to schoolchildren, Harlemites described drug users as enemies of the public and deemed them worthy of contempt, ostracism, and, sometimes, abuse. Many minority opponents of the program contributed to this discursive context by reluctantly conceding the nightmarish conditions in their communities and facilely adorning their righteous protestations with language dehumanizing drug users. By tightening the link between crime and addiction and vilifying drug users, African American supporters and most African American opponents of the drug laws bolstered their central public policy justification: restoring public safety by banishing junkies. They had made severe punishment for simple possession possible by depicting users as agents of blight and disorder. Rockefeller not only employed this rationale, but the angst and anger that permeated the black public sphere pervaded the blue-blooded governor's framing of the state's drug problem during the late 1960s and early 1970s. His statements were informed by the specific experiences of the black silent majority, and his lexicon borrowed from the black vernacular. Rockefeller's rhetoric was the rhetoric of the black silent majority, born of their experiences—carried on the tide of their struggle.

In order to understand fully the roots of the drug laws, it is important to interrogate the political origins of amendments to Rockefeller's proposal. While the laws' retributive quality can be attributed to the activism of the black silent majority, their final design demonstrates the influence of the state's issue network and the significance of state capacity. The final legislation included three major revisions to the original plan: (1) plea bargaining was spared; (2) life sentences were replaced by a complex sentencing structure that distinguished between first-time offenders and repeat offenders and varied prison terms according to the amount of dangerous drugs being sold or found in possession; and (3) substantial funds were appropriated for the hiring of attorneys, legal aid services, court officers, and correctional personnel and the expansion of courtroom facilities. Individuals who would have had to administer Rockefeller's original program—prosecutors, judges, and police officials—and various associations representing them rose up in opposition to it. Leveraging their expertise and reputation, they convinced Republican legislators, particularly conservatives, that the state lacked the capacity to implement the law and that its provisions, particularly the lack of plea bargaining, would have impeded their ability to investigate and prosecute drug crimes. Their objections caused Assemblyman DiCarlo, the conservative Republican chairman of the committee of jurisdiction, to introduce an alterative bill that directly responded to the critiques of the law enforcement community. Near unanimous Democratic opposition and waning Republican support limited the governor's options: either face a very public defeat on a signature issue or amend his plan. So Rockefeller amended the plan.

Finally, by focusing only on this one policy moment and dichotomizing the universe of policy outcomes (punitive vs. rehabilitative strategies), almost all analyses of the Rockefeller drug laws have failed to explain the complicated layering of new and old drug control policies that had emerged by the end of 1973. The Rockefeller drug laws represented a few new conspicuous threads in a thick, aging quilt of New York State's antinarcotics strategy. Over time, the narcotics control issue network, the governor and his ambitions, and the black silent majority constructed a complex drug control policy regime, including public and private agencies, that emphasized rehabilitation for some and not others and punishment for some and not others. The governor's electoral interests determined the timing of major new initiatives, the issue network and previous policies helped determine the broad structure of these initiatives, and the black silent majority defined who within this broad policy infrastructure were deserving of reform and who warranted punishment. Because of the conjuncture of these forces, New York State built a narcotics control policy regime that offered substantial resources, in terms of education and rehabilitation, to teenage nonwhite addicts, protected white middle-class young adults and housewives, and incarcerated black junkies and pushers.[48]

Race, Place, and the Tumultuous 1960s and 1970s

THEY BOOED HIM. They tried to silence him. They chanted, "We want Barry! We want Barry!" Delegates at the 1964 Republican National Convention did not hide their distaste for Governor Nelson Rockefeller. Somewhat tickled and a bit energized by the hostile reception, Rockefeller was undeterred. He lectured them, saying, "[The Republican Party repudiates] the efforts of irresponsible, extremist groups, such as the Communists, the Ku Klux Klan, the John Birch Society and others, to discredit our Party by their efforts to infiltrate positions of responsibility in the Party, or to attach themselves to its candidates." He praised traditional conservatism and celebrated liberal Republicanism. Referencing a previous speech, he intoned, "At that time I pointed out that the purpose of [a radical, well-financed and highly disciplined minority subverting the Republican Party was] 'wholly alien to the sound and honest conservatism that has firmly based the Republican party in the best of a century's traditions, wholly alien to the sound and honest Republican liberalism that has kept the party abreast of human needs in a changing world, wholly alien to the broad middle course that accommodates the mainstream of Republican principles.'" Every sentence infuriated the crowd. Each word antagonized them. Yet Rockefeller persevered. He warned delegates against embracing conservative extremism: "These extremists feed on fear, hate and terror. They have no program for America—no program for the Republican Party. They have no solution for our problems of chronic unemployment, of education, of agriculture, or racial injustice or strife." Constantly interrupted by a jeering crowd, Rockefeller pressed on: "There is no place in this Republican party for such hawkers of hate, such purveyors of prejudice, such fabricators of fear, whether Communist, Ku Klux Klan or Bircher. There is no place in this Republican party for those who would infiltrate its ranks, distort its aims, and convert it into a cloak of apparent respectability for a dangerous extremism." Then his time was up. The speech ended. The upset Republican crowd got what it wanted.[1]

Truth be told, Rockefeller's performance at the Republican National Convention was not purely ideological. It was also strategic. From 1961 until 1966 either John F. Kennedy or Lyndon B. Johnson topped the Gallup poll's list of "most admired Americans," and they were frequently followed by the pragmatic, moderate Republican Dwight D. Eisenhower. During the early 1960s, the United States was a center-left nation, and this fact was not lost on Rockefeller. The New York governor recognized the electoral power of the New Deal coalition and watched as liberalism, riding the tide of African American activism, swept through the nation. Rockefeller, who desperately desired to be president and who was keenly aware of the cultural milieu of the early 1960s, believed his ideological posture and support within the African American community made him a credible national candidate. Months before his controversial speech at the Convention, he even issued a press release that publicized the findings of a small poll of black editors demonstrating his appeal among African Americans. The poll indicated that African Americans prioritized civil rights and preferred Rockefeller to any other potential Republican candidate. The poll was not very kind to Barry Goldwater: "Not only did the Senator fail to receive a single vote in the 'preference of Negro voters' question, but also thirty-one of the thirty-four ballots expressed the opinion that the Negro Republican will not accept Mr. Goldwater in view of his opposition to certain civil rights proposals." Rockefeller cast his lot with African American voters: a risky gambit that did not pay off.[2]

From the perspective of contemporary politics, a Republican presidential candidate's aggressive courting of African American voters seems almost fantastical. Yet as Rockefeller excoriated racists and extremists in 1964, it was the electoral importance of urban black voters that had become common wisdom among many politicos. Indeed, it was the urban black vote that caused President Harry S. Truman to embrace, to the consternation of southern Democrats, a strong civil rights plank at the 1948 Democratic convention. In 1947 Clark Clifford, an aide to Truman, told the president that "many professional politicians" believed that "the northern Negro voter today holds the balance of power in Presidential elections" because of their concentration within the "pivotal, large and closely contested electoral states [such] as New York, Illinois, Pennsylvania, Ohio and Michigan." Clifford said that "this explains the assiduous and continuous cultivation of the New York Negro vote by Governor Dewey and his insistence that his controllable legislature pass a state anti-discrimination act." These same forces caused Richard M. Nixon to espouse moderate positions on civil rights during the 1950s. And in order to gain the support of Nelson Rockefeller during his pursuit of the presidency in 1960, Nixon forged the "Pact of Fifth Avenue," agreeing to push a serious civil rights plank at the Republican National Convention. During the 1950s and early 1960s, the geographical terrain of party competition, specifically the political importance of the industrial Midwest and Northeast and the concentration of African Americans within those areas, caused both Democrats and Republicans to move to the left.[3]

With this history as their background, the Rockefeller drug laws seem incongruous. Why did a staunch proponent of civil rights and fierce opponent of Goldwater extremism adopt policies that appear to have been a complete capitulation to the extreme ideological forces he once castigated? Why did the governor who had so boldly endorsed the old penology by signing Metcalf-Volker in 1962 unabashedly countenance the new penology in 1973? Why did he do so in 1973 and not before? One theory of Rockefeller's political transformation and the broader ideological shift in American politics starting in the mid-1960s emphasizes white backlash. Most recently employed by Michelle Alexander, this thesis argues that the perceived challenges civil rights posed to their life chances and social position caused whites to reject liberalism, which they believed had aided and abetted the erosion of their power, and to consider prisons as a way to reinstate the racial status quo. Several urban histories show that postwar local racial conflicts over issues like housing and education ignited fierce battles and fueled white disenchantment with the left. Others have connected white backlash within the crime policy arena to local conflicts produced by economic transformations. Loïc Wacquant links the "stupendous inflation in the confinement of lower-class blacks since 1973" to "the collapse of the ghetto as ethnic container and the subsequent deployment of the penal net in and around its remnants." Deindustrialization expanded the "black urban sub-proletariat," whose violence began to extend beyond urban ghettos. In response, frightened whites turned to penal policies to restore the old social order. From both perspectives, Rockefeller's renunciation of penal welfarism was the direct result of anxious white voters.[4]

Another backlash theory does not limit white concerns to either race or crime. From this perspective, civil rights, though significant, was not the sole source of the turbulent politics of the 1960s and early 1970s. A variety of issues and events made whites feel persecuted and alienated. In his seminal essay "The Rise of the Silent Majority," Jonathan Rieder, acknowledging the importance of race, writes, "What drew the disparate elements of the middle together was its restorationist impulse, its unhappiness with the directions of change in American life. If there was any single source of displeasure that shook the New Deal coalition to its core, it was the civil rights revolution." Capturing the complexity of white reactionary politics, he continues, "Race, however, was only the earliest and most powerful spur to these defections. Later, the Vietnam War cleaved through the Democratic Party and hacked it into bits." "Dynamic representation" best explains how this motley array of issues impacted politics and policy during this period. According to this approach, strategic politicians sense the arrival of a new "public mood"—a realization that comes from their reading of public sentiment and from "journalists, commentators, academics, and others" who talk "incessantly about where public opinion is going"—and the entire political system responds by enacting policies that are consistent with the new milieu. By implication, the punitive drug laws were the result of politicians anticipating an ideological reversal in the public mood.[5]

Assessing the veracity of these claims requires studying white beliefs and antidrug mobilization and interrogating the timing of shifts in the public mood. Finding and explaining white backlash requires studying surveys of white attitudes and inspecting the public and private statements of white residents, activists, and public officials in New York City, its suburbs, and upstate communities, and asking: How did whites frame and negotiate drug addiction and rising crimes rates in New York State? What role did race play in the formulation of their views? Evaluating dynamic representation requires identifying *when* the public mood moved to the right and ascertaining whether narcotics control policy in

New York State followed this shift. Ultimately, answering these questions will clarify how race and class and local and national politics shaped the development of the Rockefeller drug laws.

BY THE LATE 1960S AND EARLY 1970S, NEW YORK'S ONCE ascendant image had faded. The city's iridescent glow grew dim. It would be another decade before the Bronx would burn, before the front page of the *Daily News* would read "Ford to City: Drop Dead," and before *Warriors* would immortalize the city's dystopic present, but Gotham was in bad shape. New York's decline was not singular but part of a broader transformation of industrial cities in the Northeast and Midwest. The decline of manual labor, the suburbanization of work, and the movement of people to the suburbs depleted the urban labor market, furthered segregated social spaces, and concentrated poverty and concomitant social problems within minority urban areas. Federal public policy exacerbated these trends. The Interstate Highway Act of 1956 created opportunities for whites to depart central cities; the Federal Home Loan Bank Board, the Homeowners Loan Corporation, and the Federal Housing Administration gave them the means to do so. In addition to the influx of new information-based industries and the migration of urbanites to suburbs in the South and Southwest, these programs expanded the economic power and political influence of the Sunbelt and left urban minority areas in the industrial Northeast and Midwest in dire straits.[6]

These broader economic and political transformations changed New York City. It became a dangerous place. Neither the creation of the Narcotics Addiction Control Commission (NACC) nor the passage of an involuntary commitment law slowed rising rates of drug addiction or related offenses. In fact, crime rates in New York City skyrocketed to well above national averages. In 1968 the city's violent crime rate was almost four times the national average: the rate for murder and nonnegligent manslaughter was nearly double the national average; the robbery rate was more than five times the national average; and the burglary rate was more than double the national average. To be fair, the Big Apple was not the only place experiencing spikes in illegal activity during this period. Crime, on average, increased throughout the United States from 1960 to 1968. Nevertheless, New York's situation was more extreme than most. Rates of increase were higher there than in the nation: whereas the national average for violent crime rose by a little over 50 percent, the city's average rose by a little over 450 percent.[7]

City averages, though striking, conceal important neighborhood-level variation, disparities that were alarming but not at all surprising. Not all communities experienced the city's decline in the same way. Some survived mostly unscathed; some were ruined. Industrial forces that once made the city great eventually created jobless enclaves in minority communities. Public works that once served as testaments to Gotham's prosperity soon constructed "slums" of hardship and despair. Residential segregation and exploitative landlords compounded these troubles and secured the boundaries and fate of these "dark ghettos." In these islands of distress and disorganization, crime thrived. Put simply, black and Puerto Rican neighborhoods were much more dangerous than white neighborhoods. Homicide rates in white working-class precincts (Canarsie, Brooklyn), white middle-class areas (Bayside, Queens), and white upper-class precincts (Upper East Side) were dramatically lower than in precincts in minority communities. For example, the homicide rate in one Harlem precinct (the 28th) was over twenty-six times the rate in the Upper East Side, almost fifty times the rate in the most dangerous precinct in Bayside, and almost forty times the rate in Canarsie. Vital statistics verify these trends. African Americans suffered over 50 percent of deaths by homicide from 1966 to 1976 while constituting a minority of the city's population. Similarly, robbery rates were much higher in nonwhite areas. The robbery rate for the 28th Precinct in Harlem was six times the rate in the Upper East Side, ten times the rate in Canarsie, and twenty times the rate in the most dangerous precinct in Bayside.[8]

The city's narcotics problem was distributed in similar ways. In 1970 blacks constituted only 19 percent of New York City's population, but from 1966 until 1976 they suffered around 50 percent of drug-related deaths. That number rose to almost 60 percent in 1972. Moreover, African American addiction was concentrated within a few neighborhoods. Data collected by the NACC and the New York City Narcotics Registry reveal that few cases of opiate use were reported in working-class white neighborhoods like Bay Ridge or in middle-class white neighborhoods like Maspeth–Forest Hills. In contrast, opiate use was extremely high in predominantly black and Puerto Rican neighborhoods. Yet even among nonwhite neighborhoods, opiate use in Central Harlem was exceptionally high.[9]

White and black attitudes toward crime reflected actual experiences. In a 1969 statewide survey of 6,105 individuals commissioned by the NACC, respondents from "excellent" white-collar neighborhoods, a description determined by the interviewer, worried about property crime but did not express much concern for violent street crime. Almost 50 percent listed "burglary" and 32 percent listed "vandalism" as top problems facing their neighborhoods, while only 19 percent listed "poor police protection" and 18 percent listed "drug use" as top problems. Respondents from predominantly blue-collar neighborhoods also did not rate public safety concerns very highly. About 33 percent listed "vandalism," while 26 percent said "unsafe streets" and 21 percent said "drug use." Respondents from slum neighborhoods, however, were much more concerned about public safety: 54 percent listed "drug use" and 52 percent listed "unsafe streets" as the top issue facing their neighborhoods. In New York City, much higher proportions of individuals living in black and Puerto Rican areas listed "unsafe streets" as a problem in their neighborhoods: almost 60 percent from Manhattan North (the area covering Harlem), 60 percent from South Bronx–Morrisania, and 58 percent from East Central Brooklyn (the area covering Bedford-Stuyvesant). At the same time, only 39 percent of individuals from North-West Queens and only 27 percent from Bay Ridge–Flatbush listed "unsafe streets." These survey data and crime statistics indicate that, contrary to many contemporary analyses, whites in New York did not have an outsized fear of crime: the unique experiences of their communities shaped their attitudes.[10]

Because the NACC survey mostly asked about public safety concerns in neighborhoods, it did not sufficiently situate these issues within the broader, tumultuous politics of the time. Fortunately, the following year the *New York Times* polled registered voters in the state on a variety of issues. Largely corroborating the findings of the NACC survey, the results also suggest that values in addition to experiences shaped how white and black New Yorkers reacted to the events of the time. Forty-three percent listed "ending the war in Vietnam" as the main issue or problem facing the country; 26 percent listed inflation, followed by drugs (24 percent), student unrest (18 percent), crime (15 percent), and discrimination (10 percent). When asked to list the problems facing their communities, New York voters said drugs (19 percent) and crime (19 percent) were their top concerns, followed by high taxes (15 percent), pollution (9 percent), schools (9 percent), inflation (8 percent), sanitation (7 percent), and unemployment (6 percent). New Yorkers did not express much uneasiness about or exasperation at civil rights activism; they worried about a host of economic and quality-of-life issues. Instead of being engulfed by the powerful tides of national politics, whites were able to navigate these troubled waters with a certain degree of precision, as they distinguished between the pressing issues facing the nation and those facing their community.[11]

Although whites in New York City certainly grew more conservative over the course of the 1960s, the broad racial category obscures critical nuances that complicate the white backlash narrative. In the *New York Times* survey, 63 percent of all the respondents and 64 percent of those from union families, 70 percent of whom lived in New York City, described themselves as members of the "silent majority." But when asked whether they believed any groups were being treated unfairly, only 12 percent said "working men" or "the lower middle class," while 22 percent said "Negroes," which challenges the idea that the silent majority was primarily a racialized identity embraced by working-class whites antagonized by civil rights activism. Additionally, ideological orientation and issue salience varied across ethnic groups. While only 13 percent of Roman Catholics identified as "liberal," only 16 percent of Jews identified as "conservative." In fact, 77 percent of Jewish respondents reported being registered Democrats, 55 percent identified as liberal, and 76 percent gave Nixon a negative approval rating. Irish Americans, probably because of their overrepresentation in law enforcement, rated student protests as the issue of most concern to them; 27 percent of Irish Americans mentioned this issue, while only 19 percent of the entire sample mentioned it. Although some students of the period have highlighted "simmering white discontent," nonwhites voiced the most discontent of any group. Only 16 percent expressed being "very happy" compared to 35 percent of the total sample, and only 19 percent reported that things were going "very" or "fairly well" compared to 30 percent of the entire sample. The source of their disquiet was clear: 33 percent of nonwhites identified drugs and crime as major issues, while only 18 percent of the entire sample mentioned either drugs or crime.[12]

None of this is to claim that the city was devoid of racial strife during the late 1960s and early 1970s. Rather, it suggests that these moments of conflict must be understood on their own terms rather than treated as inexorable consequences of the racial order or neoliberalism and that these terms were defined by the policy arena in which clashes occurred and by the interests and values of the groups embroiled in those controversies. For example, African Americans and Jews remained committed partners in New York City's liberal coalition until the Ocean Hill–Brownsville school controversy in 1968. That is when Mayor John Lindsay's experiment in "community control" of schools and racial succession in neighborhoods sparked conflicts between black residents and activists and the Jewish-dominated teachers union. Many Jewish teachers forswore their liberal ideals to protest a policy they viewed as a threat to their material interests. In 1966 the Civilian Complaint Review Board created another racial flashpoint. At the urging of some civil rights organizations and liberal groups, like the NYCLU and the Liberal Party, Lindsay established an independent review board to investigate complaints against police officers. Opponents of the board, including the Patrolmen's Benevolent Association and the Conservative Party, gathered enough signatures for a referendum abolishing the board. In November 1966 the board went down by a large margin: about 63 percent New Yorkers voted to abolish the board, and only 36 percent voted to save it. Although whites largely opposed the board, white attitudes depended on actual experiences, ethnic background, and class. Based on one poll, 83.1 percent of Catholics voted against the board, while Jews were somewhat split, with 55 percent opposing the board and 40.2 percent supporting it. This variation is not surprising given that 54 percent of Catholic respondents had relatives or close friends on the police force, while only 24 percent of Jewish respondents reported such connections. In regard to class, college-educated whites split 50-50 on the referendum. While class did not produce dramatically different views among Catholics, it had a significant effect on the policy preferences of Jews. Almost 55 percent of college-educated Jews and about 63 percent of Jewish professionals supported the board. Finally, despite the support of some civil rights organizations, such as the Congress for Racial Equality, the coalition was led by the ACLU.[13]

While ethic conflict over the Civilian Complaint Review Board deserves attention, white Catholics, as the polls show, were far more concerned by student protests. Although many white ethnic police officers certainly did not hold positive views toward the black communities they policed, they reserved much of their ire for student protesters, who represented a public safety threat and derogated the values they held dear. In a survey of police officers in Chicago, Boston, and Washington, D.C., in 1967 almost two-thirds listed "demonstrations" as "the main cause of violence these days." "This 'rebellion of the police,'" Seymour Martin Lipset wrote, "is a response to their being faced with 'confrontation tactics' by student and black radical militants." Based on his analysis of several police surveys, Lipset concluded, "Most policemen are conservative, conventional, upwardly mobile working-class supporters of the American Way, who aspire for a better life for their families."

> To find the scions of the upper middle class in the best universities denouncing them as "pigs," hurling insults which involve use of the most aggressive sexual language, such as "Up against the wall, Mother F—," throwing bricks and bags of feces at them, is much more difficult to accept than any other situation which they have faced. Police understand as normal the problems of dealing with crime or vice. They may resent violence stemming from minority ghettos, but this, too, is understandable and part of police work. But to take provocative behavior from youths who are socially and economically much better off than they and their children is more than the average policeman can tolerate.

Police officers, many living the great American immigrant story and believing that hard work and virtue yielded success, watched as the decadent and dishonorable behavior of the "scions of the upper middle class" suffered few negative consequences, and they felt powerless to stop it. According to them, noble American institutions (e.g., courts and universities) failed to discipline and punish this behavior and frequently sided with the privileged malcontents that rejected them.[14]

Together these surveys tell a very important story. Instead of validating the simple backlash story, in which whites resentful of civil rights gains left the Democratic Party, these results reveal that the reactions of white ethnic New Yorkers to the social and political events of the period were narrowly tailored to the specific threats they encountered because of place, ethnicity, and class position, and their values more than racial attitudes influenced how they interpreted these events. To the extent that white ethnics worried about crime, their qualms were products of particular patterns of illegal activities in their neighborhoods instead of racial politics. Also, how white ethnics interpreted the turbulent events of the era depended upon their moral codes. The social conservatism of white Catholics caused them to view the antics of student protesters with contempt. The liberalism of Jews, particularly Jewish professionals, caused them to view the Nixon administration with great disdain. Furthermore, resentment among some white ethnics over black challenges to their power did not bleed into crime policymaking. The surveys do not indicate a desire among white ethnics to deploy police and prisons to maintain the old racial order or to suppress a population of surplus black labor. The evidence makes two things very clear: racial issues were not high priorities for either blacks or whites, and African Americans and Puerto Ricans were far more concerned than whites about drugs and violent crime.[15]

Perhaps it is necessary to look beyond the liberal "melting pot" to find white backlash to urban crime. By the end of the 1960s, the rest of the state was experiencing a growing drug problem. The number of accidental deaths in New York State, excluding New York City, rose from 9 in 1960 to 142 in 1971. In Erie County, which includes Buffalo, the number rose from 9 in 1969 to 21 in 1971. Other data confirm these trends. The number of individuals with an upstate residence that received treatment at facilities operated by or affiliated with the NACC increased from 262 in 1968 and 1969 to 689 in 1970 and 1971. Erie County, Monroe County, which includes Rochester, and Onondaga County, which includes Syracuse, had the largest number of residents at NACC facilities. Although these numbers pale in comparison to the rates of drug addiction and drug-related deaths reported in New York City, specifically Harlem, it is quite possible that the increase sparked concern in upstate New York. The 1969 NACC survey, however, suggests otherwise. Unlike respondents from Manhattan North, not many interviewees from Buffalo, Rochester, Syracuse, Utica, or Troy listed public safety issues as a problem in their neighborhood. In all these areas, the problem mentioned most often was vandalism. Only 9 percent of respondents from Buffalo and 5 percent of respondents from Rochester mentioned drug use.[16]

Moreover, whites did not view their drug problem through a racial lens. In 1970 Governor Rockefeller held drug forums in cities throughout the state, including in Monroe County, Syracuse, and Utica, and these forums were not hotbeds of white backlash. In fact, the tone was mostly progressive. One speaker in Utica complained about the lack of rehabilitation within prisons for people arrested for drug crimes: "There is no rehabilitation. As a matter of fact, there is nothing for [a prisoner] to do but sit there and learn about crime for 24 hours a day. He does not know about stealing and other things, but he learns. And there is nothing mentioned about drugs the whole time there. There is nothing done except for sitting there away from society and getting mad at it." At the forum in Monroe County, one speaker outlined an aggressive program devoted to education, rehabilitation, and follow-up care. He said that given the failures of the NACC, "it is necessary to reorganize thoughts on this problem realizing that drug abuse is merely a symptom of emotional turmoil and not the central problem itself." He also advocated making a variety of resources available, including "job placement [services], family planning agencies, Planned Parenthood and venereal disease [re]sources, as well as access to legal resources to inform these troubled individuals of their rights under the law." His comments were greeted with applause. In Syracuse, a women told the governor to stop arresting young men just hanging around and instead "bust" the "big pushers" and to help addicts solve the personal problems that drove them to abuse drugs.[17]

At these forums, African American junkies and pushers never emerged as bugaboos. If attendees did not attribute abuse to social conditions, they either blamed the breakdown of the family or a permissive culture. Some people argued that parents were not paying enough attention to their children. One attendee argued that "[t]he drug users have become drug users because they have not received the leadership, the inspiration, and the education that they should have from their parents." Joseph A. Piccola, sheriff of Oneida County, blamed working mothers: "[W]hen wives and mothers work—perhaps they have to, perhaps they shouldn't have to—but when they do, they are removed from their children, perhaps when they are going to school, perhaps when they are coming home from school, when mother ought to be there." He ended by saying, "Perhaps the breadwinner should earn enough so that mother can be at home with the family. Working mothers may be a contributing factor." Others blamed addiction on the moral decline of American culture. They blamed television, psychedelic posters, and coffee houses, among others things, for creating long-haired, bell-bottom-wearing, ill-mannered youth drawn to illegal narcotics. Some decried the tolerant attitudes of middle-class parents. In fact, during a hearing of New York State's Joint Legislative Temporary Commission to Evaluate the Drug Laws in Buffalo in October 1970, Mike Amico, the sheriff of Erie County, chastised the white middle class for its lenient approach to white middle-class drug users. He asked, "There is a great deal of talk these days about legalizing marijuana in this country. Why is there so much talk today?" Responding to his rhetorical question, the sheriff opined, "Perhaps we should examine the class of persons who are affected by the marijuana laws. Ten and 20 years ago it was primarily those from the ghetto who were affected by the marijuana laws. Today it's the college student, the high school student, the middle and upper class American who is affected. Could it be that the law was okay for the ghetto but terribly wrong for middle class America? . . . I think middle class America better start disciplining its children and regulating itself rather than attempting to change the laws to suit its present whims." In Monroe County, the speaker who promoted rehabilitation and social services also criticized permissive parents, remarking, "Abuse of medications is not a new problem. What is new, however, is its acceptance within the middle and upper class white American communities. The problem might not have achieved its national prominence had it remained confined to the ghettos and slums of our urban communities."[18]

Perhaps it is necessary to study how the suburbs of New York City rather than upstate communities interpreted drug addiction and crime. Aided by discriminatory housing programs and possibly motivated by racial animus, many working- and middle-class whites retreated to the suburbs to escape city life, enjoy their consumers' republic, and build their version of the American dream. Federal housing and transportation policies and economics reconfigured the social composition of these communities. By 1957, 500 companies had left New York City for the suburbs of Long Island, Westchester County, and Fairfield County, Connecticut. While the city saw an increase in executive and clerical employment, the number of individuals working in manufacturing declined from 590,000 in 1947 to 520,000 in 1957. At the same time, employment in suburban factories and offices climbed from under 2 million to about 2.5 million. In 1965 James J. McFadden, acting labor commissioner, said that the city "had reached a dead end so far as future industrial growth and jobs were concerned" and suggested that New Yorkers "might be better off seeking jobs in the suburbs and New Jersey." People followed the jobs. While the city's population declined by 1.4 percent between 1950 and 1960, the population of Nassau County rose by 93.3 percent and the population of Suffolk County rose by 141.5 percent. Additionally, by the late 1960s drug addiction had begun to spread to the suburbs of New York City. The number of drug-related deaths in Suffolk County increased from 3 in 1969 to 11 in 1971. In Nassau County, that number climbed from 13 to 31. Westchester County also experienced a rapid rise in the number of drug-related deaths: only 5 were reported in 1969, but two years later the county witnessed 43 drug-related deaths. Given all of this, it is quite possible that whites within these suburban communities saw drug addiction as a "contagion" born in creeping black ghettos and spread by malevolent black and Puerto Rican pushers, and it is quite possible these anxieties rather than the overtures of the black silent majority shaped the discursive context from which the drug laws emerged.[19]

Because of the growing spatial separation between whites and racial minorities and the concentration of the drug problem within minority communities, whites' material interest in harsher drug penalties, though conceivable, is not readily apparent. Spatial separation meant suburbanites faced unique problems and understood them on their terms instead of blaming their misfortunes on the ghetto "other." The results of the NACC survey substantiate this proposition. In 1969 vandalism was the top issue: 27 percent of respondents in New York City suburbs listed it as a problem facing their neighborhood. The next top two issues were burglary (21 percent) and drug use (15 percent). Suburbanites also distinguished the drug problem in their communities from the crisis facing inner-city communities. In 1966 Frank G. Straub, leader of the Kiwanis Club of Hopewell Junction in Dutchess County, wrote Senator Robert Kennedy to request "stringent laws" and "mandatory sentences" for "dope peddlers." Straub also noted that "the drug and narcotic problem has not become acute in Dutchess County [as it has] in other, more densely populated areas in our state and nation." Moreover, suburban whites understood their unique drug challenges. A 1971 NACC survey of 7,500 individuals in New York State indicated that barbiturates and some stimulants were much more prevalent than heroin in the suburbs. In 1966 William Cahn, district attorney for suburban Nassau County, told the Joint Committee on Narcotics and Drug Addiction, "I am concerned about the young people in my community. I am concerned about the growing addiction problem." "Dope" did not worry Cahn as much as barbiturates: "There is little chance, in my humble opinion, that a youngster would first go to heroin. . . . [The pusher], therefore, has resorted to new gimmicks in order to start the youngsters on the road toward addiction. Narcotics-based cough medicines and all sorts of barbiturate pills. This is now the problem in my community of Long Island. Pills are far more accessible and far cheaper."[20]

White suburbanites supported rehabilitation and viewed harsh sentences for dealers as ways to protect their children rather than guard their community against blacks and Puerto Ricans. In December 1965 the Birchwood Elementary School PTA delivered a petition signed by members urging legislators to "enact the necessary legislation requiring maximum sentencing for narcotics pushers." They suggested that "a minimum 20 year sentence for first offenders convicted of narcotics pushing should be mandatory." In 1966 one mother wrote Senator Bernard Smith, a Republican from Suffolk County, "[A] Northport boy . . . is now in an institution for drug addicts. He was an extremely handsome boy who also had an excellent future. The latest news about him is that he climbs the walls and jumps through windows. The doctors suspect brain injury. . . . How I cried when I learned of this boy's plight. You see, Senator Smith, this boy was once a boy scout in my husband's troop. We knew him since he was five years old." In 1966 Nassau Court Judge Elizabeth Bass Golding said, "We should be treating at least 500 youngsters—and perhaps a lot more." Judge Golding also promoted educational programs in public schools to "actually teach youngsters what they're blundering into if they experiment with pills or glue." In 1969 David Millman, superintendent of the Hauppauge Public Schools in Suffolk County, informed Senator Smith that the Hauppauge Board of Education would appreciate his support for "any legislation that would provide stronger court imposed penalties to persons convicted of selling narcotics to minors" and "legislation that would provide increased support for narcotics research, control and rehabilitation."[21]

In 1966 the *Long Island Press* published a series of articles on the spread of drug addiction to the suburbs that powerfully captures how class rather than race affected how whites in Nassau and Suffolk counties framed and negotiated this new challenge. Leonard Victor, the author of the widely read series, emphasized the class orientation of the "new" victims of drug abuse. The first article was entitled "Kids from 'Fine Families' among Thousands Hooked." Victor interviewed several drug users and found that "they all came from 'good addresses' in Forest Hills, Great Neck, Huntington, Lawrence and Hollis—not the slums." Suffolk County District Court Judge Floyd B. Sarison said, "Starting late in 1964, we began to witness a brand-new wave of middle-class and rich young addicts." Although Victor and white suburbanites described addiction as "spreading" from "the slums," specifically minority communities in New York, they did not literally mean that black or Puerto Rican junkies and pushers carried the disease to pristine communities and infected their innocent children. Put simply, they did not consider black or Puerto Rican addicts and dealers threats. One article in the series was entitled "It Was Easy to Buy Deadly Pills on LI."

To be clear, they did not completely dismiss urban neighborhoods as a source of illegal narcotics. Suffolk's police commissioner said, "We can't pretend that we're sheltered 'way out East.' Young people have too much mobility these days. If they can't get drugs here, they're only two hours from [drug sources in] Jamaica, Brooklyn, Greenwich Village or Harlem." The commissioner placed the onus on middle-class white youths instead black and Puerto Rican pushers: these teenagers and college students were agents who were freely choosing to engage in this illicit activity. Victor argued that drugs were being spread through the middle-class social networks of white youths. He reported, "To capture pushers in the multi-million dollar narcotics trade, police can pose as adult pushers. But they are powerless to penetrate high school and the private parties in the playrooms of respectable homes." In a subsequent article, Victor repeated this claim, complaining that the police could not infiltrate "the decent living rooms and playrooms of suburbia where teenagers take pills and smoke marijuana."[22]

Likewise, many white suburbanites did not blame the spread of addiction in their neighborhoods on predatory black pushers or contagious black junkies. Instead, they argued that the broader culture and family life had pushed many "fine" young people into addiction. Victor indicated that there was a "reoccurring" theme in all of his talks with young drug users: "They all hate their parents." He quoted one young woman who complained about her domineering father. Edna, "from a swank Suffolk estate," told Victor, "[My father] never showed the slightest sign of love or affection for me. And my mother was a dishrag who was afraid to raise her voice, even to me . . . let alone to my father." Don said of his parents, "Loathe 'em. My father is so damn busy making money I've never gotten well acquainted with the man. My mother's such a community do-gooder she's forgotten that charity begins at home." In his explanation for the spread of drug addiction to "good addresses," Dr. Henry Bill, director of Pilgrim State Hospital in Suffolk County, said that too many parents "either ignore their children or want too much from them" and argued that addiction was "only a symptom, like alcoholism, of the real disease, which is a lessening of moral restrictions in a sanctionless society that turns freedom into license." In 1970, at a drug forum Rockefeller held in Garden City, Dr. Celia S. Deochin, member of the Nassau County Drug Abuse and Addiction Commission, also blamed the culture, saying, "I think we have to do something about the so-called American way of life, in which there is a lack of adult role models from TV on down."[23]

This indigenous construction of drug addiction within suburbs also shaped how legislators from these areas understood the growing crisis. During the debate over involuntary commitment in 1966, Senator Smith remarked, "I come from a small community far removed from Bedford-Stuyvesant. We woke up this year with a [narcotics problem] involving the young of the community, people from families of modest income, and this is a problem that has been near to me for a number of years." Republican senator Edward Speno from Nassau County said of drug users, "We are talking about the people with whom we live and they do not necessarily live in cold tenements or back houses. Some of them come from the split levels in my own community. There is no color line, no religious line, no income line and every parent in this room shudders at the thought his son or daughter may one day experience the needle." Senator Speno stated, "I was brought to this subject in a number of ways and sought to be identified with this legislation primarily by reason of the astonishing revelation to me and my colleagues in Nassau County of the unusually large incidence of drug addiction and experimentation with drugs by young people as first disclosed in a series of articles that appear[ed] in the *Long Island Press* in its 'Spotlight on Long Island Addicts,' . . . then by a series of articles that appeared in the *Newsday* . . . long series of [in-depth] articles . . . pointing to specific situations of involvement of citizens of my community with this horrible disease." For suburban whites, drug users and dealers did not refer solely to urban blacks. Their worries emerged from their unique experiences: the threats that "goof balls" and "pep pills" posed to white working- and middle-class teenagers rather than the threats that black junkies and pushers posed to their children.[24]

How white legislators understood the drug problem in minority communities was dramatically influenced by African Americans members of the chamber. For example, in 1970 the governor announced that he would ask the Office of Crime Control and Planning to coordinate federal, state, and local campaigns against drug trafficking and abuse and would ask the State Investigation Committee to conduct hearings on and evaluate law enforcement's response to drug dealing. Republican senate majority leader Earl W. Brydges, of Niagara Falls, credited Waldaba H. Stewart, the African American Democratic senator from Brooklyn, with raising these issues and educating the legislature:

> I think, as far as I'm concerned, the springboard, the taking off point, for this program was the debate we had in the Senate the other day, initiated by Senator Stewart, on the other side of the aisle, in which he pointed out some facts—which are matters of almost first impression with me—I had no idea the degree to which he could document the actual drops [places where drugs or money are left] within the area in which he lives, and this was followed by a conference . . . with the Commissioner of Police of New York City, which was initiated by Senator Goodman in which, again, Senator Stewart and others documented the extent that you could document something like this, the fact that there were areas known to him where narcotics where customarily bought and sold.

Stewart, reflecting on his efforts as well as the politics of the moment, remarked, "I don't care whether this is an election-year program or not. . . . The statement by the Governor, even if it is made only in reaction to statements made on this floor, shows somebody is listening." And they were listening. Brydges's salutary words were not an empty gesture but an accurate depiction of the agency and reach of black legislators. Less than a week before Rockefeller's announcement, at the end of a sleepy, ordinary senate session, Stewart stood up and gave an "angry" speech that "quickly [commanded] the attention of other Senators." He impugned the New York Police Department for inaction: "A year ago I identified one dozen drops [places where drugs are sold] . . . in my Senatorial district. . . . I took these drops to the local police captains . . . then to the Commissioner of Police of the City of New York and asked them to use their police power to get these drop locations removed. . . . To this date these drops are still there." According to Stewart, law enforcement officials told him that they were "trying to get the big boys." To this the Brooklyn senator responded, "[M]y people will not take as an answer anymore that you are trying to get to the big boys." This time his pleas did not fall on deaf ears. Senator John H. Hughes, a Republican from Syracuse and chairman of the crime committee, rose in support of the senator from Brooklyn, saying, "[Senator Stewart is] looking for action and the action is not forthcoming. We'll be pleased to come into your district and have a hearing." Hughes also recounted testimony he heard during a hearing of his committee in Harlem that year: "The accusations were that policemen not only were not enforcing the law . . . but were being paid. I suggested to [Police Commissioner Leary] that this was a very serious charge . . . made by responsible people." Following these speeches, the senate unanimously passed a resolution calling for a legislative inquiry into the possible "dereliction of duty" of police in Bedford-Stuyvesant.[25]

In addition to personal experiences and the mobilization of the black silent majority, the policy preferences of white Republican politicians were also shaped by their own ideology and values. As the legislative history of the drug laws reveals, several members of the state's Conservative Party had principled objections to Rockefeller's original plan. They offered a dramatically different causal story for New York's drug problem. In 1970 a position paper on narcotics by the Conservative Party candidate for governor, Paul L. Adams, described drug addiction as a dangerous disease "which has ravaged the ghettos for years" and "is spreading at an alarming rate from ghetto to suburb, from college campus to junior high school, even, tragically, into elementary schools." Adams's policy statement placed a great deal of attention on drug addiction in the ghettos but did not condemn blackness. It appropriated the framing fashioned by the black silent majority: "By no means are all, or even almost [all], or even a majority, or even very many ghetto residents narcotics addicts. The vast majority is not. But the spread of narcotics and the rampant crime in its wake have made stable life in the ghetto virtually impossible." Adams stated that the people of Harlem were deeply concerned about drug traffic because, "as the Reverend Dempsey, a Harlem clergyman, told the committee, unless the traffic in drugs is stopped, the entire younger generation in Harlem is doomed." Instead of blaming the state's drug problem on Harlem, Adams focused on the broader international drug trade. To be clear, he advocated "special and dramatic measures" to protect New Yorkers from the disease of drug addiction, stressing the need to take "addicts off the street" and to impose maximum sentences on pushers. Nonetheless, neither addicts nor pushers were the main "enemy." Adams blamed the state's narcotics problem primarily on organized crime and international drug trafficking. The second sentence of his document read, "Simple arithmetic shows that the mob is producing more addicts for the drug market much faster and more efficiently than we can rehabilitate them." Adams argued that the "addict in the street did not consciously choose the life of degradation to which his addiction condemns him," and, as a result, the conservative gubernatorial candidate advocated going after "the source."[26]

Ultimately, the hidden and public transcripts of whites in New York reveal that they did not supply Rockefeller with the casual story that undergirded the drug laws. Whites in New York City, upstate, and the suburbs were far less concerned about drug addiction and crime than were racial minorities in urban neighborhoods. To the extent they worried about crime, they focused much more on property crimes and vandalism than violent crime. To the extent that a white backlash occurred in New York City, it was more specific than general, as it was isolated to the specific policy arenas in which blacks and certain white ethnic communities were drawn into conflict. The available survey evidence does not indicate that these clashes drove white ethnics to blame blacks for crime and drug addiction. Rather, the evidence suggests that white interest in crime was animated by actual experiences rather than racial anxieties. In 1970 whites throughout the state were far more bothered by Vietnam and Nixon than black crime or civil rights, and the views of whites mobilized around the drug issue were shaped by class and values rather than their position within the racial order.

While there is little evidence to suggest that local white backlash determined drug policy in New York, it is possible, especially given Rockefeller's presidential ambitions, that the narcotics control policy succumbed to the power of a national political culture suffused with white racial resentment. Evaluating this hypothesis requires identifying changes in the public mood and assessing whether Rockefeller's politics and drug policy responded to those shifts. Between 1950 and 1963 there was only one article in the *New York Times* mentioning "white backlash." That number rose to 157 in 1964 before hitting an all-time high in 1966 with 214 articles. In September 1966, pollster Louis Harris sensed that white backlash to the "black power movement" could be "decisive" in the upcoming elections in November: "[I]t can tear the Democratic party apart at the seams in the North where traditionally, low income whites and low income Negroes must be on the same side. . . .

Today they're not on the same side over civil rights. This could cost the Democrats and cost them heavily." The elections that year confirmed Harris's assessment. After Goldwater's monumental defeat in 1964, 1966 brought the Republican Party good fortune: it saw a net gain of three Senate seats, 47 House seats, and eight governorships. Ronald Reagan, the conservative Republican candidate for governor of California, beat the odds by defeating incumbent Democratic governor Edmund Brown and leading Republicans to a near sweep of the state's major offices. Brown attributed his defeat in part to "white backlash." Commenting on his victory, the governor-elect remarked, "It seems to be all over the country. The people seem to have shown that maybe we have moved too fast, and want to pause and reconsider the course we've been following." Given all of this, it is not surprising that Rick Perlstein identified 1966 as the crucial pivot point in American political development, writing, "If it hadn't been for the shocking defeats of a passel of LBJ liberals blindsided in 1966 by a conservative politics of 'law and order,' things might have turned out differently; Nixon might have run [in 1968] on a platform not too different from that of the LBJ liberals instead of one that cast them as American villains."[27]

Even so, the ideological shift in American political culture in 1966 neither explains Rockefeller's behavior nor New York State's narcotics control policies during the mid-1960s. Despite a general recognition of white discontent, Rockefeller aggressively courted many African American activists. In 1965, at the urging of Jackie Robinson, the governor met with an "ad hoc committee to discuss problems of [the] Negro community." The group included Bill Booth, the state NAACP chairman; Rev. Sandy Ray, minister of the Corner Stone Baptist Church; Al Duckett, an aide to Martin Luther King; and Rev. George Lawrence from Antioch Baptist Church. The purpose of the meeting was to hear the grievances of the local black community but also to identify people for state positions. In 1966 Rockefeller asked a veritable who's who of the black commu-

*Jackie Robinson
with Governor
Rockefeller, 1966.
(New York State
Archives. Governor.
Public information
photographs,
1910–1992,
2006–2008.
13703-83, Box 3,
Number 1140.*

nity to join his Committee on Urban Affairs, including Reverend
Dempsey, A. Philip Randolph, Rev. Bill Jones, Reverend Lawrence,
Reverend Ray, Mrs. Anna Hedgeman, Kenneth B. Clark, and
James R. Lawson. If a racialized political environment played a pivotal role in Rockefeller's calculations, the governor would not
have expended so much effort on the African American community and the punitive drug laws would have appeared earlier. Although the governor enacted involuntary commitment in 1966, it
was not consonant with the perceived revolution in white sentiment as it also contained a significant rehabilitative element. Thus
while the old penology had begun to wane in New York State by

1966, it had not completely withered away, and its diminished influence was the product of the black silent majority rather than the white one.[28]

Although some name 1968 as the turning point in American political culture, new national trends did not alter Rockefeller's style. In 1968, during his unsuccessful bid for the Republican nomination for president, the governor's strategy suggested that he still believed his liberal reputation would have been an asset in a general election. And he was not alone. Many shrewd political observers thought there was room in the Republican presidential primary contest for a liberal candidate. For some, the debate at the time was whether that candidate was going to be Michigan governor George Romney or Rockefeller. For others, the choice was clear: Rocky. The *Saturday Evening Post* reported, "[T]he idea persists that Rockefeller—the same divorced Eastern Establishment liberal who was venomously booed by a hysterical Republican National Convention in 1964—may be his party's key to the White House in 1968." One "venerable Republican" said, "They've got to make up their minds that they have to nominate Nelson if they want to win. There is no other way." In early January 1968 Maryland governor Spiro Agnew, who would later become Nixon's vice president, initiated a "Draft Rockefeller" campaign in "response to the groundswell of public opinion that I have seen developing." At the beginning of 1968, Melvin Laird, the powerful chairman of the House Republican Caucus, who backed Goldwater in 1964, believed Rockefeller represented the best chance for Republicans to win the presidency and pick up seats in the House. He reasoned that the New York governor was the "strongest Republican candidate with disenchanted Democrats and independents." A survey of congressional Republicans showed that 53.1 percent said that Rockefeller would be the strongest candidate, while only 37.7 percent picked Nixon. Reagan was the top choice for vice president (56.9 percent). The polls supported these assessments. A Gallup poll taken in late 1967 showed Rockefeller leading President Johnson by fourteen points, while Nixon led him by four and Romney led him by three. A Harris Poll taken in early 1968 showed a much more competitive race: Rockefeller and Johnson were tied. The same poll showed Nixon losing to the president by eight points, Romney losing by thirteen, and Reagan losing by fourteen.[29]

When Rockefeller entered the contest, he did not shun his liberal bona fides. After the assassination of Robert F. Kennedy, Rockefeller's campaign provided a home for the hopeful and progressive energies that animated Kennedy's message. In his classic journalistic account of the 1968 campaign for president, famed political reporter Theodore H. White observed:

> Once one joined Rockefeller on his June and July excursions around the country, one could see that he had similarly repealed the laws of partisanship. Or else the assassination had done so. For as I joined him, still mourning from the Kennedy campaign, I felt at home again—the gaiety and zest of the campaign were the same. The hunger for a hero was the same. . . . The same young people followed Rockefeller as had followed Kennedy in throngs as he traveled; the same heavy mixture of Negroes who wanted a champion made his rallies come alive. . . . And the crowds responded to all of Rocky's speeches with the same emotional undertones as the Kennedy crowds.

In June 1968 Rockefeller took out an ad in forty-one newspapers across the country, including black newspapers, that alluded to race riots and the crime problem in slums. In bold letters, the title was "To Burn or Not to Burn." Reminiscent of George C. Wallace, it stated, "Detroit, Newark, Watts, which once blazed on our TV screens, [smolder] now in our minds. What do these people want?" The tone, however, quickly changed. It became hopeful—and progressive: "In the ashes of Washington, a slum child answered: 'I would like my street to look like a brand new neighborhood with changed people who are friendly to others.'" The ad continued, "I say that our cities can be saved. . . . [But] they will not be saved by men who read rousing speeches about crime control—and say nothing about gun control." Ultimately, the ideological sensibilities and political coalitions that defined his strategy in 1964 continued to do so in 1968.[30]

Over time, Rockefeller had begun to exhibit some ideological movement to the right, but the transformation was not thorough. Although local politics made him more conservative during the 1970 gubernatorial contest, they did not influence his drug policy. When Rockefeller decided to run for an unprecedented fourth term as governor in 1970, Democratic polls exposed his weaknesses in four policy areas: taxes, narcotics, mass transportation, and aid to cities. These political headwinds pushed "High Tax Rocky" to the right. Rockefeller's local political fortunes increasingly rested in the hands of disgruntled white ethnics. The governor told friends that "he could not hope to hold the 35% of Jewish and Negro votes his polls showed him he had received in the past and that he would have to make up for them by increasing his vote in places like Bay Ridge and Buffalo." So he aggressively wooed Italian politicians, including Mario Procaccino, and was "more likely to be photographed nibbling pasta than knishes." At the press conference in which Procaccino publicly declared his support for Rockefeller, the governor thanked and embraced him, an act that did not go unnoticed within the black community. A few days later, before Rockefeller's address to 100 Black Men, an association of prominent African American males, Jackie Robinson told the governor's aides to prepare for a question about the endorsement. Despite the need to appeal to conservative Italian voters, the narcotics control policies the governor proposed in 1970 were not as punitive as his 1973 drug laws. From 1966 until 1973, on the advice of the state's issue network, Rockefeller vetoed several attempts to increase penalties for drug possession and sales and expanded rehabilitative resources.[31]

In the early 1970s Rockefeller had begun to notice that the American population was not in the same ideological place it was when he excoriated extremists in 1964 or when he adopted Kennedyesque optimism in 1968. Republican attitudes in the early 1970s clarify the governor's electoral constraints. In 1971, 27 percent of Republican voters wanted Spiro Agnew to return as Nixon's running mate. That number rose to 43 percent in 1972. Reagan scored second place in both years, with 19 percent and 20 percent, respectively. In 1971 Rockefeller was tied with John Connally, secretary of the treasury, for fourth place; only 10 percent listed either the governor or the secretary. Rockefeller's odds improved in 1972: with the support of 14 percent of Republican voters, he climbed to third place right after Reagan. In August 1973 a Gallup poll revealed that 22 percent of Republican voters wanted to see Agnew nominated as the Republican candidate for president. Another 22 percent listed Reagan, and 13 percent listed Rockefeller. After an investigation and indictment forced Agnew to resign as vice president in early October 1973, initial polling suggested that his departure would create a competitive race for the Republican nomination. A poll conducted just before his resignation showed that Reagan was the second choice of 29 percent of Agnew supporters. Almost 20 percent selected Rockefeller, and 16 percent selected Connally. In a survey of Republican county chairmen conducted in early 1974, 39 percent selected Reagan for their party's nomination in 1976, while 24 percent selected Vice President Gerald Ford and only 12 percent selected Rockefeller. This survey also revealed regional variation: Reagan led in all regions, but his highest levels of support came from the West (47 percent) and the South (46 percent). In the Midwest, Reagan scored 39 percent, and both he and Rockefeller received 28 percent in the East. Ford came in second in the West, South, and Midwest. Thus polling from 1972 until early 1974 reveals that, if Rockefeller still desired the Republican nomination, Reagan was the man to beat, and, in order to beat him, Rockefeller needed to improve his ratings in the South and the Southwest.[32]

Only these political dynamics can explain the ideological orientation of Rockefeller's original drug proposal and its specific timing. In March 1972 Rockefeller ran into William Fine, president of a department store and chairman of a drug rehabilitation program, at a party. The governor asked Fine to visit Japan to learn why that nation had one of the lowest addiction rates in the world. Fine agreed, flew to Japan, spent a weekend meeting with health officials, and returned "with the apparent secret to the Japanese success against drugs—life sentences for pushers." He submitted his report to the governor but received no response for two months. At another party attended by Fine, Rockefeller, and Reagan, Fine and the California governor discussed the trip. Reagan asked for the report, and Fine asked Rockefeller for permission to share the report with him. Rockefeller refused. As Persico explains, "This thunderbolt was to be hurled by him." Interestingly, Reagan, who as president assumed leadership over the War on Drugs in 1982, was also partly responsible for the war's first major offensive: the Rockefeller drug laws. As the aging governor of New York contemplated his last attempt at the presidency, he believed, based on polling evidence, that the governor of California was the only thing standing between him and the White House. After Fine informed Reagan about the results of his fact-finding mission in Japan, Rockefeller knew that he could not afford to let Reagan propose life sentences for narcotics crimes and own this issue in the eyes of conservative Republican primary voters. This was his issue. His policy. His time.[33]

While racial discord was a crucial component of this cultural moment, it would be a mistake to conflate the conservative politics that determined the harshness and timing of Rockefeller's drug laws with racial backlash. It would be an error to depict the Republican primary voters with whom Rockefeller sought to ingratiate himself as racist former Democrats, as compatriots of Bull Connor or George Wallace. Many backlash white voters remained in the Democratic Party for many years. Although more white southerners voted Republican in presidential elections from 1964 onward, it was not until the middle of Reagan's presidency that more southern whites began identifying as Republicans than Democrats. Tradition and the power of incumbency kept the Democratic Party a force in southern politics until the Republican takeover of Congress in 1994. Many communities outside of the South's black belt had a tradition of racial moderation and had been more concerned with economic issues. The dramatic transformation of the South, propelled by federal policies and economic modernization, only deepened these political impulses by creating white-collar suburban enclaves whose politics were defined more by material concerns and cultural matters than by Jim Crow. Based on his study of the grassroots activism of the white silent majority in the Sunbelt South during the late 1960s and early 1970s, Matthew Lassiter reports that "The southern base of the Republican party always depended more on the middle-class corporate economy than on the top-down politics of racial backlash." He also notes, "During an era of social crisis and racial turmoil, the GOP voters in the suburbs and the Wallace voters in the countryside would not fit comfortably into a stable political coalition."[34]

Similarly, it is important to disentangle the history of the New Deal coalition from the history of the conservative movement. Civil rights activism and the policy choices of Democratic political elites certainly upset the fragile alliance of southern whites, midwestern and northeastern white ethnics, and African Americans. But the conservative movement, which had not died in the aftermath of the Great Depression, followed its own trajectory. Kim Phillips-Fein writes, "If we shift our focus from cultural to economic issues, it becomes clear that the origin of modern conservative politics and ideology predates the 1960s. And in this sense the roots of the movement's triumph can be found in the disaffection of people very different from the white working-class conservatives who are so often seen as central to its rise." The economic transformation of the Sunbelt and local religious life produced middle-class, suburban hotbeds of traditional, antigovernment conservatism. Lisa McGirr demonstrates that, unlike white middle-class reformers in New York, these "suburban warriors" stood "united in their opposition to liberal 'collectivism'—the growing tendency of the state to organize social and economic life in the name of the public welfare and the social good," and they opposed "what they perceived to be a decline in religiosity, morality, individual responsibility, and family authority." This Republican constituency championed a "culture of control," but not for racial purposes. Civil rights and riots occasionally quickened its authoritarian sensibilities, but racial conflict did not invent them. In other words, the politics that compelled Rockefeller to cull the punitive notions of the black silent majority did not rise from the ashes of the New Deal coalition, which was consumed by civil rights. They were forged in the enduring embers of the conservative movement, which were heated by economic expansion and religious fervor.[35]

FOR SOME, THE ROCKEFELLER DRUG LAWS EMBODIED THE authoritarian sensibilities the governor of New York once so eloquently derided. For others, the measures constituted a spectacular repudiation of the racial liberalism he once symbolized. By the end of 1973, liberal New Yorkers had begun to view Rockefeller as the epitome of the reactionary politics of the "silent majority"—the white silent majority, that is. Liberals held him responsible for the gruesome Attica massacre, a prison riot that ended with the deaths of twenty-nine inmates and ten hostages. And with the passage of the controversial drug laws, an icon of liberal Republicanism assumed a prominent place within backlash narratives—an infamous position within the history of mass incarceration. Although race was a crucial feature of postwar American political development, Nelson Rockefeller encountered in the late 1960s and early 1970s a political terrain dramatically transformed by federal policies and economic forces. The balance of political power within American politics no longer rested in the industrial Midwest and Northeast. By the time Rockefeller previewed his infamous drug laws, the analysis in Clark Clifford's memo to President Truman was out of date: the trenches of American partisan conflict had been dramatically reconfigured by the movement of whites to the suburbs of New York and the advance of suburban warriors in the Sunbelt. In both cases, values and class, more so than race, defined how these communities interpreted their experiences with drugs and crime.

The same racialized public policies and economic forces that constructed the "dark ghetto" shielded middle-class whites and working-class white ethnics in New York City from the violence and vice of the "black urban sub-proletariat," and, as a result, their views toward drugs were defined by their actual experiences and values rather than racial panic. Although rising crime rates caught the attention of all New Yorkers, anticrime attitudes varied across neighborhoods and social groups. Given neighborhood-level patterns of drug abuse and violent crime, African Americans and Puerto Ricans were far more concerned. Whites across the city were exposed to different crime threats, and they complained more about property crime than either drugs or violent crime. Moreover, while racial minorities consistently listed drugs and crimes as their top concerns, whites gave other issues, such as student protests and taxes, higher ratings. Contrary to the claims of Wacquant and others, whites in the city did not clamor for prisons or more severe criminal sentences. They did not need to. The "ethnic container" that was the ghetto never collapsed. Because whites were never in any real danger, they had other things on their minds.

There is very little evidence that whites in the city turned to the new penology in order to guard their position within the racial order. Survey evidence shows that racial minorities more than whites, including those who considered themselves members of the silent majority, felt aggrieved and resentful. African Americans certainly challenged their influence in a variety of policy realms, but these battles never culminated in a grassroots, white working-class movement for more prisons. In order to understand the limited impact of white backlash within the city during this period, it is important to disaggregate these ethnic conflagrations. Because of New York City's unique history of ethnic diversity and because the city's political system provided "both a conduit for neighborhood political expression and a supply of entry-level positions," ethnic power was dispersed across neighborhoods and policy spheres. Consequently, the African American pursuit of greater representation and influence involved some ethnic groups at some moments and not others. There were also class differences. Notwithstanding the Ocean Hill–Brownsville school controversy, upper-income Jews remained liberal. Irish police officers harbored resentment toward both racial minorities and upper-class student protesters, whose behavior they considered affronts to the values to which they faithfully adhered. Furthermore, these disparate battles between blacks and working-class white ethnics never congealed into a broader racial war, and they clearly did not push the city's drug program to the right. City officials continued to espouse the old penology, and local politicians, including members of law enforcement, most sensitive to the electoral pressures of white backlash consistently opposed harsh drug penalties and waged a fierce battle against the Rockefeller drug laws.[36]

Racialized housing policies and urban deindustrialization established a color line that protected suburban whites from the "black urban sub-proletariat." The urban black poor neither jeopardized their life chances nor endangered their consumers' republic. As a result, their attitudes toward drugs were shaped by their actual experiences and values rather than either racial stereotypes or racial resentment. While the black silent majority defined junkies as outside the boundaries of their community and U.S. citizenship, middle-class whites in upstate counties and in the suburbs of New York City viewed drug users as members of "good families." Instead of treating addicts as the "other," middle-class whites depicted these users as daughters, sons, and neighbors. Because they believed that addicts were victims of either poor parenting or the broader culture, they advocated for rehabilitation. Yet some members of these communities protested these liberal views. Many officials, particularly those from white ethnic backgrounds, derided parental leniency—the way white middle-class mothers and fathers coddled instead of punished wayward children who already had been given all the chances in the world. These suburbanites did not want law enforcement to storm minority neighborhoods; they wanted the police to invade the "playrooms of respectable homes."

The hidden and public transcripts of white legislators show that the conservative shift in New York State's narcotics control policy responded to the framing of Harlem's black silent majority instead of the attitudes of middle-class suburban whites. Like many of their constituents, white state legislators were able to distinguish between the nature of narcotics problems in their communities and the nature of the problems in Harlem and other minority neighborhoods. Their comments during legislative debates and the text of their position papers indicate that black leaders, like Reverend Dempsey and Senator Stewart, taught them about "the reign of criminal terror" in minority neighborhoods and described in vivid detail the prisons of despair that junkies, pushers, and other "thugs" had forced "decent citizens" to live in. Various documents reveal that black leaders pleaded with white legislators to extend the penal arm of the state into their "dark ghetto." And these white officials frequently obliged. As politicians with their own ideas and goals, leaders of the Conservative Party also followed their own ideology when assessing the state's narcotics problem and determining appropriate prescriptions, which led them to be far more troubled over international drug trafficking and organized crime than junkies and low-level pushers in Harlem and other minority communities. Observing their small-government philosophy and heeding the wishes of local law enforcement, members of the Conservative Party also forced Rockefeller to curtail his draconian plan in 1973. In the end, the cumulative effect of these dual local discourses and the mobilization of New York's black silent majority, white silent majority, and issue network was the development of a narcotics control policy regime that punished poor black users and low-level dealers, spared white middle-class housewives and young adults, and attempted to save very young children.

Of course, Rockefeller's ambitions also shaped the ideological direction and timing of drug policy in New York State. Because of his presidential aspirations, it is quite plausible that a racialized national political culture forced the governor to adopt a radical policy that would incarcerate large numbers of African Americans. The evidence, however, does not support this claim. Not only did the drug laws not arrive immediately after either 1966 or 1968, years when analysts at the time and historians since have claimed that American culture was reconstructed by white racial animus, but the governor also did not immediately alter his presidential strategies. Eventually, Rockefeller sensed a new mood within the Republican Party. He witnessed the enthusiasm with which party activists embraced Ronald Reagan. They wanted Barry in 1964, but they had fallen in love with the conservative governor of California in the early 1970s. Rockefeller realized he needed to make a change, and so change he did. By 1973, his ideological conversion was complete, and the content and timing of his original drug proposal was a direct reflection of his need to compete against the new conservative icon. It is unlikely that Rockefeller's ideological makeover in the early 1970s was geared to the general mood of the national electorate. He had always believed that the greatest impediment to his pursuit of the presidency was the Republican primary voter rather than the American median voter.

Historians and other analysts who have emphasized the power of the racialized public mood that emerged in the late 1960s miss two important dynamics. Explanations of mass incarceration emphasizing white backlash to black activism of the 1960s and early 1970s unwisely reduce the history of the period to the politics of race. Civil rights was one of many issues that jolted the social, political, and moral foundations of American society. Although Rieder's nuanced account of the white silent majority supplies a correction, his formulation of the silent majority lacks conceptual precision. How a cornucopia of concerns functioned politically varied across geographical, class, ethnic, and ideological boundaries. The white silent majority in New York did not emerge incorporeal from a cultural milieu molded by the media or Machiavellian elites. It came from matter. It was motivated by specific, tangible concerns at home and at work rather than a phantasmic racial threat. Furthermore, "dynamic representation" makes much more sense in the context of low-information politicians: without knowing the attitudes and policy preferences of specific groups, politicians might rely on conventional wisdom as a guide. Yet Rockefeller was ahead of his time in his use of polling and public relations experts. The data he generated allowed him to ascertain and target the fears and aspirations of particular communities.[37]

Finally, Rieder's conception of the silent majority unduly removes working- and middle-class blacks from the "restorationist" American middle. African Americans are unidimensional: they are defined as a cohesive group, single-mindedly driven by race. In contrast, whites are treated with greater analytic care: Rieder stresses their multiple grievances, permits class differences, makes room for morality and ideology, and emphasizes historical contingency. Black politics exists as a mere foil to the interests, values, and aspirations of working- and middle-class whites. However, taking the interests, values, and aspirations of both working- and middle-class whites and blacks seriously and locating them both within particular places clarifies the tumultuous politics of the late 1960s and early 1970s, especially drug policy development in New York State. From the black silent majority in urban black belts to the white silent majority in the suburban Sunbelt, the politics that defined the punitiveness and timing of the Rockefeller drug laws as well as the broader narcotics control regime was rooted in the politics of class rather than the politics of race.

Conclusion

"Liberal Sentiments to Conservative Acts"

AFRICAN AMERICAN LEADERS, organizations, and newspapers across the country "noted with great interest the tough new
drug law" passed in New York in 1973. Col. Leon H. Washington,
publisher of the *Los Angeles Sentinel*, greeted the Rockefeller drug
laws with cautious optimism. He surmised, "Only time will tell
how effective this tough anti-drug law will [be in decreasing] the
drug problem in the state of New York. Any way you look at it, at
least Gov. Nelson Rockefeller had the guts to get a bill into law [that
is] designed to take many in the drug business off the streets."
Other black newspapers were more ambivalent, weighing the punitive elements of the law against the costs of drug trafficking and
addiction. "Dope in the community," Baltimore's *Afro American*
stated, "has become a nasty problem. . . . Police seem not to be able
to solve it, to some degree because many of them have their hands
out for payoffs. To the average citizen the prevalence of dope means
their families are threatened on every turn. Children could become
victims, addicts steal and kill and the costs to taxpayers and property owners are mushrooming." The gravity of the drug crisis, the
editorial reasoned, obviated the potential hazards of the law and

the potentially perverse political calculations of the governor. In terms of the latter, the editorial stated, "One thing, whether for political reasons or otherwise, Gov. Rockefeller is attempting to do something about the problem." In regard to the former, it stated, "If Gov. Rockefeller's new law shows any progress in curbing the problem, maybe some of its questionable aspects can be compromised on civil and human rights. . . . If nothing else, the New York law may provide some new directions on which tactics might be best used to curb the drug menace."[1]

H. Carl McCall, chairmen of the editorial board of the *Amsterdam News*, was more circumspect and offered suggestions for "living with the new law." He clearly understood the potential costs: "Overcrowding of the prisons, magnifying an already intolerable situation in penal institutions, seems to be a sure [result]." Yet he added, "However one feels about the new drug law, it is on the books for the moment, and we have to live with it. But we don't have to sit idly by and watch the steps of implementation once more neglect the needs, desires and true representation of the Black and Puerto Rican communities." Even so, McCall was clear-eyed about Rockefeller's motivations, emphasizing the governor's noticeable ideological shift from "liberal sentiments to conservative acts." He argued that, in order to brandish his conservative bona fides with Republican primary voters, the governor "followed his crushing of [the] Attica protest with crackdowns on welfare clients and a toughening up of narcotics legislation."[2]

As McCall predicted, the Rockefeller drug laws produced a dramatic expansion of New York State's prison population and the mass incarceration of people of color, particularly blacks and Latinos from New York City. In 1973 there were 14,679 felony drug arrests; by 1989, that number had risen to an astounding 62,293. Although the number of felony drug arrests declined to 40,209 in 2008, that figure was still almost triple the total the year Rockefeller signed his punitive program into law. In 1973 there were 843 felony drug commitments to prison; that number rose to 11,225 in 1992. Total commitments dropped to 5,190 in 2008, but that number was still more than six times the total in 1973. Drug offenders represented only 11 percent of the state's prison population in 1973; that proportion rose to an all-time high of 35 percent in 1994 before dropping to 20 percent in 2008.[3]

The racial disparities are undeniable. In 1980, 32 percent of individuals incarcerated for drug offenses were white, 38 percent were African American, and 29 percent were Latino. In 1992, the year the state reported the highest number of felony drug commitments to prison, 5 percent of individuals incarcerated for drug offenses were white, 50 percent were African American, and 44 percent were Latino. In 2006, 25 percent of adults committed to prison from New York City were from areas that held only 4 percent of the city's adult population. Over 50 percent of those individuals were committed for drug offenses, and 97 percent were African American or Latino. The human costs are also unmistakable. As critics predicted, the Rockefeller drug laws led to overcrowding in New York's prisons, filled those penal institutions with racial minorities, and failed to curb drug addiction and crime. Physicians for Human Rights and the Fortune Society conducted interviews with fifty men and women who served at least one year in a New York state prison for a nonviolent drug offense. Their findings were sobering: "All respondents spoke about the misery of incarceration. Whether the difficulty of separation from family, the dangerous conditions to which they were exposed, the abuse they witnessed or the emotional toughening they underwent, respondents described lives of often petty crimes and addiction interrupted—but not ameliorated or resolved—by incarceration." They reported, "Families lose sons, brothers, husbands and fathers; communities lose potential leadership and economic power, schools lose parental involvement."[4]

Accounts of mass incarceration have accurately described the odious consequences of punitive crime policies. But regarding the origins of these policies, the record has been incomplete, taking snapshots of policy enactments, ignoring the voice and agency of working- and middle-class African Americans, and reducing political institutions and processes to the reproductive power of either racism or neoliberalism. Policies have histories that need to be traced and explained. *Black Silent Majority* has unearthed the complex conjuncture of historical and institutional factors that have defined postwar crime policies and generated these deplorable outcomes and has found that attending to multiple African American voices enriches our understanding of the intricate and cacophonous postwar politics of punishment.[5]

AFTER THE END OF WORLD WAR II, INTERNATIONAL DRUG trafficking resumed and wreaked havoc upon African American communities in New York City. The confluence of the malignant and robust heroin trade and the depressed and racialized market for low-skilled labor caused many poverty-stricken African Americans, like *Dope*'s Louie, to seek "junk" in order to feel "great" and "free" and caused some entrepreneurial and sinister individuals, like *Dope*'s Porse, to sell the drug in order to make a living. For these reasons, the dual scourges of heroin addiction and crime befell African American neighborhoods much more so than white neighborhoods. Drug-related arrests, surveys of self-reported drug use, and statistics on individuals receiving treatment in state-sponsored or affiliated programs indicate that higher proportions of African Americans than whites were heroin users from the end of the war until the 1970s. While each individual measure carries its own descriptive limitations, vital statistics, the most reliable data, confirm these trends, revealing that higher proportions of African Americans than whites died from drug-related causes over the same period. The data also show that black drug-related deaths were concentrated in minority neighborhoods, especially Harlem.

Similarly, crime rates shot up in black neighborhoods during the 1960s and 1970s. Crime rates climbed throughout the city, but the highest rates of increase occurred within minority communities, like Harlem and Bedford-Stuyvesant. African Americans constituted a minority of the city's population but represented about half of all homicides. Neighborhood context defined individuals' exposure to certain illegal acts; their expressed concerns were not abstract but born of the unique nature of crime in their communities. The black silent majority was much more alarmed about drug addiction and violent crime than its white analogue. While working- and middle-class whites worried about vandalism and property crime, working- and middle-class African Americans sought an end to the "reign of criminal terror" in their neighborhoods.

It is certainly important to take stock of the concepts and ideas espoused by policy experts and public officials. The disposition of working- and middle-class African Americans notwithstanding, a racialized construction of black criminality could have imbued the criminological theories of members of the state's issue network and hindered the enactment of liberal prescriptions for New York's drug epidemic. It is quite plausible that the concentration of drug addiction within minority communities interacted with racial stereotypes to prompt a shift from penal welfarism to the culture of control in New York State. Yet the legislative histories of major and minor narcotics control policies from the late 1940s until 1973 belie this proposition. Public transcripts—hearing testimonies, press releases, newspaper reports, speeches, and studies conducted by legislative committees, public officials, and civic organizations—and letters and internal memoranda indicate that few, if any, policy activists or public officials in New York State drew on racial notions to diagnose the addiction problem facing the United States during the 1950s and 1960s. White liberal politicians, civic leaders, and public officials in the state's narcotics control network, including

Sylvia Singer, Rev. Norman Eddy, Dr. Paul Zimmering, and Senator Manfred Ohrenstein, drew on scientific evidence and their class-inflected progressive ideology to diagnose the growing menace of heroin addiction. For young black drug addicts, like Charlie Reed and Walter Vandermeer, and old black drug addicts, like Louie in *Dope*, white reformers and liberals remained dutiful guardians of the old penology from the end of World War II until the passage of the drug laws.

During the 1940s Harlem leaders and white reformers articulated identical explanations for Harlem's crime situation, but, because different material interests and moral imperatives animated their views, their public statements diverged as the evolution of the American racial order and economic system placed working and middle-class blacks in a promising yet precarious social context. During the early 1940s, black and white middle-class leaders stood side by side to rebuke mainstream newspapers for reporting on crime and delinquency in a manner that reinforced racist ideas while discounting the structural origins of criminal behavior, particularly joblessness and racial discrimination. While white reformers were motivated by progressive values, the black middle class, wary of the white gaze, emphasized the perfectibility of man in public in order to guard against validating notions of black inferiority, which they believed represented the greatest impediment to equal rights. In private, as the crime threat to "prominent citizens" and "hard-working mothers" rose, they discussed individual character and values and advanced the need for more discipline.

Beginning in the early 1960s, working- and middle-class African Americans and white reformers began to describe the "junkyard by the sea" very differently, and their anticrime explanations and prescriptions started to conflict. White reformers and liberal politicians did not experience the daily indignities of ghetto life, so in public and private they consistently championed criminologies of the welfare state. For some, this stance was an article of faith or a tenet of their social philosophy. For others, it was a product of consequentialist reasoning, based on their reading of the available evidence or their professional expertise. Because urban black crime never threatened their public safety or social position, their fidelity to their values and expertise remained unshakable. In contrast, the consequences of drug policy for users and government agencies mattered less to working- and middle-class African Americans than the consequences for their personal welfare. Their policy preferences were shaped by their desire to defend private spaces, recapture public spaces, and restore their peace of mind. Additionally, working- and middle-class African Americans drew upon the moral content of indigenous class categories and exploited the language of citizenship to make sense of the threats to their safety. When crime rates climbed, they disregarded the old penology and publicly embraced the new one. According to them, contumacious junkies and pushers were operating outside of bounds of "decent" society and spurning the law with reckless abandon, and the evil purveyors of junk and a "derelict army of addicts" were ruining the community and the life chances and lifestyles of citizens. They had shed much blood, sweat, and tears to compel the United States to extend to them rights denied, and, as a result, they boasted political gains and saw a consumers' republic rise from the concrete. Consequently, they believed junkies and pushers were abjuring the obligations of citizenship, undercutting their political and social progress and closing off their access to consumer goods. Drug addicts trying to finance a quick fix pilfered the symbols of their thin yet meaningful success: television sets, fur coats, and the hubcaps on their Cadillacs.

Junkies and pushers were not the only individuals working- and middle-class African Americans wished to displace. Surveys show that, in addition to drug addiction and crime, Harlemites also worried about "bad kids" and "drunks on the streets." Many Harlemites felt overwhelmed by the brokers of all types of violence and vice. In 1959 the *New York Age* drafted a lengthy list of outcasts deserving eviction from the community: "recidivists," "junkies," "dope pushers," "muggers," "prostitutes," "pimps," "trespassers," "loiterers," and "crap-game organizers." In 1962 Mrs. Mary Smith of West 145th Street was sick of hearing "filth and profanity" every time she walked the streets. By 1966 Mrs. Miller of 125th Street had begun to believe that the "middle class Negro" was surrounded by "the rampant poverty-ridden element." Langston Hughes's Jesse B. Simple found a solution: a "new land" "for all the un-nice, upset, disturbed, hopped-up, wine soaked people who cannot and do not and will not and *won't* act nice."[6]

Irrepressible black-on-black violence and liberalism's perceived intransigence in the face of this new fact of urban life gave life and purpose to the black silent majority. The "silent" in the movement's appellation functioned as both a critique and a call to arms. As a critique, the trope scolded some working- and middle-class African Americans for sitting idly by as a willful minority infringed upon their rights and transgressed social norms. As a call to arms, the trope urged working- and middle-class African Americans to tell it like it is. For many working- and middle-class African Americans throughout the country, the trope of the silent majority effectively captured their frustration and alienation. They felt abandoned by the dominant institutions of society, especially legislatures, courts, and the police, that seemed to neglect their basic need for security, which they also considered a civil right. The black silent majority maintained that U.S. citizenship entailed both rights and responsibilities, and they firmly believed that they had earnestly fought for their rights and fulfilled their responsibility by living upstanding, middle-class lives defined by work, probity, and service. So they felt dejected by liberalism, which they believed had disregarded their striving and pain and had come to the defense of a minority of malcontents, including criminals, white student protestors, black militants, and the poor, who constantly flouted sacred liberties and mocked, without reprisal, the laws and norms to which they faithfully adhered. These tensions boiled over during the debate over the Rockefeller drug laws. In 1973 the black silent majority and white liberals depicted the state's drug problem and the governor's antidrug program in starkly different terms. While working- and middle-class African Americans grew frustrated with the persistence of crime, members of the state's issue network were buoyed by slight decreases in rates of drug addiction. While members of the state's issue network, white reformers and law enforcement officials, derided the governor's proposal for its perceived abridgment of civil liberties and impracticality, members of the black silent majority castigated white "bleeding hearts" for not considering how junkies were eroding their civil rights and making their neighborhoods unlivable. They blasted white liberals for their reliance on statistics and sociology and their dismissal of the public safety threat posed by drug addiction and trafficking. According to the black silent majority, white liberals, from their privileged perch within the racial order, suffered from ideological vainglory and a class-based myopia, which led them to fight on behalf of addicts and pushers rather than the city's working- and middle-class black citizens.

While much of the literature on mass incarceration has been slow to acknowledge the punitive impulses of African Americans, some authors who have contend that aggressive policing and other harsh measures are part of a panoply of policies that also include social programs. Indeed, this is how Charles Hamilton depicted the black silent majority: as hard-working African Americans with middle-class aspirations, values, and fears who are more liberal than their white counterparts and, in terms of crime policy, tend to view themselves as members of a racial community and to embrace structural explanations for criminal behavior and support less punitive solutions. The question is not whether African Americans supported punishment at the expense of structural solutions but the conditions under which this occurred. The issue is not *whether* but *when*. During the late 1950s and early 1960s, working- and middle-class African Americans supported Metcalf-Volker and advocated for more hospital beds for drug users. At this point, the "Zombie-eyed junkie" was more of an inconvenience than an emergency. As *Dope* depicts, residents could ignore junkies and vagrants and treat them as cautionary tales. By 1966 junkies had begun to imperil the property and persons of working- and middle-class Harlemites. Consequently, the black silent majority in New York supported involuntary commitment, a policy that permitted the expulsion of addicts from the streets while promising rehabilitation. Thus the program balanced the normative predispositions and the public safety needs of the black silent majority. By 1973 junkies had become more than an imposition, and the "un-nice" had become unbearable. In community meetings and town halls, residents set aside sociology and their liberal affinities. They begged for aggressive policing and punitive policies to banish unsavory characters, alleviate their perturbation, and return commerce and community back to normal.[7]

While the black silent majority had not completely abandoned penal welfarism by the early 1970s, they had restricted access to its benefits. The tragic death of Walter Vandermeer and the dramatic rise in juvenile addiction prompted women's groups, like MAD, and other civic associations to lobby public and private agencies for hospital beds for young drug users and more programs to combat juvenile addiction. In response, from 1966 until 1973 the state funded several educational programs that warned young people about the dangers of illegal drugs. Walt's tragic story not only inspired a play; it shaped policy, even becoming a module in New York City's Department of Education's antidrug curriculum. The state also implemented or subsidized a variety of programs to house and treat juvenile drug users. The "perfectibility" of children was not an absolute principle: there was no definitive age level separating the redeemable from the damned. These determinations depended on the nature of the threat. Members of the black silent majority had no compunction revoking the deservedness of teenage and child loiterers and muggers. According to frightened residents, these young people were not simply misguided; they were just plain mean. And, as a result, youthful offenders were incapable of reform, and merited punishment.

Perhaps the retributive attitudes and regulatory practices of working- and middle-class African Americans evidence the strength of Antonio Gramsci's concept of hegemony. Instead of focusing on direct forms of coercion, hegemony draws attention to the ways in which ruling classes operating though the institutions of civil society can exert moral and intellectual influence over subordinate groups and sustain their consent to the dominant values of society and to their own oppression. Following this logic, the morality of the black silent majority emulated the bourgeois values of the ruling classes and, as such, existed to manufacture consent to the status quo. This idea is not beyond the pale: Harold Cruse and Charles Hamilton formulated similar arguments. This theory, however, relies on the false assumption of a unitary public sphere. Power can both control and evict, and exclusion can cleave space for the construction of ideologies and practices that are independent of the prevailing social order. Moreover, these removed settings, or what Nancy Fraser calls "subaltern counterpublics," can serve as sites of autonomous political action. "In stratified societies," Fraser writes, "subaltern counterpublics have a dual character. On the one hand, they function as spaces of withdrawal and regroupment; on the other hand, they also function as bases and training grounds for agitational activities directed toward wider publics. . . . It is precisely in the dialectic between these two functions that their emancipatory potential resides." As Fraser's notion of "subaltern counterpublics" implies, post-Reconstruction segregation—ironically, Jim Crow—propelled the production of a distinct black public sphere, in which African Americans formulated critiques of Jim Crow and mobilized against it. Lawrence W. Levine's classic study of the black oral tradition shows that the ideas and practices of blacks within these subaltern black counterpublics do not mimic the dominant culture. Instead, African Americans rejected some ideas and practices and appropriated and modified others. Levine's work implies that the black silent majority did not paraphrase power: their language was homegrown and their appeals for stern measures were authentic.[8]

The relationship between the subaltern black counterpublic and the bourgeois public sphere varied with the historical development of American racism and the interests and ideologies of black activists and residents. At the nadir in American race relations, middle-class African Americans revised Victorian ideology and fused it with indigenous notions of self-help and reform, and post-Reconstruction black civil society preserved these class-based values. Despite this independence, the "agitational activities" that emerged from subaltern black counterpublics were fashioned with an eye toward the ideologies of the bourgeois public sphere. During the Roaring Twenties, middle-class blacks gave birth to the New Negro in order to trumpet the humanity and worth of African Americans. After their experiment with the New Negro ended, middle-class blacks continued to pay heed to the white gaze. When Harlem's "crime wave" began to infiltrate the bourgeois public sphere in the early 1940s, middle-class black activists publicly attacked media sensationalism and charged it with trafficking in outdated racial stereotypes, and they expounded structural theories of crime in order to counter claims of the innate inferiority of black people. Yet in the privacy of Harlem's subaltern counterpublic, they secretly brooded over delinquency and fixated on values, family structure, and the lack of discipline within schools and homes. Interestingly, fear of the white gaze did not make them more punitive; it made them appear more progressive than they actually were.

Historical socioeconomic and cultural shifts fundamentally reconfigured the politics of black-on-black crime. New York's bourgeois public sphere—at least the corner devoted to studying and debating drug addiction and crime—grew more progressive. A new generation of liberal white do-gooders entered and dominated this policy arena. Much less Protestant as a group than their forebearers, these educated middle- and upper-class men and women were no less evangelical in their devotion to evidence-based social reform. While some of their predecessors might have condemned blackness, these policy experts, activists, social workers, and public officials blamed the postwar rise in drug addiction and crime on poverty and racial discrimination. Simultaneously, working- and middle-class African Americans became less fearful of the white gaze. From the 1940s until the 1950s, they experienced tangible progress. Everyone from Brother Johnson to Adam Clayton Powell Jr. welcomed and praised new redevelopment projects, the increase in numbers of elected and appointed black officials, black professionals, and greater working- and middle-class African American participation in the consumer culture. Working- and middle-class Harlemites had forged a new fate, one not linked to the fate of the urban black poor. They had become less invested in civil rights and more concerned about public safety. Beliefs about black-on-black crime once shielded in the subaltern counterpublic were now being expressed publicly, in everyday talk as well as opinion polls, editorials, cartoons, songs, and plays. Instead of parroting the sociological and epidemiological consensus among members of the state's predominantly white narcotics control network, working- and middle-class Harlemites spoke their own truth. They repurposed the communal spaces and institutional forms used as "bases and training grounds for agitational activities" during struggles for equal rights to broadcast their predicament, share indigenously constructed frames, and push for immediate and drastic solutions. Because of Reverend Dempsey's crusade and other grassroots efforts, working- and middle-class African Americans penetrated this policy arena and managed to influence how white politicians from suburban and rural areas of the state understood the drug problem in minority communities. Over time, Rockefeller, who was no pioneer of punishment, began to recite their grievances, appropriate their language, and echo the discourse of their movement.

The evidence does not indicate that working- and middle-class African Americans' shift from "liberal sentiments to conservative acts" was the result of their succumbing to the hegemony of the white ruling class. To the contrary, a rich array of sources show that, especially during the late 1960s and early 1970s, the black silent majority offered an alternative to the criminologies of the welfare state espoused by the white middle-class reformers who had monopolized the debate over drug addiction and crime during the 1950s and the early 1960s. Many minority legislators voted against the drug laws, and survey evidence indicates that, driven by their own interests and ideologies, they were at odds with the communities they represented. In general, many black political elites were much more optimistic about the current state and future of Harlem than the people they represented. For other minority elected officials, the bourgeois public sphere, as it had during the 1940s, made them more liberal than their constituents. African American politicians like Percy Sutton, whose political aims required the support of white liberals and Democratic leaders, expressed ideas in white-dominated public spaces that contradicted pleas they heard during meetings and marches in their communities. Furthermore, contrary to Hamilton's "patron-recipient relationship" theory, Dempsey and other grassroots activists did not alter their views or tamp down their antidrug, anticrime mobilization because of the receipt of government funds. They had been agitating for punitive policies before the governor made funds available for his antidrug policies. In fact, the politics of involuntary commitment in 1966 indicate that it was white reform organizations and some white politicians, like Mayor Lindsay, that began to embrace punitive solutions in order to secure state funding.[9] Nevertheless, neither the discourse of the black silent majority nor the claims of the state's narcotics control network was determinative. Neither can explain the timing of major narcotics control legislation in New York State. Capacity constraints and the political interests of governors and other state legislators influenced *when* dramatic changes in narcotics control policy occurred. The presence or absence of sufficient capacity influenced whether and when politicians and officials adopted certain policy proposals. At the same time, budgetary constraints were both "perceptual" and real. Depending on their priorities, politicians could marshal arguments for or against the barriers the budget imposed on certain policy initiatives. How public officials interpreted capacity constraints depended on their institutional position and political interests. Capacity concerns mattered more for bureaucrats charged with executing drug policy than for elected officials who merely had to vote for or sign legislation. Those in elective office had greater opportunities to avoid blame by attributing policy failures to agency heads, other governmental levels, and even the beneficiaries of social policies (i.e., drug users), but a bureaucrat's role in the administration of programs was traceable. Worried about risks to their reputations and institutions, agency heads were more likely to prioritize capacity concerns, and these considerations shaped how they approached new policy initiatives.[10]

The effect of capacity constraints also depended on the political context—both the level of public attention and gubernatorial ambitions. When drug addiction was not at the top of the agenda, governors and legislators responded to the issue network by enacting incremental policy shifts, forming investigatory committees, or placing blame on the federal government. Agency heads successfully scuttled several plans by convincing Governors Dewey and Harriman that their organizations lacked sufficient capacity to implement comprehensive legislation. Although activists and increasing rates of drug addiction kept the issue on the agenda during Dewey's and Harriman's tenures in office, neither politician felt enough political pressure to ignore resource limitations. Both simply shifted blame onto the federal government. By 1962 a number of key political variables had changed: a poll-sensitive Nelson Rockefeller had become governor and was facing reelection, and reformers had built a formidable statewide network of civic groups. Led by Senator Metcalf, the issue network negotiated a policy that in the abstract met the goals of the rehabilitative ideal but did not provide adequate resources to support it. To spare the expense of creating a new department and to gain the support of agency heads worried that a new department would compete against their organizations for scarce state resources, the coalition charged the Department of Mental Hygiene with the execution of the program. This compromise meant that the responsibility for implementation fell on bureaucrats whose primary interests and expertise were not in the area of narcotics control. By 1966 the policy venue had moved from the issue network to the governor's office. Rockefeller's aides, informed by the causal story promulgated by working- and middle-class African American activists, cognizant of the wishes of vested interests and limited by available capacity, designed a program for involuntary commitment that would pass legislative muster but would face significant challenges and delays during the implementation phase.

The limitations of narcotics control programs established in 1962 and 1966 set the stage for subsequent policy development. Because officials who were not invested in the program's success and refused to fight for more resources were placed in charge of Metcalf-Volker and because it did not offer sufficient incentives for drug users to select treatment or stay in voluntary commitment, the program faltered. Due to this policy failure and the causal story of addiction promoted by Dempsey and others, blame did not fall on Metcalf-Volker. It fell on junkies, who, according to Dempsey and working- and middle-class Harlemites, just did not want to act right. Consequently, the black silent majority turned to involuntary commitment in order to forcibly remove drug users from the streets and compel them to submit to treatment. Because the design of the legislation slowed the implementation of the program, it did not provide working- and middle-class Harlemites any immediate relief. Residents continued to fear their commute to and from work, churchgoers continued to fear attending worship services, and business owners continued to fear opening their shops. So Dempsey's crusade continued and the pleas of working- and middle-class African Americans became more strident. Shorn of any commitment to rehabilitation for adult drug users and other criminal offenders, the black silent majority turned exclusively to the police and prisons for their salvation. They foisted a hard bargain on drug users, "hoods," and other social outcasts: submit to the norms of traditional black civil society without the guarantee of structural reforms or face prison time.

Because explanations for the drug laws usually operate at a macro level, they get some parts of this story right while missing crucial details. As dominant accounts assert, Republican Party politics played a seminal role in the formulation of the controversial antidrug program. But by not attending to the specific political movements that emerged, these explanations write the organizing of working- and middle-class African Americans out of the history of the drug laws and misconstrue the preferences and motivations of working- and middle-class whites in New York and throughout the country. From the corners of urban black neighborhoods rather than the cul-de-sacs of middle-class white suburban neighborhoods, a backlash to liberal drug approaches emerged in the 1960s and early 1970s. Working- and middle-class African Americans in

Harlem, caught in the throes of the urban crisis, shifted the discursive terrain in New York in favor of policy prescriptions that punished the irresponsible, distinguished them from good citizens, and sought to control junkies, pushers, and thugs. While individuals from both black and white communities mobilized on behalf of severe penalties for pushers, African Americans activists viewed junkies very differently than whites did. Whites in the suburbs of New York City and in upstate communities—places like Suffolk Country and Monroe County—described addicts as the sons and daughters of good families gone astray; they were more concerned about "pep pills" and "goof balls" than hard drugs. Working- and middle-class African Americans were much more concerned about hard drugs, increasingly treated junkies as the "other," and mobilized on behalf of polices that would remove the "other" from their lives. By the mid-1960s drug policies in New York State had begun to align with criminological notions conjured by working- and middle-class African Americans instead of reflecting the values of working- and middle-class whites.

Although it would be naïve to dismiss the riotous racial politics of the late 1960s and early 1970s, it would also be analytically unwise to miss the cultural nuances of these battles and their effects on drug policy development in New York State. While crime and drugs fomented tension between working- and middle-class African Americans and the urban black poor, the desire of working- and middle-class African Americans to control policy implementation within their communities and to place more blacks in positions of power within city government instigated conflict between them and certain whites. Ethnicity, class position, and values determined the spatial and professional exposure of certain whites to racial threats and their policy preferences. Italians remained conservative because of their cultural background and their marginalization within the Irish-dominated Democratic political machine in New York. The Irish-dominated police force found themselves at odds with both the urban black poor whom they policed and the upper-class white student protestors they were forced to control. Working-class Jews viewed the Ocean Hill–Brownsville school conflict as a threat to their social position, but upper-income Jews remained faithful to their liberal sensibilities. The legislative history of the drug laws shows that many state legislators representing white ethnics prone to backlash in other policy arenas fought Rockefeller's original proposal. Informed by their own ideology and the expertise of law enforcement officials, members of the state's Conservative Party, an early institutional incarnation of the New Right in New York, leveraged their influence within the Republican Party to lessen the punitiveness of the program. The conservative politics that induced Rockefeller's ideological transformation and influenced the timing of his original drug control proposal were not defined by southern Dixiecrats or aggrieved white working-class voters in the industrial Midwest and Northeast. They were defined by "suburban warriors" in the Sunbelt, whose activism was inspired by their white-collar experiences and their evangelical faith.

Dominant accounts of the Rockefeller drug laws completely miss the contours of the pastiche of narcotics control policies that had emerged in New York State by 1973. The Rockefeller drug laws represented a few new conspicuous threads in a thick, aging quilt of New York State's antinarcotics strategy. By focusing on this one policy moment, many studies of the Rockefeller drug laws miss a much deeper history and cannot explain the complicated layering of new and old drug control policies that emerged between the late 1940s and the early 1970s. While the passage of the Rockefeller drug laws constituted a sharp punitive turn, the carceral state that emerged from this moment mixed the old and new penology. Although the lack of capacity and will prevented the enactment of a comprehensive, well-financed medical approach to addiction, members of the issue network successfully achieved incremental changes that expanded rehabilitative resources in the state. In between the passage of major drug-control initiatives, New York governors and the mayors of New York City, in response to the mobilization of the issue network, sponsored experimental treatment programs and antidrug education strategies, financed, through executive action, modest increases in the number of hospital beds available for drug users, and made funds available to private agencies offering treatment and aftercare, including methadone maintenance. Moreover, during the drafting of the 1966 involuntary commitment bill, private agencies and municipal governments received resources to implement their own versions of penal welfarism. The layering of punitive sentences and rehabilitative programs administered by government and voluntary agencies produced a carceral regime in New York State that attempted to maintain social order by punishing some (those deemed threats to "decent citizens") and reforming others (children and those users willing to submit to treatment). Instead of experiencing a drastic and clean break with the old penology, modern crime policy, because of the lingering political influence of liberal experts and administrators in public and private agencies, witnessed the significant yet incomplete retrenchment and privatization of penal welfarism.[11]

While the carceral regime that emerged in New York State after 1973 might seem to conform to neoliberal logic, its specific developmental path points to a different inheritance. *Black Silent Majority* has revealed that use of private agencies in the fight against drug addiction and crime was rooted in real capacity deficits, perceived budgetary limitations, and the ways both shaped political context and constrained policy options. When pressured by interest group activism to adopt some type of rehabilitative scheme, governors and mayors of New York City frequently responded by exploiting preexisting capacity within public and private agencies, and these actions created feedback mechanisms whereby the beneficiaries of new funding streams subsequently mobilized to protect and expand those resources. Thus the privatization of some aspects of drug policy in New York State was a product of actual state structure rather than a belief in the limits of state power or the perceived virtues of market-oriented strategies. Moreover, practices within voluntary organizations that emphasized monitoring, assessment, and accountability were not a consequence of neoliberal thinking but were borrowed from older progressive notions of evidence-based social policy and good government reform. The white middle-class individuals lobbying for and administering these programs were not neoconservatives. They were old-fashioned do-gooders.[12]

H. CARL MCCALL WAS PRESCIENT. HE WAS RIGHT ABOUT THE consequences of the drug laws, and he was partially right about the laws' origins. The story of the infamous Rockefeller drug laws cannot be fully told without recognition of the governor's shift from "liberal sentiments to conservative acts." But *Black Silent Majority* has uncovered so much more. Drug policy development in New York State from the end of World War II until 1973 was also defined in part by the "liberal sentiments" of white reformers and white conservatives—just not in the way usually portrayed in the literature. The former labored unremittingly to establish a drug program consistent with the old penology. When they succeeded in 1962 with Metcalf-Volker, these liberals struggled to broaden the program and adopt new therapies. They jealously guarded their advancements after their criminological model came under vicious assault in 1966 and 1973. Though not vociferous advocates of the old penology, white conservatives fought to soften the blow of the new carceral regime they glimpsed in Rockefeller's original proposal.

Black Silent Majority is also in the unenviable position of furnishing a history that shows that working- and middle-class African Americans are partially responsible for the mass incarceration of black sons, brothers, husbands, and fathers and the misery they endured while committed to penal institutions in New York. To be clear, the model of black politics featured here is not unusual, as it builds on and revises both social scientific linked-fate theories and historical accounts of black class categories. While economic position certainly matters in the construction of African American class identities, it interacts with definitions of virtue to create a historically variable matrix of shared class understandings. Like linked-fate approaches, this model of black politics connects individual African American interests to evolving racial orders and economic systems and post-Reconstruction African American civil society in which those interests are framed and negotiated. This book, however, shows that the black counterpublic remained a stolid repository for traditional morality instead of being an incubator of racial solidarity. As historical studies of black class politics reveal, indigenous class-based values can be conservative, stressing individual responsibility, or progressive, promoting the perfectibility of man. Whether and when working- and middle-class African Americans deployed either facet of their values depended on the nature of the threats posed to their social position. This is where some of the descriptive claims of the new Jim Crow thesis and arguments about neoliberalism are extremely useful: the economic freedoms and social rights afforded working- and middle-class blacks because of the long struggle for civil rights, deindustrialization that closed off the labor market to unskilled, uneducated blacks, and persistent racial segregation placed the dispossessed and the recently empowered in constant contact and conflict. As Kenneth Clark documented in his study of postwar Harlem, chronic joblessness and racial segregation cultivated antisocial behaviors that posed significant risks to the citizenship and consumers' re-public working- and middle-class Harlemites had begun to enjoy in the late 1950s. They responded to these threats by drawing on the darker side of their morality, blaming individuals instead of so-cial structure, seeking punishment instead of reform.[13]

At the heart of this story is the breakdown of racial soli-darity—the suspension of brotherhood and the persecution of the "hood." But this is not altogether surprising. Within the historical context of Jim Crow, racial solidarity made sense: working- and middle-class African Americans and the urban black poor shared similar constraints on their political rights and economic liberties. But times changed. By the 1950s day-to-day interactions with the victims of racial domination and economic exploitation made a greater impression on working- and middle-class African Ameri-cans than their impersonal relationship with the increasingly in-visible agents of those structural forces. While group consciousness had been a formidable shield against Jim Crow and the prepotency of the white gaze, it stumbled in the face of the advancements of working- and middle-class African Americans. In this new histor-ical context, defined by political and economic opportunity and a "reign of criminal terror," racial bonds became like gossamer. Ev-eryday folks like Mrs. Miller of 125th Street and Mrs. Bernice Simms of W. 121st Street, business owners like George Ellis of Degeorge Ladies', Men's, and Children's Wear and beautician Mrs. Cleo Weber, and politicians and activists like Rev. Oberia Dempsey and Mark Southall began to confront black foes—tangible threats with sinew and souls. They were "muggers," "rapists," and "murderers." They were monsters who had thrown the commu-nity into chaos and endangered the safety and jeopardized the hard work and aspirations of working- and middle-class African Amer-icans. So the black silent majority spoke. It organized. It abandoned liberalism, embracing harsh sentences and aggressive policing methods in order to end their nightmare and restore the benefits of their newly won citizenship. In the end, we cannot understand the postwar politics of punishment without understanding the African American shift from "liberal sentiments to conservative acts." The carceral state did not arise like the sun at an appointed time: the black silent majority was present at its making.

Notes

Acknowledgments

Index

Notes

Preface

1. The Innocence Project, http://www.innocenceproject.org; Rand Paul and Patrick Leahy, "Rand Paul and Patrick Leahy: Join Us to Do Away with Mandatory Minimums," *US News & World Report*, August 2013, 1; Mark Appuzo, "Unlikely Allies Push for a Liberalization of Sentencing Laws," *New York Times*, March 3, 2014, A13; Aviva Shen, "Three States Dump Major Private Prison Company in One Month," *Think Progress*, June 21, 2013; Isaiah 61:1 (King James Version).

2. Glenn C. Loury, "Listen to the Black Community," *Public Interest*, no. 117 (1994): 33–37, 35.

3. Lisa L. Miller, "The Invisible Black Victim: How American Federalism Perpetuates Racial Inequality in Criminal Justice," *Law & Society Review* 44, nos. 3–4 (2010): 805–842.

Introduction

1. Nelson A. Rockefeller, *Public Papers of Nelson A. Rockefeller, Fifty-Third Governor of the State of New York* (Albany: New York State, 1973), 650.

2. "The Politics of Drugs," *New York Times*, January 9, 1973, 38; "Comment," *New Republic* 168, no. 4 (1973): 9–13; Lesley Oelsner, "Governor's Drug Plan Draws Anger, Cautious Applause and a Sense of Anguish," *New York Times*, January 4, 1973, 29; New York (State), *To Minutes of Transcript of a Public Hearing of the Senate and Assembly Standing*

Committees on Codes, Held in Hearing Room B, New Legislative Office Building, Albany, N.Y., on February 13, 1973 (White Plains, NY: O'Neill Reporting, 1973), 3.

3. New York (State), *To Minutes of Transcript*, 652.

4. Ibid., 657–658.

5. Ibid., 665.

6. Robert McG. Thomas Jr., "New Drug Laws Scored in Harlem," *New York Times*, February 3, 1973; Amy Plumer, "Albany Notes," *New York Amsterdam News*, May 12, 1973; *The Imperial Rockefeller*, 1970s–early 1980s, Drafts, undated, Series 2, Box 31, Folder 2, Joseph E. Persico Papers, 1910–2003, M. E. Grenander Department of Special Collections & Archives, University at Albany; Joseph E. Persico, *The Imperial Rockefeller: A Biography of Nelson A. Rockefeller* (New York: Simon & Schuster, 1982). Interestingly, neither that line nor any similar claim made it into the final draft of the manuscript.

7. "Report of the Anti-Crime Committee of the New York Branch NAACP," Wilcox Collection, Spencer Research Library, University of Kansas; Maurice Carroll, "N.A.A.C.P. Deplores Harlem 'Terror,' " *New York Times*, December 13, 1968, 1.

8. NAACP, "Report of the Anti-Crime Committee."

9. Ibid.; Douglas Robinson, "Senate in Albany Votes Abolition of Death Penalty," *New York Times*, May 13, 1965, 1; Sidney H. Schanberg, "Governor Signs Loan-Shark Bill, Making Criminal Usury a Felony," *New York Times*, June 9, 1965, 35.

10. New York State, *Report of the New York State Joint Legislative Committee on Crime* (Albany: The Committee, 1969), 279; M. S. Handler, "Harlem Officials Testify on Crime," *New York Times*, February 21, 1969, 50.

11. Roy Wilkins, "New Trend Developing in Black Communities," *Afro American*, January 13, 1968, 2; Paul Delaney, "Blacks, in Shift, Organize to Combat Rise in Crime: A Grass Roots Flavor Crusade Begun by Mayor," *New York Times*, November 13, 1974, 22; Charlayne Hunter, "Blacks Are Developing Programs to Fight Crime in Communities," *New York Times*, February 23, 1976, 14; Charlayne Hunter, "Blacks Organizing in Cities to Combat Crimes by Blacks," *New York Times*, February 22, 1976, 1; Don Snyder, "Senior Citizen Passes Out Auto Stickers," *Los Angeles Times*, October 5, 1969, SG7; Jack V. Fox, "Too Many Fears Paralyze Black Action," *Chicago Defender*, January 19, 1974, 16; "What You Can Do to Combat Crime," *Ebony*, January 1975, 116;

"Beulah Baptist Church Plans Drug Seminar," *Atlanta Daily World*, August 11, 1972, 2; "Big Bethel Sponsors Drug 'Rap' Session," *Atlanta Daily World*, January 3, 1971, 1.

12. Jewell Chambers, "Fearful Residents Talk about City Crime," *Afro American*, January 27, 1968, 1; *Afro American* quoted in J. A. Parker and Allan C. Brownfeld, *What the Negro Can Do about Crime* (New Rochelle, NY: Arlington House, 1974), 52–53; William Raspberry, "Drug Addicts: Victims or Victimizers?," *Washington Post*, March 9, 1973, A27; Hunter, "Blacks Are Developing Programs to Fight Crime in Communities," 14; Delaney, "Blacks, in Shift, Organize to Combat Rise in Crime," 22; Hunter, "Blacks Organizing in Cities to Combat Crimes by Blacks," 1; Fox, "Too Many Fears Paralyze Black Action," 16.

13. Roy Walmsley, "World Prison Population List, 8th edition," International Centre for Prison Studies, School of Law, King's College London, 2009; "New Incarceration Figures: Thirty-Three Consecutive Years of Growth," Sentencing Project, December 2006, http://www.sentencingproject.org:80/doc/inc_newfigures.pdf; Marc Mauer and Ryan S. King, "Uneven Justice: State Rates of Incarceration by Race and Ethnicity," Sentencing Project, July 2007, http://www.sentencingproject.org/doc/publications/rd_stateratesofincbyraceandethnicity.pdf; Mary Pattillo, David F. Weiman, and Bruce Western, *Imprisoning America: The Social Effects of Mass Incarceration* (New York: Russell Sage Foundation, 2004); Devah Pager, *Marked: Race, Crime, and Finding Work in an Era of Mass Incarceration* (Chicago: University of Chicago Press, 2007); Megan Comfort, *Doing Time Together: Love and Family in the Shadow of the Prison* (Chicago: University of Chicago Press, 2008); Bruce Western, *Punishment and Inequality in America* (New York: Russell Sage Foundation, 2007); Christopher Uggen and Jeff Manza, *Locked Out: Felon Disenfranchisement and American Democracy* (Oxford: Oxford University Press, 2006); Vesla M. Weaver and Amy E. Lerman, "Political Consequences of the Carceral State," *American Political Science Review* 104, no. 4 (2010): 817–833.

14. James A. Inciardi, *Handbook of Drug Control in the United States* (New York: Greenwood Press, 1990); Desmond S. King and Rogers M. Smith, *Still a House Divided: Race and Politics in Obama's America* (Princeton, NJ: Princeton University Press, 2011), chapter 8; Michael H. Tonry, *Malign Neglect: Race, Crime, and Punishment in America* (New York: Oxford University Press, 1995); Dan Baum, *Smoke and Mirrors: The War on Drugs*

and the Politics of Failure (Boston: Little, Brown, 1996); Lawrence D. Bobo and Victor Thompson, "Unfair by Design: The War on Drugs, Race, and the Legitimacy of the Criminal Justice System," *Social Research* 73, no. 2 (2006): 445–472; Doris Marie Provine, *Unequal under Law: Race in the War on Drugs* (Chicago: University of Chicago Press, 2007); Patrick A. Langan, *Historical Statistics on Prisoners in State and Federal Institutions Yearend 1925–86* (Washington, DC: U.S. Dept. of Justice, Bureau of Justice Statistics, 1988).

15. Marie Gottschalk, "Hiding in Plain Sight: American Politics and the Carceral State," *Annual Review of Political Science* 11 (2008): 235–260; "City Called 'Haven' for Drug Addicts," *New York Times*, February 15, 1947, 17; David T. Courtwright, *Dark Paradise: A History of Opiate Addiction in America* (Cambridge, MA: Harvard University Press, 2001), 151. For broader historical examinations of the "drug war," see Kathleen Frydl, *The Drug Wars in America, 1940–1973* (Cambridge, UK: Cambridge University Press, 2013); David F. Musto, *The American Disease: Origins of Narcotic Control* (New Haven, CT: Yale University Press, 1973); Arnold H. Taylor, *American Diplomacy and the Narcotics Traffic, 1900–1939: A Study in International Humanitarian Reform* (Durham, NC: Duke University Press, 1969). A few studies have taken a long view of drug and crime policy development in New York: Eric C. Schneider, *Smack: Heroin and the American City* (Philadelphia: University of Pennsylvania Press, 2008); Vanessa Barker, *The Politics of Imprisonment: How the Democratic Process Shapes the Way America Punishes Offenders* (Oxford: Oxford University Press, 2009); Arthur Pawlowski, "New York State Drug Control Policy during the Rockefeller Administration, 1959–73," PhD dissertation, State University of New York at Albany, 1984. *Black Silent Majority* builds upon and revises these excellent accounts by excavating the role that African Americans played in the transformation of drug policy in New York from 1948 until 1973.

16. Michelle Alexander, *The New Jim Crow: Mass Incarceration in the Age of Colorblindness* (New York: New Press, 2012), 21–22.

17. David Harvey, *A Brief History of Neoliberalism* (Oxford: Oxford University Press, 2005); Loïc Wacquant, "From Slavery to Mass Incarceration: Rethinking the 'Race Question' in the United States," *New Left Review*, 2nd series, 13 (February 2003): 40–61, 48–49, 51. See also Loïc Wacquant, *Punishing the Poor: The Neoliberal Government of Social Insecurity* (Durham, NC: Duke University Press, 2009).

18. Michael C. Dawson, *Behind the Mule: Race and Class in African-American Politics* (Princeton, NJ: Princeton University Press, 1994); Elijah Anderson, *Code of the Street: Decency, Violence, and the Moral Life of the Inner City* (New York: Norton, 1999).

19. James A. Morone, *Hellfire Nation: The Politics of Sin in American History* (New Haven, CT: Yale University Press, 2003).

20. Herbert Blumer, "Race Prejudice as a Sense of Group Position," *Pacific Sociological Review* 1, no. 1 (1958): 3–7; Evelyn Brooks Higginbotham, *Righteous Discontent: The Women's Movement in the Black Baptist Church, 1880–1920* (Cambridge, MA: Harvard University Press, 1993); Stemson quoted in Khalil Gibran Muhammad, *The Condemnation of Blackness: Race, Crime, and the Making of Modern Urban America* (Cambridge, MA: Harvard University Press, 2010), 187, 189, 190.

21. For a discussion of joblessness and ghetto-related behaviors, see William Julius Wilson, *When Work Disappears: The World of the New Urban Poor* (New York: Vintage, 1997).

22. Nelson A. Rockefeller, *Public Papers of Nelson A. Rockefeller, Fifty-Third Governor of the State of New York* (Albany: New York State, 1969), 297, 302–303, 528–529, 555; Nelson A. Rockefeller, *Public Papers of Nelson A. Rockefeller, Fifty-Third Governor of the State of New York* (Albany: New York State, 1970), 31. For a discussion of the potential autonomy of political institutions and processes, see Theda Skocpol, "Bringing the State Back In: Strategies of Analysis in Current Research," in *Bringing the State Back In*, ed. Peter B. Evans, Dietrich Rueschemeyer, and Theda Skocpol (Cambridge, UK: Cambridge University Press, 1985); James G. March and Johan P. Olsen, "The New Institutionalism: Organizational Factors in Political Life," *American Political Science Review* 78, no. 3 (1984): 734–749.

23. Deborah A. Stone, "Causal Stories and the Formation of Policy Agendas," *Political Science Quarterly* 104, no. 2 (1989): 281–300; Malcolm M. Feeley and Jonathan Simon, "The New Penology: Notes on the Emerging Strategy of Corrections and Its Implications," *Criminology* 30, no. 4 (1993): 449–474, 450, 455; David Garland, *The Culture of Control: Crime and Social Order in Contemporary Society* (Chicago: University of Chicago Press, 2001); Hugh Heclo, "Issue Networks and the Executive Establishment," in *The New American Political System*, ed. Anthony King (Washington, DC: American Enterprise Institute, 1978), 104. For studies of the influence of issue networks, see Paul Pierson, *Dismantling*

the Welfare State? Reagan, Thatcher, and the Politics of Retrenchment (Cambridge, UK: Cambridge University Press, 1994); Daniel P. Carpenter, *The Forging of Bureaucratic Autonomy: Reputations, Networks, and Policy Innovation in Executive Agencies, 1862–1928* (Princeton, NJ: Princeton University Press, 2001). See also Lisa L. Miller, *The Perils of Federalism: Race, Poverty, and the Politics of Crime Control* (Oxford: Oxford University Press, 2008); Lisa L. Miller, "Rethinking Bureaucrats in the Policy Process: Criminal Justice Agents and the National Crime Agenda," *Policy Studies Journal* 32, no. 4 (2004): 569–588.

24. John W. Kingdon, *Agendas, Alternatives, and Public Policies* (Boston: Little, Brown, 1984).

25. Lee Rainwater, "Crucible of Identity: The Negro Lower-Class Family," *Daedalus* 95, no. 1 (1966): 172–216, 174.

26. Jürgen Habermas writes, "The bourgeois public sphere may be conceived above all as the sphere of private people come together as a public; they soon claimed the public sphere regulated from above against the public authorities themselves, to engage them in a debate over the general rules governing relations in the basically privatized but publicly relevant sphere of commodity exchange and social labor." Jürgen Habermas, *The Structural Transformation of the Public Sphere: An Inquiry into a Category of Bourgeois Society* (Cambridge, MA: MIT Press, 1989), 36. James C. Scott, *Domination and the Arts of Resistance: Hidden Transcripts* (New Haven, CT: Yale University Press, 1990); Melissa V. Harris-Perry, *Barbershops, Bibles, and BET: Everyday Talk and Black Political Thought* (Princeton, NJ: Princeton University Press, 2004).

Chapter 1: Rights and Wreckage in Postwar Harlem

1. David Levering Lewis, *When Harlem Was in Vogue* (New York: Penguin, 1997); Kenneth B. Clark, *Dark Ghetto: Dilemmas of Social Power* (New York: Harper & Row, 1965).

2. Maryat Lee, "Dope," in *The Best Short Plays, 1952–1953*, ed. Margaret Mayorga (New York: Dodd, Mead, 1953), 87–107; "Narcotics Play Listed," *New York Times*, April 21, 1951, 19; Eugene Kinkead, "Sixteen," *New Yorker*, November 10, 1951, 44–65; "Dope in Church," *Jet*, December 20, 1951; "Children in Peril," *Life*, June 11, 1951.

3. Lee, *Dope*, 106.

4. Ibid., 97–98.

5. Ibid., 102–104.

6. Kinkead, "Sixteen"; "Dope in Church"; "Children in Peril"; William W. French, *Maryat Lee's EcoTheater* (Morgantown: West Virginia University Press, 1998), 20; Woodie King, *The Impact of Race: Theatre and Culture* (New York: Applause Theatre & Cinema Books, 2003), 37–38.

7. Clark, *Dark Ghetto;* Gilbert Osofsky, *Harlem: The Making of a Ghetto; Negro New York, 1890–1930* (New York: Harper & Row, 1966).

8. James Weldon Johnson, *The Book of American Negro Poetry* (New York: Harcourt, Brace, 1931), 7. For a discussion of the New Negro movement, see Alain Locke, *The New Negro* (New York: Simon & Schuster, 1997); Henry Louis Gates Jr. and Gene Andrew Jarrett, *The New Negro: Readings on Race, Representation, and African American Culture, 1892–1938* (Princeton, NJ: Princeton University Press, 2007).

9. Nathan Irvin Huggins, *Harlem Renaissance* (New York: Oxford University Press, 1971), 4–5; Langston Hughes, *The Big Sea: An Autobiography* (New York: Hill and Wang, 1963), 228; Alain Locke quoted in Osofsky, *Harlem,* 187. For a discussion of the social conditions in Harlem during the 1930s, see Charles H. Robert, *The Negro in Harlem: A Report on Social and Economic Conditions Responsible for the Outbreak of March 19, 1935* (New York: Mayor's Commission on Conditions in Harlem, 1936); Myrtle Evangeline Pollard, "Harlem As Is," vol. 1: "Sociological Notes on Harlem Social Life," BAA and MBA thesis, College of the City of New York, 1936; Franklin O. Nichols, *Harlem Housing* (New York: Citizens' Housing Council of New York, 1939). See also National Urban League, *Racial Problems in Housing* (New York: National Urban League, 1944); National Council of Negro Women, *Disease, Death, Delinquency Are Bred in Slums* (Washington, DC: National Council of Negro Women, 1945). It is important to note that others have criticized arguments about the failure of the Harlem Renaissance. The argument presented here is not about the wholesale failure of the Harlem Renaissance. Rather, it is about the class biases of the movement. For critiques of the failure narrative, see Ann Douglas, *Terrible Honesty: Mongrel Manhattan in the 1920s* (New York: Farrar, Straus and Giroux, 1995); Houston A. Baker, *Modernism and the Harlem Renaissance* (Chicago: University of Chicago Press, 1987).

10. "250 More Police in Harlem to Stamp Out Crime Wave," *New York Times,* November 8, 1941, 23; "Columnist 'Spanked' for Slant on Harlem," *Afro American,* December 6, 1941, 9; "Tragedy in Harlem," *New York Times,* November 8, 1941, 18; Dominic I. Capeci, "Fiorello H. La

Guardia and the Harlem 'Crime Wave' of 1941," *New York Historical Society Quarterly* 64, no. 1 (1980): 7–29.

11. Editorial, *New York Age*, December 13, 1941, 7; "Juvenile Delinquency," *New York Age*, November 29, 1941, 6; Claude McKay, "New Crime Wave Old Story to Harlemites: Poverty Brings Prostitution, 'Muggings,' Robberies," *New Leader*, November 29, 1941, 5.

12. Memorandum from Roy Wilkins to Walter White, November 10, 1941, Box II: A298, Folder 4, Part II: General Office File, 1940–1956, National Association for the Advancement of Colored People records, 1842–1999, Library of Congress, Washington, DC; "Statement by the NAACP Board of Directors," November 11, 1941, Box II: A298, Folder 4, Part II: General Office File, 1940–1956, National Association for the Advancement of Colored People records, 1842–1999, Library of Congress, Washington, DC; "Crime Smear," *Crisis*, December 1941, 375; Richard Wright, *Native Son* (New York: Harper & Bros, 1940).

13. "Better Harlem Schools Committee Maps to Contend with Critical Situation," *New York Age*, January 2, 1943, 2; "Harlem Denies 'Mugging' Wave," *Brooklyn Daily Eagle*, April 5, 1943, 2; Albert Deutsch, "Crime News," *Afro American*, January 16, 1943, 7; "Says Harlem Crime Is Overemphasized," *Gazette and Daily*, March 23, 1943, 2; "8 Held in Rape Case," *New York Times*, April 2, 1943, 23; "2 Youths Convicted of 'Mugging' Attack," *New York Times*, April 2, 1943, 23; "Time Features 'Negro' Muggings but Plays Down Mass Rape of White Girl by 13 Whites," *New York Age*, April 10, 1943, 1.

14. Michael Carter, "The Truth about Crime in New York's Harlem," *Afro American*, May 8, 1943, 14.

15. Letter of Invitation to Crime Conference, February 6, 1943, Box II: A298, Folder 4, Part II: General Office File, 1940–1956, National Association for the Advancement of Colored People records, 1842–1999, Library of Congress, Washington, DC.

16. Letter from Hulan E. Jack to Walter White, February 17, 1943, Box II: A298, Folder 4, Part II: General Office File, 1940–1956, National Association for the Advancement of Colored People records, 1842–1999, Library of Congress, Washington, DC; Minutes of Harlem Crime Conference, Harlem YMCA, February 20, 1943, Box II: A298, Folder 4, Part II: General Office File, 1940–1956, National Association for the Advancement of Colored People records, 1842–1999, Library of Congress, Washington, DC.

17. Minutes of Harlem Crime Conference.

18. Letter from Adam Clayton Powell Jr. to Walter White, February 16, 1943, Box II: A298, Folder 4, Part II: General Office File, 1940–1956, National Association for the Advancement of Colored People records, 1842–1999, Library of Congress, Washington, DC; Minutes of Harlem Crime Conference.

19. George S. Schuyler, "The World Today," *Pittsburgh Courier*, September 23, 1944, 1; Charles V. Hamilton, *Adam Clayton Powell, Jr.: The Political Biography of an American Dilemma* (New York: Atheneum, 1991), 152; "Powell's Church Wars on Hoodlums," *New York Times*, June 16, 1944, 21.

20. Eric C. Schneider, *Smack: Heroin and the American City* (Philadelphia: University of Pennsylvania Press, 2008); Billie Holiday, William Dufty, and Vincent Pelote, *Lady Sings the Blues* (Harmondsworth, UK: Penguin Books, 1984); Jill Jonnes, *Hep-Cats, Narcs, and Pipe Dreams: A History of America's Romance with Illegal Drugs* (New York: Scribner, 1996); Mayme Hatcher Johnson and Karen E. Quinones Miller, *Harlem Godfather: The Rap on My Husband, Ellsworth "Bumpy" Johnson* (Philadelphia: Oshun, 2008); Shane White, *Playing the Numbers: Gambling in Harlem between the Wars* (Cambridge, MA: Harvard University Press, 2010); Ron Chepesiuk, *Gangsters of Harlem: The Gritty Underworld of New York's Most Famous Neighborhood* (Fort Lee, NJ: Barricade Books, 2007); Paul L. Crawford, Daniel I. Malamud, and James R. Dumpson, *Working with Teen-age Gangs: A Report on the Central Harlem Street Clubs Project* (New York: Welfare Council of New York City, 1950); "Dope Victims Tell Sordid Stories," *Daytona Beach Morning Journal*, June 27, 1951, 5; "Youth Drug 'Epidemic' Cited at Crime Probe," *Spokane Daily Chronicle*, June 26, 1951, 1; Paul Zimmering et al., "Heroin Addiction in Adolescent Boys," *Journal of Nervous and Mental Disease* 114, no. 1 (1951): 19–34, 20–21.

21. Claude Brown, *Manchild in the Promised Land* (New York: Simon & Schuster, 2012); Rev. Oberia D. Dempsey quoted in Charles V. Hamilton, *The Black Preacher in America* (New York: Morrow, 1972), 190–191; "Dope Claims Young Addict's Buddy," *New York Age*, August 4, 1951, 1; "Hot Spots of Sin," *Jet*, January 24, 1952, 18–22; Langston Hughes, "Drug Addiction," *Chicago Defender*, December 22, 1956, 9.

22. U.S. House of Representatives, *Traffic in, and Control of, Narcotics, Barbiturates, and Amphetamines: Hearings before a Subcommittee of the Committee on Ways and Means, House of Representatives, Eighty-fourth Congress on Traffic in, and Control of, Narcotics, Barbiturates, and Amphetamines: October 13, 14, 18, 19, November 4, 7, 8, 10, 11, 14, 16, 17, December 14, 15, 1955,*

and January 30, 1956 (Washington, DC: Government Printing Office, 1956), 478.

23. Laymond Robinson Jr., "Our Changing City: Harlem Now on the Upswing," New York Times, July 8, 1955, 25.

24. O. S. McCullum, "Brother Johnson Put in 2 Cents," New York Age, July 21, 1951, 5.

25. Hubert J. O'Gorman, Negro Professionals in New York City, 1950 and 1960 (New York: Urban Research Center, Hunter College, 1965); Martha Biondi, To Stand and Fight: The Struggle for Civil Rights in Postwar New York City (Cambridge, MA: Harvard University Press, 2003), 237. Also see Theodore J. Lowi, At the Pleasure of the Mayor: Patronage and Power in New York City, 1898–1958 (New York: Free Press of Glencoe, 1964); John O'Kearney, "Which Way Harlem? Unity on a Key Issue," Nation, October 27, 1956, 347–348, 348.

26. Lizabeth Cohen, A Consumers' Republic: The Politics of Mass Consumption in Postwar America (New York: Knopf, 2003); E. Franklin Frazier, Black Bourgeoisie (Glencoe, IL: Free Press, 1957); Fact Finders Associates, Inc., Survey of the New York City Negro Market Made among 2,075 Families in Manhattan, Brooklyn, Bronx, Queens and Richmond (New York: Fact Finders Associates, 1952); Quick Facts about Selling the Negro Market: Where the Most Changes Are Taking Place; A Handy Guide for National Advertisers and Advertising Agencies (New York: Associated Publishers, 1952); Baltimore, America's 5th Largest Negro Market: A Report on the Characteristics of the Baltimore Negro Market, Its Buying Habits and Brand Preferences in 1945 (Baltimore: Baltimore Afro-American, 1946); The New Philadelphia Story: A Report on the Characteristics of the Philadelphia Negro Market, Its Buying Habits and Brand Preferences in 1945; From a Survey by the Research Company of America, N.Y. (Philadelphia: Philadelphia Afro-American, 1946); Research Company of America, Report on Characteristics of the Washington Negro Market: Its Product Buying and Brand Preferences in 1945 (Washington, DC: Research Company of America, 1946); Pittsburgh Courier Publishing Company and Harold C. Falkoff, Consumer Analysis of the Pittsburgh Negro Market, 1950–1951: A Study of Buying Habits, Brand Preference, and Ownership (Pittsburgh: Pittsburgh Courier, 1951); Merchandising Survey of Packaged Laundry Soap, Toilet Soap, Shortening, Pipe and Drain Cleaners and Glass and Window Cleaners in the Negro Market (Chicago: Johnson, 1953); "The U.S. Negro, 1953," Time, May 11, 1953, 58.

27. Ludlow W. Werner, "Across the Desk," New York Age, June 17, 1944, 6.

28. U.S. House of Representatives, *Traffic in, and Control of, Narcotics, Barbiturates, and Amphetamines*, 479.

29. Richard L. Lyons, "Former Rep. Emanuel Celler Dies," *Washington Post*, January 16, 1981, B5; "Drug Penalties," *Washington Post*, July 19, 1951, 10; "Narcotics Penalty Stiffened in House," *New York Times*, July 17, 1951, 16.

30. Clark, *Dark Ghetto*, 34; Harlem Urban Development Corporation, *A Profile of the Harlem Area: Findings of the Harlem Task Force* (New York: Harlem Urban Development Corporation, 1973). For a discussion of black employment and the public sector, see Virginia Parks, "Revisiting Shibboleths of Race and Urban Economy: Black Employment in Manufacturing and the Public Sector Compared, Chicago 1950–2000," *International Journal of Urban and Regional Research* 35, no. 1 (2011): 110–129. For a discussion of minority representation in public sector employment in New York City, see Martin Shefter, *Political Crisis, Fiscal Crisis: The Collapse and Revival of New York City* (New York: Basic Books, 1985).

31. HARYOU, *Youth in the Ghetto: A Study of the Consequences of Powerlessness and a Blueprint for Change* (New York: HARYOU, 1964); Milton Helpern and Yong-Myun Rho, "Deaths from Narcotism in New York City: Incidence, Circumstances, and Postmortem Findings," *New York State Journal of Medicine* 66, no. 18 (1966): 198; U.S. Senate, *Organized Crime and Illicit Traffic in Narcotics, Hearings before the Permanent Subcommittee on Investigations of the Committee on Government Operations* (Washington, DC: U.S. Government Printing Office, 1964), 760.

32. James Baldwin, "Fifth Avenue, Uptown: A Letter from Harlem," *Esquire*, July 1960.

33. Kenneth Bancroft Clark, *The Negro Protest: James Baldwin, Malcolm X, Martin Luther King Talk with Kenneth B. Clark* (Boston: Beacon Press, 1963), 4–5.

34. U.S. Congress, *Federal Role in Urban Affairs, Hearings, Eighty-ninth Congress, Second Session [Nineteeth Congress, First Session]* (Washington, DC: Government Printing Office, 1966), 1149–1150; "Ghetto Testimony before Senate Draws Mixed Harlem Reaction," *Amsterdam News*, September 3, 1966, 1; Marjorie Hunter, "Senators Hear of Life in the Ghetto," *New York Times*, August 30, 1966, 29.

35. U.S. Congress, *Federal Role in Urban Affairs*, 1115–1116.

36. "Ghetto Testimony before Senate Draws Mixed Harlem Reaction," 1.

37. Ibid.

38. Melissa V. Harris-Perry, *Barbershops, Bibles, and BET: Everyday Talk and Black Political Thought* (Princeton, NJ: Princeton University Press, 2004), 22; John F. Kraft, *A Report of Attitudes of Negroes in Various Cities: Prepared for the Senate Subcommittee on Executive Reorganization* (New York: Kraft, Inc., 1966).

39. "Interview # 3," "She," Box 128, Folder 5; "Interview 1," Box 128, Folder 4; "Interviews Conducted with Residents of 114th Street," Box 128, Folder 5; all in Kenneth Bancroft Clark Papers, Manuscript Division, Library of Congress, Washington, DC.

40. Langston Hughes, "Simple Is Heard All over the World," *Chicago Defender*, November 20, 1965, 10; Langston Hughes and Donna Sullivan Harper, *The Later Simple Stories* (Columbia: University of Missouri Press, 2002), 202.

41. Hughes and Harper, *The Later Simple Stories*, 259; Langston Hughes and Donna Sullivan Harper, *The Return of Simple* (New York: Hill and Wang, 1994), 126.

42. Gilbert Osofsky, *Harlem: The Making of a Ghetto: Negro New York, 1890–1930*, 2nd ed. (New York: Harper & Row, 1971), 189–201.

43. Cohen, *A Consumers' Republic*; Michael B. Katz, *Why Don't American Cities Burn?* (Philadelphia: University of Pennsylvania Press, 2012). For a discussion of race and housing policy and politics, see Ira Katznelson, *When Affirmative Action Was White: An Untold History of Racial Inequality in Twentieth-Century America* (New York: Norton, 2005); Thomas J. Sugrue, *The Origins of the Urban Crisis: Race and Inequality in Postwar Detroit* (Princeton, NJ: Princeton University Press, 1996); Arnold R. Hirsch, *Making the Second Ghetto: Race and Housing in Chicago, 1940–1960* (Cambridge, UK: Cambridge University Press, 1983); Douglas S. Massey and Nancy A. Denton, *American Apartheid: Segregation and the Making of the Underclass* (Cambridge, MA: Harvard University Press, 1993).

Chapter 2: Black Junkies, White Do-Gooders, and the Metcalf-Volker Act of 1962

1. Eugene Kinkead, "Sixteen," *New Yorker*, November 10, 1951, 44–65.

2. Ibid., 44–48.

3. Ibid., 60; "Named to Court Post: Mrs. Sylvia Singer Put on Domestic Relations Bench," *New York Times*, March 4, 1955, 32.

4. "Rocky Asks Hospital Care for Young Narcotics Addict," *Wellsville (NY) Daily Reporter*, January 22, 1962, 2; "Rocky Urges All-Out War on

Narcotics," *Times Record*, January 22, 1962, 1; New York State, *Public Papers of Nelson A. Rockefeller* (Albany: State of New York, 1962), 367.

5. *Report of the Sub-Committee on Crime and Delinquency of the City-Wide Citizens' Committee on Harlem* (New York: City-Wide Citizens' Committee on Harlem, 1942).

6. Letter from Vito Marcantonio to Walter White, November 12, 1941, Box II: A298, Folder 4, Part II: General Office File, 1940–1956, National Association for the Advancement of Colored People records, 1842–1999, Library of Congress, Washington, DC; "Harlem Crime Wave Called Nonexistent," *New York Times*, November 18, 1941, 15; "Crime Wave Seen as Social Problem," *New York Times*, November 8, 1941, 23; "Better Jobs Needed to Solve So-called Harlem Crime-Wave," *New York Age*, January 3, 1942; " 'Crime Wave' Publicity Causes Wide Activity in an Effort to Find a Solution to Problem," *New York Age*, November 22, 1941, 1.

7. "East Harlem Revisited," *Union Seminary Quarterly Review* 5, no. 1 (1949): 25–29; Benjamin Alicea, "Christian Urban Colonizers: A History of the East Harlem Protestant Parish in New York City, 1948–1968," PhD dissertation, Union Theological Seminary, 1990; "Religion: Concrete Vineyard," *Time*, August 29, 1955; "Churches in Rented Stores," *New York Times*, April 26, 1949, 27; "Pastor in Harlem Hunts Violations," *New York Times*, October 31, 1949, 42; *The Menace of Narcotics to the Children of New York: A Plan to Eradicate the Evil; Interim Report* (New York: Welfare Council of New York City, 1951), iii; "Curb on Narcotics Sought for Youth," *New York Times*, December 22, 1950, 42; Letter from Senator Halpern to Thomas E. Dewey, February 22, 1951, and letter from Jack B. Weinstein to Mr. Shapiro, February 23, 1951, Series 7, Box 20, Folder 2, Thomas E. Dewey Papers, Department of Rare Books, Special Collections and Preservation, Rush Rhees Library, University of Rochester.

8. "Woman Urges Civic Action on Narcotics," *Toledo Blade*, December 3, 1951, 18; "N.Y. Official Denies Racial Link in Dope," *Jet*, May 29, 1952, 20; Conference on Drug Addiction among Adolescents, *Conferences on Drug Addiction Among Adolescents . . . Held at the New York Academy of Medicine, on November 30, 1951 and March 13 and 14, 1952* (New York: Blakiston, 1953); Paul Zimmering et al., "Heroin Addiction in Adolescent Boys," *Journal of Nervous and Mental Disease* 114, no. 1 (1951): 19–34, 20–21.

9. Jack Dalton, "The Tattler," *New York Age*, December 9, 1950, 6; "Harlem Cop Thwarts Plot to Rob Youth, Grabs Trio," *New York Age*, January 27, 1951, 3; "Harlem Dope Drive Net Users, Tools," *New York Age*, December 16, 1950, 7; "Artist and Model Jailed in Raid on 'Laboratory,'" *New York Age*, June 16, 1950, 27; "Cops Nip Huge Harlem Dope Mill," *New York Age*, May 5, 1951, 2; "Harlem Rally for Dope War Set by Brown," *New York Age*, June 9, 1951, 3; "Hot Spots of Sin," *Jet*, January 24, 1952, 22; "New York's Children Accuse . . . ," *Life*, June 25, 1951, 22–23; Willie Bryant, "Locality Mayor Lauds Cop on Vice Cleanup," *New York Age*, August 28, 1954, 1.

10. "Would Curb Addicts," *New York Times*, February 5, 1947, 48.

11. Greenwich House Records, Tamiment Library and Robert F. Wagner Labor Archive, Elmer Holmes Bobst Library, New York City; "$120,000,000 for City Housing Approved in Referenda Bills," *New York Times*, April 8, 1947, 29; New York State, *Public Papers of Thomas E. Dewey: Fifty-First Governor of the State of New York, 1947* (Albany: State of New York, 1947), 236; "Dewey Signs Bills to Aid Children," *New York Times*, April 19, 1949, 19; New York State, *Public Papers of Thomas E. Dewey: Fifty-First Governor of the State of New York, 1949* (Albany: State of New York, 1949), 236; "More Realistic Narcotics Laws Have Bogged Down for Many Years," *Buffalo Courier Express*, June 27, 1961.

12. "Narcotics Study Ordered by Mayor," *New York Times*, December 12, 1950, 36; "Drug Addiction by Teen-agers," *Brooklyn Daily Eagle*, December 15, 1950, 10.

13. "Urge Center to Cure Young Dope Addicts," *Brooklyn Daily Eagle*, January 22, 1951, 3; "Ask Non-Penal Institutions for Teen-age Addicts," *Brooklyn Daily Eagle*, February 9, 1951, 6; "Text of Narcotics Report and Proposals for More Drastic Penalties," *New York Times*, February 8, 1951, 18.

14. *Interim Report; Drug Addiction among Teenagers* (New York: Mayor's Committee on Drug Addiction, 1951); "Action Is Outlined in Narcotics Fight," *New York Times*, July 17, 1951, 16.

15. Letter from Jack B. Weinstein to Governor Thomas E. Dewey, February 24, 1951, and letter from Seymour Halpern to Governor Thomas E. Dewey, February 22, 1951, Series 7, Box 20, Folder 2, Thomas E. Dewey Papers, Department of Rare Books, Special Collections and Preservation, Rush Rhees Library, University of Rochester; "8 Bills at Albany Ask Narcotics War," *New York Times*, January 19,

1951, 18; "Speed the Drug Inquiry," *New York World-Telegram*, February 15, 1951; "More Drug Legislation," *New York World-Telegram*, February 23, 1951; "Curb on Narcotics Weighed at Albany," *New York Times*, February 21, 1951, 20.

16. "Chief Magistrate Target at Albany" *New York Times*, March 15, 1951, 33; Richard J. Roth, "Narcotics Probe Head Has an 8-Year Lead on Job," *Brooklyn Daily Eagle*, May 6, 1951, 27; "Legislature Votes Narcotics Study," *New York Times*, March 17, 1951, 21; "Dewey Approves Narcotics Inquiry," *New York Times*, April 6, 1951, 40; New York State, *Public Papers of Thomas E. Dewey: Fifty-First Governor of the State of New York, 1951* (Albany: State of New York, 1951), 298; *Governor's Bill Jacket: 1951 Chapter 528* (New York: New York Legislative Service, 1951); *Governor's Bill Jacket: 1951 Chapter 529* (New York: New York Legislative Service, 1951); *Governor's Bill Jacket: 1951 Chapter 530* (New York: New York Legislative Service, 1951); MacNeil Mitchell, "Letter to Governor Thomas E. Dewey," March 26, 1951, in *Governor's Bill Jacket: 1951 Chapter 530*; Richard G. Denzer, "Letter to Lawrence E. Walsh," March 29, 1951, in *Governor's Bill Jacket: 1951 Chapter 530*.

17. "City to Establish Addicts' Hospital," *New York Times*, July 1, 1951, 1; "Medicine: Hospital in the River," *Time*, July 14, 1952; "Governor and Mayor Expected to Agree on Plan for Narcotics Hospital Set-up," *New York Times*, November 14, 1951, 27; Warren Weaver, "Dewey Drafts New Approach to City-State Narcotic Curbs," *New York Times*, October 15, 1951, 1.

18. "Goldstein Plan to Meet Drug Peril Deserves Action by Legislature," *Brooklyn Daily Eagle*, January 16, 1952, 12; "Parents First Line of Attack in War on Child Drug Addicts," *Brooklyn Daily Eagle*, June 14, 1951, 14; Sid Frigand and Ken Johnston, "Youth, 17, Admits He Took Peddler's Proceeds in Bets," *Brooklyn Daily Eagle*, June 13, 1951, 1; "Growing National Horror," *Troy (NY) Record*, June 20, 1951; "6,000 Teen-agers Said Dope Addicts," *Daily Messenger*, June 15, 1951; "The Narcotics Horror," *New York Times*, June 14, 1951, 26; "Public Awakening," *New York Times*, June 16, 1951, 14; "State Seeks 'Cure' for Prison Addicts," *New York Times*, June 17, 1951, 37; Leo Egan, "Goldstein Asks Stiff Narcotic Law with Life for Three-Time Offender," *New York Times*, January 14, 1952, 1; "Narcotics Use by Teen-Agers to Be Studied, Dewey Says," *Oneonta (NY) Star*, June 12, 1951, 1; Nathaniel L. Goldstein, *Narcotics, a Growing Problem, a Public Challenge, a*

Plan for Action: A Report (Albany: New York State, 1952), 9; *Governor's Bill Jacket: 1952 Chapter 632* (New York: New York Legislative Service, 1952); *Governor's Bill Jacket: 1952 Chapter 415* (New York: New York Legislative Service, 1952); *Governor's Bill Jacket: 1952 Chapter 8* (New York: New York Legislative Service, 1952); New York State, *Public Papers of Thomas E. Dewey: Fifty-First Governor of the State of New York, 1952* (Albany: State of New York, 1952).

19. Henry Epstein, *Perspectives on Delinquency Prevention* (New York: Office of the Mayor, 1955), 24; "Javits Reports Rise in Use of Narcotics," *New York Times*, September 4, 1955, 1; Jacob K. Javits, *Narcotic Addiction in New York, 1955: Growing Problem; Report* (Albany: New York State Dept. of Law, 1955).

20. "Harriman Asks New Center for Dope Addicts," *Post-Standard* (Syracuse), February 18, 1956, 18; "Harriman Asks for War on Narcotics," *Times Record*, February 17, 1956, 13; William Stringfellow, *My People Is the Enemy: An Autobiographical Polemic* (New York: Holt, Rinehart and Winston, 1964), 71; *Report of the State of New York Joint Legislative Committee on Narcotic Study* (Albany: State of New York, 1959), 92–93; Warren Weaver, "2 Parties Start Narcotics Drive," *New York Times*, February 9, 1956, 21; Vincent F. Condello, assistant to the mayor, "Memorandum to Lt. Gov. DeLuc et al.," February 17, 1956, in *Governor's Bill Jacket: 1956 Chapter 526* (New York: New York Legislative Service, 1956); "Anti-Dope Bill Signed by Harriman," *Troy (NY) Record*, April 18, 1956, 1; Warren Weaver, "Governor Spurs Narcotics Fight," *New York Times*, April 12, 1956, 22; Office of the District Attorney of New York County, "Memorandum to Daniel Gutman, Counsel to the Governor," February 24, 1956, in *Governor's Bill Jacket: 1956 Chapter 526*.

21. U.S. Congress, *Drugs in Our Schools: Hearings, Ninety-Second Congress, Second Session* (Washington, DC: Government Printing Office, 1972), 96; Theodore Rosenthal and Leona Baumgartner, "A Summary of Statistical Data of Habitual Drug Use in New York State," Table A, Robert F. Wagner Documents Collection, Julius C. C. Edelstein Series, Box 060237, Folder 3, La Guardia and Wagner Archives, Fiorello H. La Guardia Community College/CUNY, Long Island City, New York; *Minutes of the Public Hearing Held at the Association of the Bar on November 25, 1957* (New York: Certified Reporting, 1957); "15 in State Named to Fight Narcotics," *New York Times*, July 16, 1956, 23; "Narcotic Hearings to Open," *New York Times*, November 24, 1957, 45; "Narcotics Study

Scores Ineptness," *New York Times*, February 10, 1958, 9; *Second Interim Report of the State of New York Joint Legislative Committee on Narcotic Study* (Albany: State of New York, 1958), 13; "Narcotics Conference," 1954, vinyl record, Anna Kross Papers, MS-173, Box 18, Folder 4, American Jewish Archives, Cincinnati, Ohio.

22. "Church Program," *Bridgeport (CT) Telegram*, February 1, 1955, 36; "The Rev. Norman Eddy, 93: Ministered to East Harlem," *New York Times*, July 1, 2013, A17; Dan Wakefield, "In Spanish Harlem," *Image*, no. 2 (1992); see also Dan Wakefield, *Island in the City: The World of Spanish Harlem* (Boston: Houghton Mifflin, 1959); Eric C. Schneider, *Smack: Heroin and the American City* (Philadelphia: University of Pennsylvania Press, 2008), 130; Mayor Robert F. Wagner Jr. quoted in Samuel Roberts, "'Rehabilitation' as Boundary Object: Medicalization, Local Activism, and Narcotics Addiction Policy in New York City, 1951–62," *Social History of Alcohol and Drugs* 26, no. 2 (2012): 147–169, 159; Emanuel Perlmutter, "Narcotics Laws Called Too Weak," *New York Times*, December 4, 1957, 46; "Sometimes Only the Pusher Takes the Kids Seriously," *Village Voice*, February 19, 1958, 3; "Village Plans City's First Community Addicts' Center," *Village Voice*, April 8, 1959, 1; "Narcotics Council Formed," *Village Voice*, July 20, 1958, 30; "Turkey or Therapy?," *Village Voice*, January 21, 1959; "Hospital Aid for Addicts Asked by Community Group," *Village Voice*, October 29, 1958, 3; "Human Treatment for Drug Addicts Asked by City Group," *Village Voice*, December 17, 1958, 1; "Narcotics Expert Scores Anslinger," *New York Times*, February 8, 1959, 55; "Drug Addiction Conference Backs Legislative Proposal," *Village Voice*, February 11, 1959, 3.

23. "City Plan Asked to Help Addicts," *New York Times*, March 16, 1959, 33; East Harlem Protestant Parish, "The Beginning of Action," New York State Council of Churches Records, Box 17, Folder: Narcotics, Special Collections Research Center, Syracuse University; "Addiction Project Due," *New York Times*, March 17, 1959, 6; "Leaders Protest on Narcotic Care," *New York Times*, March 28, 1959, 36; Laymond Robinson, "Mayor to Confer on Aid to Addicts," *New York Times*, April 29, 1959, 35; East Harlem Protestant Parish, "The Beginning of Action"; Laymond Robinson, "Hospitals to Treat Addicts," *New York Times*, June 5, 1959, 29; "Progress and Pitfall," *Village Voice*, June 10, 1959, 4.

24. New York State Council of Churches, "Memorandum No. 27," March 5, 1962, New York State Council of Churches Records, Box 17, Folder:

Narcotics, Special Collections Research Center, Syracuse University; "Two Good Bills," *Village Voice*, March 18, 1959, 4; New York State, *Public Papers of Nelson A. Rockefeller* (Albany: State of New York, 1959); Emma Harrison, "State Task Force Set Up on Addicts," *New York Times*, November 6, 1959, 1; East Harlem Protestant Parish, "The Beginning of Action"; "Names and Addresses of the Members of the Governor's Special Task Force on Narcotics Addiction," New York State Council of Churches Records, Box 17, Folder: Narcotics, Special Collections Research Center, Syracuse University; *Proceedings of the Conference on Post-Hospital Care and Rehabilitation of Adolescent Narcotic Addicts, Hotel Sheraton-Ten Eyck, Albany, New York, January 8, 1960, January 9, 1960* (New York: Governor's Task Force on Addiction, 1960), 9–11; *New York Medicine* 16 (1960): 453.

25. Paul A. Hoch, "Letter to Senator Austin W. Erwin, Chairman, Senate Committee on Finance," March 17, 1960, in *Governor's Bill Jacket: 1960 Chapter 530*; "Budget Report," April 8, 1960, in *Governor's Bill Jacket: 1960 Chapter 530*; "Department of Mental Hygiene" April 12, 1960, in *Governor's Bill Jacket: 1960 Chapter 530*; "Church Plea Made for Narcotics Bill," *New York Times*, March 28, 1960, 31; Helen M. Harris, "Letter to Nelson A. Rockefeller," April 6, 1960, in *Governor's Bill Jacket: 1960 Chapter 530*; New York State, *Public Papers of Nelson A. Rockefeller* (Albany: State of New York, 1960), 489. "Governor Signs Bill on Addicts," *New York Times*, April 18, 1960, 36.

26. "Narcotic Reforms Blocked," *Buffalo Courier Express*, June 29, 1961; *Journal of the Senate of the State of New York, at Their One Hundred Eighty-Fourth*, vol. 1 (Albany, NY: Williams Press, 1961), 2352.

27. "Citizen Units at Hearing Oppose Closing Addicts' Hospital Here," *New York Times*, August 11, 1960, 16; Norman Eddy, "Letter to Friends," December 5, 1960, New York State Council of Churches Records, Box 17, Folder: Narcotics, Special Collections Research Center, Syracuse University; "Hogan Aide Offers Plan to Treat Addicts as Sick, Not Criminals," *New York Times*, November 11, 1960, 25; New York Council on Narcotics Addiction, "State of Aims for 1963," Robert F. Wagner Collection, Julius C. C. Edelstein Series, Box O60255, Folder 1, "Chronological File," La Guardia and Wagner Archives, La Guardia Community College, Long Island City, New York; "Memorandum," October 5, 1961, George R. Metcalf, Box 46, "Meeting Oct. 6, 1961 N.Y.C," M. E. Grenander Department of Special Collections & Archives, University at Albany.

28. Letter from Paul H. Hoch to George R. Metcalf, March 8, 1961, and letter from George R. Metcalf to Richard H. Kuh, April 7, 1961, Box 13, Folder: Narcotics Correspondence, 1961, George R. Metcalf Papers, M. E. Grenander Department of Special Collections & Archives, University at Albany.

29. "Memorandum from Harry O'Donnell to Robert McManus," July 16, 1952, Reel 42, Rockefeller Gubernatorial Papers, First Administration, 1959–1962, New York State Archives, Cultural Education Center, Albany; "Join the War on Dope," *Journal-American*, January 14, 1962.

30. "Minutes: Meeting on Narcotics Control Legislation," October 6, 1961, Box 46, "1961, New York City October 6 Meeting," and "Letter from Paul D. McGinnis to George R. Metcalf," November 8, 1961, Box 13, "Narcotics Legislation," George R. Metcalf Papers, M. E. Grenander Department of Special Collections & Archives, University at Albany; Robert M. Quigley, "Assembly Report," *Daily Messenger*, March 27, 1962, 8; New York State, *Public Papers of Nelson A. Rockefeller* (1962), 367; "Minutes: Meeting on Narcotics Control Legislation," November 3, 1961, Series 4, Box 3, Folder 21, Julius Volker Papers, M. E. Grenander Department of Special Collections & Archives, University at Albany; "Minutes: Meeting on Narcotics Control Legislation," December 21, 1961, Box 13, "Narcotics Legislation," George R. Metcalf Papers, M. E. Grenander Department of Special Collections & Archives, University at Albany.

31. *Senate Debate Transcripts 1962, Chapter 204* (New York: New York Legislative Service, 1962); "Minutes: Meeting on Narcotics Control Legislation," Box 46, "Meeting Oct. 6, 1961 N.Y.C," M. E. Grenander Department of Special Collections & Archives, University at Albany.

32. Senator Metcalf quoted in Schneider, *Smack*, 131; *Senate Debate Transcripts 1962, Chapter 204*, 1399; "The Great Need," *Journal-American*, January 23, 1962, 14; "Clinch the Cure," *Journal-American*, January 24, 1962, 26; "Letter from Kenneth B. Keating to 'Friend,'" February 12, 1962, Box 14, Folder 3, Kenneth Barnard Keating Papers, Department of Rare Books, Special Collections and Preservation, Rush Rhees Library, University of Rochester.

33. Meeting Agenda, Health Committee, Harlem Neighborhoods Association, Inc., January 26, 1961, Box 6, Folder 9, Harlem Neighborhoods Association Records, 1941–1978, Schomburg Center for Research in Black Culture, New York City; "Letter from Lloyd E. Dickens to Nelson

Rockefeller," February 13, 1962, Series 13682–78, Reel 42, Rockefeller Gubernatorial Papers, First Administration, 1959–1962, New York State Archives, Cultural Education Center, Albany; "James Watson, 79, Judge of U.S. Court of International Trade Succumbs," *Jet*, October 1, 2001, 55; *Senate Debate Transcripts 1962, Chapter 204*, 1405.

34. U.S. Senate, *Juvenile Delinquency (the Effectiveness of the Juvenile Court System): Hearings before the Subcommittee to Investigate Juvenile Delinquency of the Committee on the Judiciary, United States Senate, Eighty-Sixth Congress First Session, Pursuant to S. Res. 54, Eighty-Sixth Congress, Investigation of Juvenile Delinquency in the United States, February 12 and 13, 1959* (Washington, DC: Government Printing Office, 1959), 10; John P. Shanley, " 'Junkyard by the Sea,' Documentary Film, Interviews Victims of Habit," *New York Times*, January 13, 1961, 59; "Drug Addiction in New York TV Feature," *Amsterdam News*, January 7, 1961, 12.

35. "Mark T. Southall, Leader in Harlem," *New York Times*, June 30, 1976; "Mark Southall Dead, Former Assemblyman," *Amsterdam News*, July 3, 1976; Murray Illson, "Addiction Spread in Harlem Scored," *New York Times*, December 9, 1961; "Southall Hits Drugs in Harlem," *Amsterdam News*, December 16, 1961; "Statement Submitted by Mark T. Southall," and "Letter from Mark T. Southall to William J. Ronan," March 27, 1962, and "Petition and Resolution," Series 13682–78, Reel 42, Rockefeller Gubernatorial Papers, First Administration, 1959–1962, New York State Archives, Cultural Education Center, Albany; "Cops, the Numbers, and Respect," *New York Age*, July 25, 1959, 9; "Clean Out This Scum," *New York Age*, September 5, 1959, 6; "Problems Neglected?," *Miami News*, August 3, 1961, 1; "H. E. Jones Urges Fight on Dope Evil," *Pittsburgh Courier*, October 20, 1962, 2.

Chapter 3: Reverend Dempsey's Crusade and the Rise of Involuntary Commitment in 1966

1. "Asst. Pastor Invested at Mt. Lebanon," *Amsterdam News*, November 14, 1953, 19; Letter to J. H. Jackson, June 23, 1958, Martin Luther King Papers Project, Stanford University, Stanford, CA; Clarence Taylor, *The Black Churches of Brooklyn* (New York: Columbia University Press, 1994); "Non-Partisan Group Slates Mass Meeting," *New York Age*, September 26, 1953, 1; "O. D. Dempsey," Part III, Youth File, 1956–1965, Box III, Folder E54, Speakers, General, 1956–1960, National Association for the Advancement of Colored People Records, 1842–1999, Library of

Congress, Washington, DC; "'Give Until It Hurts' Plea of Concord Men," *New Journal and Guide*, November 22, 1952, 5; "Rev. Dempsey Is Going to Washington," *Amsterdam News*, September 1, 1962, 6; *Mr. Smith Goes to Washington*, Columbia Pictures, 1939; "Rev. Dempsey Fan," *Amsterdam News*, July 20, 1957, 8; "Rev. Dempsey Is Mayor of Harlem," *Amsterdam News*, October 31, 1959, 1; "Rev. Dempsey to Have Day," *Amsterdam News*, May 27, 1961, 27; Cheryl Perry, "For Dempsey," *Amsterdam News*, April 22, 1961, 11; Bill Slater, "Adam Fails to Leave Abyssinian," *Afro American*, December 15, 1962, 2; Ralph J. Bunche and Jonathan Scott Holloway, *A Brief and Tentative Analysis of Negro Leadership* (New York: New York University Press, 2005).

2. Earl Brown quoted in Samuel M. Johnson, *Often Back: The Tales of Harlem* (New York: Vantage Press, 1971), 16, 60–61; "Launch Crusade on Foul Mouth Hoodlums," *Amsterdam News*, November 28, 1959, 5; "Forms Improvement Group: Harlem Businesswoman Set to Clean Up Area," *Pittsburgh Courier*, November 25, 1961, 3; "Evangelical Rally Continues in Harlem," *Pittsburgh Courier*, July 21, 1962, 16.

3. *Proceedings: White House Conference on Narcotic and Drug Abuse, September 27 and 28, State Department Auditorium, Washington, D.C.* (Washington, DC: Government Printing Office, 1962); *Minutes of the Public Hearing Held at the Association of the Bar on November 25, 1957* (New York: Certified Reporting, 1957); Committee on Narcotics Control, "Minutes of Meeting," February 27, 1958, Box 93, Folder 36, Greenwich House Records, Tamiment Library and Robert F. Wagner Labor Archive, Elmer Holmes Bobst Library, New York City; "15 in State Named to Fight Narcotics," *New York Times*, July 16, 1956, 23; "Narcotic Hearings to Open," *New York Times*, November 24, 1957, 45; "Crowd Overflows Pompei Hall to Hear Narcotics Official, Others," *Village Voice*, January 15, 1958, 1; Stephen Klaidman, "Harry Anslinger, Narcotics Chief," *Washington Post*, November 18, 1975, A20; U.S. House of Representatives, *Traffic in, and Control of, Narcotics, Barbiturates, and Amphetamines: Hearings before a Subcommittee of the Committee on Ways and Means, House of Representatives, Eighty-fourth Congress on Traffic in, and Control of, Narcotics, Barbiturates, and Amphetamines: October 13, 14, 18, 19, November 4, 7, 8, 10, 11, 14, 16, 17, December 14, 15, 1955, and January 30, 1956* (Washington, DC: Government Printing Office, 1956), 1118; U.S. House of Representatives, *Treasury–Post Office Departments Appropriations*

for 1960: Treasury Department, the Tax Court of the United States, Hearings before the Subcommittee of the Committee on Appropriations, House of Representatives, Eighty-sixth Congress, First Session (Washington, DC: Government Printing Office, 1959), 129.

4. U.S. House of Representatives, *Traffic in, and Control of, Narcotics, Barbiturates, and Amphetamines*, 527–528; "New Approach on Narcotics," *Milwaukee Journal*, February 19, 1964, 20.

5. *McKinney's Session Laws of New York* (St. Paul, MN: West, 1966), chapter 192; John Sibley, "State Senate Votes Rockefeller Plan for Compulsory Treatment of Addicts," *New York Times*, March 29, 1966, 19; "Plan to Try Drug Program," *Kansas City Times*, February 3, 1966, 31; "Solons Get Bill to Curb Narcotics," *Times Record*, February 23, 1966, 17.

6. William F. Buckley Jr., "Rocky and the Drug Plan," *Wellsville (NY) Daily Reporter*, March 8, 1966, 2; John Sibley, "Fight on Addicts Brews in Albany," *New York Times*, February 3, 1966, 50; John Sibley, "State Tries New Answer to Riddle: How to Cure Addiction," *New York Times*, April 3, 1966, E5; "Joint Statement by Assemblyman Jerome Kretchmer and State Senator Manfred Ohrenstein on Governor Rockefeller's Program on Narcotics," February 23, 1966, Record Series B1952-08, Box 19, Folder: Narcotics 1973, Manfred Ohrenstein Papers, New York State Archives, Cultural Education Center, Albany.

7. "Recommendations of the New York State Commission of Investigation concerning Narcotics Addiction in the State of New York," March 24, 1966, Series 1, Box 6, Folder 6, Bernard C. Smith Papers, M. E. Grenander Department of Special Collections & Archives, University at Albany; "Tragic Failure," *Journal-American*, May 2, 1963, 20; Mayor's Temporary Narcotics Commission of New York City, "Summary of Papers and Discussion Presented at the Gracie Mansion Conference held at the New York Hilton Hotel, February 3–5, 1965," Robert F. Wagner Collection, Julius C. C. Edelstein Series, Box 060301, Folder 23, La Guardia and Wagner Archives, La Guardia Community College, Long Island City, New York; *Report of the Joint Legislative Committee on Health Insurance Plans, 1962* (Albany: Joint Committee on Health Insurance Plans, 1963).

8. Irving Spiegel, "Mayor Asks U.S. for Narcotics Aid," *New York Times*, June 4, 1963, 16; "Invitation to Reception at Gracie Mansion," June 3, 1963, Box 060237, Folder 6, Julius Edelstein Series, Robert F. Wagner

Collection, La Guardia and Wagner Archives, La Guardia Community College/CUNY, Long Island City, New York.

9. James Booker, "The Political Pot," *Amsterdam News*, June 9, 1962; James Booker, "The Political Pot," *Amsterdam News*, June 30, 1962; James Booker, "The Political Pot," *Amsterdam News*, December 8, 1962.

10. "Petition and Resolution," Series 13682–78, Reel 42, Rockefeller Gubernatorial Papers, First Administration, 1959–1962, New York State Archives, Cultural Education Center, Albany; "Rocky Pledges State Action to Curb Narcotics in Harlem," *Pittsburgh Courier*, March 17, 1962, 2; "Presidential Action Urged on Dope Evil," *Pittsburgh Courier*, June 16, 1962, 2; "Dempsey Gratified in His Anti-Dope Drive," *Amsterdam News*, September 1, 1962, 23.

11. "New York Political Roundup," *Pittsburgh Courier*, February 9, 1963, 3; "Rinkydinks of L.A. and N.Y. Give Check to 'Sit Down' Strike," *Los Angeles Sentinel*, July 14, 1960, B1; "Honor Ward for Fair Job Practices," *Chicago Defender*, April 1, 1961, 4; *Amsterdam News*, August 6, 1966, 11, February 3, 1968, 3, May 31, 1966, 4, March 23, 1968, 49; "Mass Meeting on Dope Hits Mark in Harlem," *Pittsburgh Courier*, July 7, 1962, 2; "Promises to Name Names at Harlem Crime Rally," *Amsterdam News*, June 9, 1962, 8; "250 Youngsters March on Crime," *New York Times*, June 24, 1962, 48; "Anti-Crime and Dope Rally in Harlem This Saturday," *Pittsburgh Courier*, May 11, 1963, 1; "FBI to Participate in Harlem Confab on Crime and Narcotics," *Pittsburgh Courier*, September 21, 1963, 1; "Rally Calls for Anti-Dope Drive," *Pittsburgh Courier*, April 25, 1964, 11.

12. Paul Crowell, "Ellis Isle Urged for U.S. Hospital," *New York Times*, January 18, 1958, 17; "Ellis Island Proposed: Harlem Leaders Seek Aid Center for Narcotics Addict," *Pittsburgh Courier*, September 7, 1963, 2; "Groups Flood Rocky with New Requests," *Amsterdam News*, April 4, 1964, 4; "'Rocky' Speaks in Harlem," *Amsterdam News*, November 20, 1965, 1.

13. "Dempsey Has Advice for Lindsay Dope Fight," *Amsterdam News*, December 11, 1965.

14. Letter from Manuel Galagarza to Mayor Lindsay, November 5, 1965, Series II, Box 89, Folder 50, John V. Lindsay Collection, Yale University Library, Manuscripts and Archives, New Haven, Connecticut; John F. Kraft, Inc., *The Report of a Survey of Attitudes of Harlem Residents*

toward Housing, Rehabilitation, and Urban Renewal (New York: J. F. Kraft, 1966), National Association for the Advancement of Colored People records, 1842–1999, Box IV: A34, Harlem, 1966–1967, Library of Congress, Washington, DC.

15. "Interviews Conducted with Residents of 114th Street," 9–10, Box 128, Folder 5, Kenneth Bancroft Clark Papers, Manuscript Division, Library of Congress, Washington, DC; John F. Kraft, Inc., *The Report of a Survey of Attitudes of Harlem Residents.*

16. Malcolm X, "Letter to A. Philip Randolph," Papers of A. Philip Randolph, Box 19, Folder: Emergency Committee for Unity on Social Problems, 1961–1962, Library of Congress, Washington, DC; A. Philip Randolph, "Letter to Friend," August 24, 1961, Papers of A. Philip Randolph, Box 19, Folder: Emergency Committee for Unity on Social Problems, 1961–1962, Library of Congress, Washington, DC; Joan Cook, "Anna Hedgeman Is Dead at 90," *New York Times*, January 26, 1990, D18; Emergency Committee for Unity on Social and Economic Problems, "Economic and Social Demands," "Program for Correcting and Preventing the Breakdown of Law-and-Order Enforcement in the Black Community," and "The Drug Menace and Preventative and Corrective Programs," April 24, 1962, Papers of A. Philip Randolph, Box 19, Folder: Emergency Committee for Unity on Social Problems, 1961–1962, Library of Congress, Washington, DC.

17. Manning Marable, *Malcolm X: A Life of Reinvention* (New York: Viking, 2011); Anna Arnold Hedgeman, *The Trumpet Sounds: A Memoir of Negro Leadership* (New York: Holt, Rinehart and Winston, 1964), 167; William P. Jones, "The Forgotten Radical History of the March on Washington," *Dissent* 60, no. 2 (2013): 74–79; Lucy G. Barber, *Marching on Washington: The Forging of an American Political Tradition* (Berkeley: University of California Press, 2002); David J. Garrow, *Bearing the Cross: Martin Luther King, Jr., and the Southern Christian Leadership Conference* (New York: Morrow, 1986); Taylor Branch, *Parting the Waters: America in the King Years, 1954–63* (New York: Simon & Schuster, 1988).

18. David F. Musto, *The American Disease: Origins of Narcotic Control* (New Haven, CT: Yale University Press, 1973), 231.

19. "Addicts Care Plan Defended by State," *New York Times*, June 25, 1964, 20; Paul H. Hoch, "State of Dealing with Narcotics Addiction," November 13, 1964, Folder 14, Box 2, Series 36.1, Wycoff, Nelson A. Rockefeller Gubernatorial Records, Rockefeller Archive Center, Sleepy Hollow, New York.

20. "Statement from the Community Council of Greater New York to the Mayor's Temporary Commission on Narcotics Addiction" and "Letter to Catherine B. Hess from William J. Punkert," April 14, 1965, Box 20, Folder 333, Council of the City of New York Collection, La Guardia and Wagner Archives, La Guardia Community College/CUNY, Long Island City, New York; Edith Evans Asbury, "Lag on Narcotics Seen by Kennedy," *New York Times*, April 25, 1965, 68; Letter from Rev. O. D. Dempsey to Senate Committee on Mental Hygiene, April 7, 1965, Committee Records, 1965, Mental Hygiene Committee, New York State Archives, Cultural Education Center, Albany; *1965 Report of the Senate Committee on Mental Hygiene on the Problem of Narcotics Addiction and Treatment to the Legislature of the State of New York* (Albany: Senate Committee on Mental Hygiene, 1965).

21. WABC, "Decision at Albany," transcript, February, 20, 1965, Committee Records, 1965, Mental Hygiene Committee, New York State Archives, Cultural Education Center, Albany; New York State, *Public Papers of Nelson A. Rockefeller* (Albany: State of New York, 1965), 347, 595–596, 624–625; New York State, *Public Papers of Nelson A. Rockefeller* (Albany: State of New York, 1966), 260; *Governor's Bill Jacket: 1966 Chapter 192* (New York: New York Legislative Service, 1966); "Teen-agers Who Use Drugs in U.S. Not Confined to Beat, Slum Groups," *Schenectady (NY) Gazette*, August 25, 1966, 2; Ben A. Franklin, "Traffic in 'Pep Pills' and 'Goofballs' Is Linked to Underworld," *New York Times*, February 1, 1965, 13; "Harris Tells House of Football Players Who Use 'Pep Pills,'" *New York Times*, March 10, 1965, 26; "Senate Votes Curb on Pep Pill Sales," *New York Times*, June 24, 1965, 37; "Pep Pills, Goof Balls Are National Scandal," *Ellensburg (WA) Daily Record*, March 16, 1965, 4; "House Committee Calls for Control over Goof Balls," *Prescott (AZ) Evening Courier*, January 9, 1970.

22. "Albany Announces Its Joint Chairmen for 36 Committees," *New York Times*, July 17, 1965, 51; *Report of the State of New York Joint Legislative Committee on Narcotic and Drug Addiction* (Albany: Joint Legislative Committee, 1966); "'Junkies' Have Made Harlem Place of Fear," *Pittsburgh Courier*, December 11, 1965, 1.

23. New York State, *Public Papers of Nelson A. Rockefeller* (Albany: State of New York, 1963); New York State, *Public Papers of Nelson A. Rockefeller* (Albany: State of New York, 1964); Press Release, January 3, 1965, Folder 14, Box 2, Series 36.1, Wycoff, Nelson A. Rockefeller Gubernatorial Records, Rockefeller Archive Center, Sleepy Hollow, New York; William

Diaz and Stephen M. David, *A Political History of the Addiction Services Agency, 1965–1970* (Bronx, NY: Institute for Social Research, Fordham University, 1971), 2; John M. Martin et al., *A Political History of the New York State Narcotic Addiction Control Commission, 1965–September 1972* (Bronx, NY: Institute for Social Research, Fordham University, 1972).

24. "Plan to Try Drug Program"; Maxwell Powers, "Drug Treatment in California," *Villager (NY)*, April 21, 1966; *New York Times*, January 6, 1966; *The Standard California Codes* (Albany, CA: Hanna Legal Publications, 1961), 425–426; " 'Rocky' Speaks in Harlem," *Amsterdam News*, November 20, 1965, 1; Meeting Agenda, Health Committee, Harlem Neighborhoods Association, Inc., January 26, 1961, Box 6, Folder 9, Harlem Neighborhoods Association records, 1941–1978, Schomburg Center for Research in Black Culture, New York City.

25. "War on Crime and Narcotics Addiction: A Campaign for Human Renewal" (Albany: State of New York, 1966); Press Release, Executive Chamber, Nelson A. Rockefeller, October 28, 1966, Department of Health Commissioner's Office Records, Series 13307-82, Box 51, Folder: Narcotics General, 1965–66, New York State Archives, Cultural Education Center, Albany.

26. "Rocky Calls for Total Drug War," *Amsterdam News*, January 8, 1966; "Governor Unveils War Plans on Narcotics," *Amsterdam News*, December 11, 1965; "All Our Fight," *Amsterdam News*, January 8, 1966; Editorials, *Amsterdam News*, December 24, 1966.

27. Gilbert Osofsky, *Harlem: The Making of a Ghetto; Negro New York, 1890–1930* (New York: Ivan R. Dee, 1996), 115; Stephen D. Glazier, *Encyclopedia of African and African-American Religions* (New York: Routledge, 2001), 1–2; Lee A. Daniels, "The Political Career of Adam Clayton Powell," *Journal of Black Studies* 2 (1973): 115–138; Cary D. Wintz and Paul Finkelman, *Encyclopedia of the Harlem Renaissance*, vol. 1 (New York: Routledge, 2004), 272.

28. *Senate Debate Transcripts 1966, Chapter 192* (New York: New York Legislative Service, 1966); Judson L. Jeffries, "The New York State Black and Puerto Rican Legislative Caucus, 1970–1988," *Afro-Americans in New York Life and History* 24, no.1 (2000): 7.

29. John Sibley, "State Tries New Answer to Riddle: How to Cure Addiction," *New York Times*, April 3, 1966, E5; Paul Hofmann, "Shops on W. 145th St. Fight to Survive Crime," *New York Times*, February 20, 1966,

1; Les Matthews, "Harlemites Decry Crime in Streets, Demand Police Act," *Amsterdam News,* March 5, 1966, 4.

30. "State's Investigators Seek Forced Care for Addicts," *New York Times,* March 28, 1966, 1; John Sibley, "State Senate Votes Rockefeller Plan for Compulsory Treatment of Addicts," *New York Times,* March 29, 1966, 19; "Senate OK's Rock's Narcotics Program," *Post-Standard,* March 26, 1966, 2; Gerry McLaughlin, "Assembly Supports Rocky's Anti-Narcotics Legislation," *Times Record,* March 31, 1966, 8; "Narcotics War OKed in Senate," *Oneonta Star (NY),* March 29, 1966, 1; *Senate Debate Transcripts 1966, Chapter 192,* 2516–2519.

31. Robert Howe Connery and Gerald Benjamin, *Rockefeller of New York: Executive Power in the Statehouse* (Ithaca, NY: Cornell University Press, 1979), 89–93; Arthur Pawlowski, "New York State Drug Control Policy during the Rockefeller Administration, 1959–73," PhD dissertation, State University of New York at Albany, 1984.

32. *Governor's Bill Jacket: 1966 Chapter 192* (New York: New York Legislative Service, 1966); Morris Kaplan, "$250-Million Plan Is Urged on State to Curb Addiction," *New York Times,* December 31, 1965, 1; "Implementation of New York State's Civil Commitment Law Criticized," *NAPAN Newsletter* 2, no. 2 (1964): 1–2; "Statement Filed by Richard H. Kuh," Box 46, Folder: Metcalf 1964, Narcotics Hearing, NYC, Nov 13, M. E. Grenander Department of Special Collections & Archives, University at Albany. For a discussion of policy venues, see Frank R. Baumgartner and Bryan D. Jones, *Agendas and Instability in American Politics* (Chicago: University of Chicago Press, 1993).

33. "Recommendations of the New York State Commission of Investigation concerning Narcotics Addiction in the State of New York," March 24, 1966, Series 1, Box 6, Folder 6, Bernard C. Smith Papers, M. E. Grenander Department of Special Collections & Archives, University at Albany; "Plan to Try Drug Program"; *Governor's Bill Jacket: 1966 Chapter 192;* "Rockefeller Launches All-Out War on Dope," *Amsterdam News,* February 26, 1966, 1; Letter from Rowena Friedmman to Nelson Rockefeller, March 30, 1966, and letter from Karl D. Zukerman to Robert Douglass, March 26, 1966, and letter from Gordon E. Brown to Nelson Rockefeller, March 24, 1966, in *Governor's Bill Jacket: 1966 Chapter 192;* M. S. Handler, "Addict Bill Asked by City and State," *New York Times,* February 4, 1966, 38; Sydney H.

Schanberg, "Rockefeller Signs Bill on Narcotics," *New York Times*, April 7, 1966, 35; Diaz and David, *A Political History of the Addiction Services Agency*, 2; Martin et al., *A Political History of the New York State Narcotic Addiction Control Commission*.

34. Bernard Weinraub, "Confinement of Addicts Proposed by Rockefeller," *New York Times*, February 24, 1966, 1; Sibley, "State Tries New Answer to Riddle," E5.

35. Letter from Herbert Berger, M.D., to Governor Nelson Rockefeller, February 18, 1962, in *Governor's Bill Jacket: 1962 Chapter 204* (New York Legislative Service, Inc, 1962).

Chapter 4: Crime, Class, and Conflict in the Ghetto

1. Daniel Patrick Moynihan, "Memo for the President," January 16, 1970, White House Central Files, Staff Member Office Files, Series III, Subject Files, Sub-series A, Subject File 1, Box 30, Folder: Negroes, Nixon Presidential Library and Museum, Yorba Linda, California; *The Negro Family: The Case for National Action* (Washington, DC: Government Printing Office, 1965).

2. "Rights Leaders' Statement on Moynihan," *New York Times*, March 6, 1970, 27; Linda Charlton, "21 Rights Leaders Rebut Moynihan," *New York Times*, March 6, 1970, 1.

3. Charles V. Hamilton, "The Silent Black Majority," *New York Times*, May 10, 1970, 201.

4. Hamilton, "Silent Black Majority." For a discussion of "linked fate," see Michael C. Dawson, *Behind the Mule: Race and Class in African-American Politics* (Princeton, NJ: Princeton University Press, 1994).

5. Mary Ellen Perry, "Black Middle Class Is Caught in a Squeeze, Says Novelist," *Oakland (CA) Post*, June 22, 1972, 15; Bill Webster, *One by One* (Garden City, NY: Doubleday, 1972).

6. Perry, "Black Middle Class Is Caught in a Squeeze," 15; Webster, *One by One*.

7. Harold Cruse, *The Crisis of the Negro Intellectual* (New York: Morrow, 1967), 90; Charles V. Hamilton, "The Patron-Recipient Relationship and Minority Politics in New York City," *Political Science Quarterly* 94, no. 2 (1979): 211–227.

8. Dennis H. Allee, "Memo to Senator Jacob Javits," November 1, 1971, Senator Jacob K. Javits Collection, Box 57, Folder: Harlem, Special

Collections and University Archives, Stony Brook University; *Living in Harlem: A Survey of Residents' Attitudes* (New York: Louis Harris and Associates, 1973), 74.

9. Robert H. Connery, *Rockefeller of New York: Executive Power in the Statehouse* (Ithaca, NY: Cornell University Press, 1979), 269; Paul Hofmann, "Crime Area Given More Protection," *New York Times*, February 26, 1966, 19; Homer Bigart, "Middle-Class Leaders in Harlem Ask Crackdown on Crime," *New York Times*, December 24, 1968, 25; Bedford-Stuyvesant Youth in Action, Inc., Senior Citizen Survey, 1966, Box 8, Folder 8, Olivia Pleasants Frost Papers, Schomburg Center for Research in Black Culture, New York Public Library.

10. Bernard McDonald, *Crime and Its Effect on Business Activity in the Bedford-Stuyvesant Community of Brooklyn, New York* (New York: Bedford-Stuyvesant Restoration Corporation, 1972); Mary H. Manoni, *Bedford-Stuyvesant: The Anatomy of a Central City Community* (New York: Quadrangle, 1973), 78–79.

11. Letter from Philip A. Smith to Robert F. Kennedy, May 4, 1965, Series: Correspondence Subject File, 1965, Box 38, Folder: Narcotics, 7/1965–8/1965, Robert F. Kennedy Senate Papers, 1964–1968, John F. Kennedy Library, Boston; "Crime among Us," *Amsterdam News*, April 17, 1971, 19.

12. Earl Caldwell, "Group in Harlem Asks More Police," *New York Times*, December 4, 1967, 1; Bigart, "Middle-Class Leaders in Harlem," 25.

13. Bigart, "Middle-Class Leaders in Harlem, 25"; *A Survey of Crime: Its Impact on Business and the Economy of Central Harlem* (New York: Small Business Chamber of Commerce of the City of New York, 1971).

14. "Memo from Wyatt Tee Walker to Nelson A. Rockefeller," August 11, 1966, Folder 1180, Box 43, Series 34.04, Nelson A. Rockefeller Gubernatorial Records, Rockefeller Archive Center, Sleepy Hollow, New York; Connery, *Rockefeller of New York*, 269; "Memo from Joe Persico to the Governor," September 11, 1970, Folder 3177, Box 78, Series 33.FA372, Nelson A. Rockefeller Gubernatorial Records, Rockefeller Archive Center, Sleepy Hollow, New York.

15. Governor's town meeting files, 1967–1972, Series B0919–82, Box 2, New York State Division of the Budget, New York State Archives, Cultural Education Center, Albany; Maria C. Lizzi, "'My Heart Is as Black as Yours': White Backlash, Racial Identity, and Italian American Stereotypes in New York City's 1969 Mayoral Campaign," *Journal*

of American Ethnic History 27, no. 3 (2008): 43–80; "Procaccino Offers Anticrime Program," *New York Times*, December 6, 1967, 31.

16. *Report of the New York State Joint Legislative Committee on Crime, Its Causes, Control & Effect on Society* (Albany: State of New York, 1969), 306.

17. Ibid., 300–302.

18. Ibid., 285–289.

19. "10,000 Attend Services for Slain New York Police," *Baltimore Afro American*, January 29, 1972, 2; Murray Schumach, "Top Police Officials Believe Black Militants Were the Slayers of Two Policemen on Lower East Side," *New York Times*, January 30, 1972, 35; Anonymous, "Show Us Your Courage," *Amsterdam News*, March 11, 1972, A4; "To a Cop on His Beat," *Amsterdam News*, February 17, 1973, A1.

20. Orde Coombs, "Three Faces of Harlem," *New York Times*, November 3, 1974, E32.

21. Ibid.

22. Charlayne Hunter, "Blacks Are Developing Programs to Fight Crime in Communities," *New York Times*, February 23, 1976, 14; Charles A. Murray, *Losing Ground: American Social Policy, 1950–1980* (New York: Basic Books, 1984), 117; *Criminal Victimization Surveys in the Nation's Five Largest Cities: National Crime Panel Surveys of Chicago, Detroit, Los Angeles, New York, and Philadelphia* (Washington, DC: U.S. Dept. of Justice, Law Enforcement Assistance Administration, National Criminal Justice Information and Statistics Service, 1975); Philip H. Ennis, *Criminal Victimization in the United States: A Report of a National Survey* (Chicago: National Opinion Research Center, University of Chicago, 1967).

23. U.S. House of Representatives, *The Improvement and Reform of Law Enforcement and Criminal Justice in the United States: Hearings before the Select Committee on Crime, United States House of Representatives* (Washington, DC: Government Printing Office, 1969), 25–26.

24. Robert Crosby and David Snyder, *Crime Victimization in the Black Community: Results of the Black Buyer II Survey* (Bethesda, MD: Resource Management Corp., 1970); U.S. House of Representatives, *The Improvement and Reform of Law Enforcement and Criminal Justice in the United States*, 25–26; Kirk Scharfenberg, "Inner City Residents Prefer 'Tough' Police," *Washington Post*, March 15, 1972, B1; Raul Ramirez "90% in Poll Call D.C. Drug Problem Serious," *Washington Post*, July 26, 1973; Crosby and Snyder, *Crime Victimization in the Black Community*.

25. Ethel Payne, "Cartoonist Depicts Horrors of Black-on-Black Crime," *Chicago Defender*, March 9, 1974, 32.

26. This analysis draws heavily from Daniel Kahneman and Amos Tversky, "Choices, Values, and Frames," *American Psychologist* 39, no. 4 (1984): 341–350.

27. "Crime Must Be Stopped," *Atlanta Daily World*, September 18, 1970, 4.

28. "Nation: The Anguish of Blacks in Blue," *Time*, November 23, 1970; "Black Cops Threatened to Jail Whites for Brutality," *Jet*, October 16, 1969, 16; Renault A. Robinson, "Rx for Black vs. Black Crime," *Chicago Defender*, July 18, 1970, 11.

29. Editorial quoted in J. A. Parker and Allan C. Brownfeld, *What the Negro Can Do about Crime* (New Rochelle, NY: Arlington House, 1974), 54.

30. William Raspberry, "What's the Compulsion to Shoot Heroin?," *Washington Post*, February 14, 1973, A15; William Raspberry, "Drug Addicts: Victims or Victimizers?," *Washington Post*, March 9, 1973, A27.

31. William Raspberry, "Racial Moderates Want to Be Heard," *Washington Post*, June 5, 1967, B1; "Wilkins Says Black Majority Is Too Quiet," *Kokomo (IN) Tribune*, May 14, 1970, 5; Lou Cannon and Al Eisele, "Black Silent Majority Applauded by Wilkins," *Independent Press Telegram* (Long Beach, CA), March 17, 1970, A16.

32. Audrey Weaver, "'Silent' Blacks Doing Slow Burn," *Chicago Defender*, August 1, 1970, 12; Lucy Nash, "Black on Black," *Chicago Defender*, August 6, 1974, 11.

33. "Attitude of Negroes on Key Questions," *New York Times*, July 27, 1964, 19; Louis Harris, "Poll Gives Views of Negro Leaders," *Spokesman-Review* (Spokane, WA), December 19, 1966, 3; "Crisis of Color," *Newsweek*, August 22, 1966; Jerry Buck, "In ABC Survey Black Panthers Are Debated," *Kentucky New Era*, April 13, 1970, 10.

34. "Black Silent Majority Meet," *Sacramento Observer*, October 22, 1970, A-9; "Silent Black Majority Now Clamoring to Be Heard," *Amsterdam News*, July 11, 1970, 1; "'Right On' . . . to What?," Box 5, Folder: Black Silent Majority Committee, 1972–1975, Stanley Scott Papers, 1971–1977, Gerald R. Ford Library, Ann Arbor, Michigan.

35. "Clay Claiborne Trial Set Jan. 31," *Washington Afro American*, January 18, 1966, 1; "Goldwater Adherents Hold Key Republican Party Jobs," *Oregon Statesman*, October 19, 1963, 4; Simeon Booker, "How Republican Leaders View the Negro," *Ebony*, March 1964, 30; "Ticker,"

Jet, November 27, 1964, 12; "Clay Claiborne Says Not Guilty in King Write-in Campaign," *Baltimore Afro American,* December 12, 1964, 20; "Clay Claiborne Freed in Vote Write-in Case," *Afro American,* June 11, 1966, 1; Dan Day, "Claiborne Sought in Vote Plot," *Afro American,* November 14, 1964, 1; Rowland Evans and Robert Novak, "GOP in Disagreement on Wooing Black Votes," *Morning Herald* (Hagerstown, MD), March 24, 1970, 4; "'Silent Majority' of Blacks Formed," *New York Times,* July 12, 1970, 23; Memo from Clay Claiborne to Ollie Atkins, October 16, 1972, "Black Progress," Box 5, Folder: Black Silent Majority Committee, 1972–1975, Stanley Scott Papers, 1971–1977, Gerald R. Ford Library, Ann Arbor, Michigan.

36. Ethel L. Payne, "Black Silent Majority Maps Anti-Violence Plan," *Chicago Defender,* October 17, 1970, 40; Simeon Book, "Ticker Tape U.S.A.," *Jet,* October 29, 1970, 11; "Black Silent Majority Blasts Rep. Dellums," *Pittsburgh Courier,* May 15, 1971, 3; "Black Raps Militants, Urges Law and Order," *Miami News,* August 8, 1972, 9; William Raspberry, "Claiborne Seeks Consensus Only," *Delta Democrat-Times* (Greenville, MS), November 22, 1970, 5; "Silent Majority Promotes Nixon," *Sacramento Observer,* August 12, 1971.

Chapter 5: King Heroin and the Development of the Drug Laws in 1973

1. Barbara Campbell, "Boy, 12, Dies of Heroin Dose in Harlem Bathroom," *New York Times,* December 16, 1969, 61.

2. "Why Did Walter Die?," *Time* 94, no. 26 (1969): 20; Campbell, "Boy, 12, Dies of Heroin Dose in Harlem Bathroom," 61.

3. Charlayne Hunter, "Heroin Victim, 12, Is Eulogized Here," *New York Times,* December 19, 1969, 92.

4. Ibid.; Bureau of Curriculum Development, New York City Board of Education, "Drug and Substance Abuse, Intermediate and Junior High School," Project No. 2508, March 1970, Senator Jacob K. Javits Collection, Box 66: "Narcotics," Folder 3, Special Collections and University Archives, Stony Brook University.

5. Thomas S. Hischak and Gerald Martin Bordman, *American Theatre: A Chronicle of Comedy and Drama, 1969–2000* (New York: Oxford University Press, 2001), 31; "King Heroin," *Ebony,* June 1971, 56–61; "Harlem Audience Finds Antipoverty Workshop's Drama on Heroin 'Right On,'" *New York Times,* March 1, 1970, 65; "'King Heroin' Tells Life of Dope Addict," *Jet,* April 8, 1971, 30; "Morality Play," *New York,* March 15, 1971, 53.

6. For the traditional history of the Rockefeller drug laws, see Julilly Kohler-Hausmann, "'The Attila the Hun Law': New York's Rockefeller Drug Laws and the Making of a Punitive State," *Journal of Social History* 44, no. 1 (2010): 71–95; Robert Gangi, "The Rockefeller Drug Laws," in *Racializing Justice, Disenfranchising Lives: The Racism, Criminal Justice, and Law Reader*, ed. Manning Marable, Ian Steinberg, and Keesha Middlemass (New York: Palgrave Macmillan, 2007); Jessica Neptune, "The Rockefeller Drug Laws and Punitive Politics," *Social History of Alcohol and Drugs* 26, no. 2 (2012): 170–191; Heather Ann Thompson, "Why Mass Incarceration Matters: Rethinking Crisis, Decline, and Transformation in Postwar American History," *Journal of American History* 97, no. 3 (2010): 703–734.

7. WCS-TV, *Newsmakers*, March 19, 1967, transcript; "Statement by Assemblyman Jerome Kretchmer and State Senator Manfred Ohrenstein," March 21, 1967, Record Series B1952–08, Box 19, Folder: Narcotics-1973, Manfred Ohrenstein Papers, New York State Archives, Cultural Education Center, Albany; Narcotics Addiction Control Commission, "Progress Report," 1967, and Press Release, January 22, 1968, and "Letter from Lawrence W. Pierce to Dr. Hollis S. Ingraham," November 4, 1966, and Press Release, January 22, 1968, New York State Department of Health Commissioner's Office Records, Series 13307–82, Box 52, Folder: New York State Narcotics Addiction Control Commission, New York State Archives, Cultural Education Center, Albany.

8. Mary Koval, Dean V. Babst, and Anthony Cagliostro, *Drug Use Rates among Young People in New York State* (New York: Narcotics Addiction Control Commission, 1973); Thomas Capone and James McLaughlin, *Incidence of Drug Addiction and Usage among School Age Population of New York City: A Report to the City Council* (New York: Bureau of Educational Research, Board of Education of the City of New York, 1970); U.S. House of Representatives, *Testimony of Michael M. Baden, M.D., Deputy Chief Medical Examiner, New York City, N.Y. "Drugs in Our Schools," Hearings before the Select Committee, House of Representatives* (Washington, DC: Government Printing Office, 1972), 96; Alfonso A. Narvaez, "Narcotics Death Called Homicide," *New York Times*, March 12, 1970, 29; "Harlem Church Forces Teen Hangout Out of Area," *Jet* 38, no. 11 (1970): 54; Martin T. Arnold, "Ex-Aide to Dr. King Appointed State's Expert on Urban Negro," *New York Times*, March 2, 1966, 38; George Dugan, "Harlem Pastor Goes into Street to

Ask Drive against Narcotics," *New York Times*, April 6, 1970, 34. Walker served as executive director of the Southern Christian Leadership Conference from 1960 to 1964.

9. "Blacks Declare War on Dope: Police, Government Inaction Prods New Yorkers to Launch Their Own Attack," *Ebony* 25, no. 11 (1970): 31–40; "Protesters Reject Addict Care Plan," *New York Times*, January 16, 1970, 22; Thomas F. Brady, "St. Luke's Yields on Drug Facility," *New York Times*, January 18, 1970, 56; Barbara Campbell, "West Side Marchers Seek More Addict Facilities," *New York Times*, March 24, 1970, 30.

10. "DC Dope March Gaining Support," *Amsterdam News*, April 4, 1970, 42; Alex Ward, "D.C. Protest Planned April 10 to Dramatize War on Drugs," *Washington Post*, March 21, 1970, B3; Les Matthews, "War Declared on Narcotics Problem," *Amsterdam News*, February 28, 1970, 3; Richard L. Madden, "Marchers Urge U.S. Act on Drugs," *New York Times*, April 11, 1972, 12; "Plan Rally against Narcotics," *Amsterdam News*, April 25, 1970, 3.

11. John Sibley, "State Police to Act on Narcotics Here," *New York Times*, February 21, 1968, 1; "TV Interview of Governor Nelson A. Rockefeller Re Narcotics Program," February 20, 1968, Folder 3781, Box 136, Series 34.11, Diane Van Wie, Nelson A. Rockefeller Gubernatorial Records, Rockefeller Archive Center, Sleepy Hollow, New York.

12. Bill Kovach, "Governor Drafts Program on Teen-Age Drug Abuses," *New York Times*, February 25, 1970, 1; "News Conference of Governor Nelson A. Rockefeller," February 24, 1970, Folder 3782, Box 136, Series 34.11, Diane Van Wie, Nelson A. Rockefeller Gubernatorial Records, Rockefeller Archive Center, Sleepy Hollow, New York.

13. New York State, *Public Papers of Nelson A. Rockefeller* (Albany: State of New York, 1968), 346–347, 494–496; New York State, *Public Papers of Nelson A. Rockefeller* (Albany: State of New York, 1970), 561–563, 1087–1091, 1365; "Methadone Grants by State, $433,000," *New York Times*, July 27, 1970, 19; "News Conference of Governor Nelson A. Rockefeller"; "Expanded Youth Narcotics Addiction Program," Folder 3794, Box 136, Series 34.11, Diane Van Wie, Nelson A. Rockefeller Gubernatorial Records, Rockefeller Archive Center, Sleepy Hollow, New York; "Joint Statement by Governor Nelson A. Rockefeller, Temporary President of the Senate Earl W. Brydges, and Assembly Speaker Perry B. Duryea," February 24, 1970, Series 13307, Dept. of

Health Commissioner's Office, Box 52, New York State Archives, Cultural Education Center, Albany.

14. "He Really Declares War on Dope," *Amsterdam News*, June 19, 1965, 6; Malcolm W. Brown, "Pastor Organizes Militia to Combat Crime in Harlem," *New York Times*, October 21, 1967, 33; "Addicts' Victims Turn Vigilante: Targets of Addicts Turning Vigilante," *New York Times*, September 23, 1969, 1; "Dope Ring Threatens to Kill Rev. Dempsey as Police Net Narrows," *New Pittsburgh Courier*, September 26, 1964, 1; Precinct 26, *Complaint Report*, April 11, 1971, New York City Police Department, NY; "Anti-Drug Pastor Assaulted," *Afro American*, April 24, 1971, 18.

15. "Addicts' Victims Turn Vigilante," 1.

16. "Harlem Residents Seek More Cops," *Chicago Defender*, December 16, 1967, 5; Homer Bigart, "Middle-Class Leaders in Harlem Ask for Crackdown on Crime," *New York Times*, December 24, 1968, 25; "Addicts' Victims Turn Vigilante," 1.

17. William E. Farrell, "State Senate Calls for Brooklyn Drug Hearings," *New York Times*, February 19, 1970, 1; "500 Attend 4 Hour Crime Hearing," *Amsterdam News*, November 18, 1972, A1.

18. "Lay That Pistol Down!," *Amsterdam News*, June 19, 1965, 16; Arnold H. Lubasch, "Harlem Likened to the Old West," *New York Times*, January 8, 1969, 48.

19. "500 Attend 4 Hour Crime Hearing," A1.

20. Charles B. Rangel, "Addiction Epidemic in Harlem," *New York Law Journal*, July 6, 1971.

21. Nelson Rockefeller, "Governor Seeks All-Out Effort on Drugs," *New York Law Journal*, December 6, 1971; Edward Jay Epstein, *Agency of Fear: Opiates and Political Power in America* (New York: Putnam, 1977); Sasha Abramsky, *Hard Time Blues: How Politics Built a Prison Nation* (New York: Thomas Dunne Books / St. Martin's Press, 2002).

22. New York State, *Minutes of Transcript of a Public Hearing of the Senate and Assembly Standing Committees on Codes, Held in Hearing Room B, New Legislative Office Building, on January 30, 1973* (White Plains, NY: O'Neill Reporting, 1973).

23. Press Release, "Blumenthal Calls Rockefeller's State of the State a Public Temper Tantrum," January 9, 1973, Record Series B1952–08, Box 19, Folder: Narcotics-1973, Manfred Ohrenstein Papers, New York State Archives, Cultural Education Center, Albany; Francis X. Clines,

"Legislature Open," *New York Times*, January 4, 1973, 1; Francis X. Clines, "Harlem Leaders Back Life Terms for Drug Sale," *New York Times*, January 23, 1973, 43; Lesley Oelsner, "Governor's Drug Plan Draws Anger, Cautious Applause and a Sense of Anguish," *New York Times*, January 4, 1973, 29.

24. *Governor's Bill Jacket: Chapter 278* (New York: New York Legislative Service, 1973); Oelsner, "Governor's Drug Plan Draws Anger," 29; William E. Farrell, "Legislators Seek a Compromise on Governor's Drug Penalties," *New York Times*, February 24, 1973, 60; William Ferrell, "D.A.'s Assail Rockefeller Drug Penalties," *New York Times*, February 7, 1973, 45; James M. Markham, "The Fight on Narcotics: End of Plea Bargaining Is Regarded as Prelude," *New York Times*, January 9, 1973, 79; Francis X. Clines, "Court Official Says Governor's Drug Plan Won't Work," *New York Times*, February 17, 1973, 35; Max H. Seigel, "Lindsay Assails Governor's Plan to Combat Drugs," *New York Times*, January 10, 1973, 1.

25. "Notes from the State Senate and Assembly Codes Committee Hearings on Governor Rockefeller's Anti-Drug Program," February, 1973, Folder 348, Box 33, Series 21.2, Rockefeller Gubernatorial Records, Rockefeller Archive Center, Sleepy Hollow, New York.

26. "Memo from Evelyn Cunningham to the Governor," January 19, 1973, Folder 354, Box 34, Series 21.2, Rockefeller Gubernatorial Records, Rockefeller Archive Center, Sleepy Hollow, New York; Simeon Booker and Carol McCabe Booker, *Shocking the Conscience: A Reporter's Account of the Civil Rights Movement* (Jackson: University Press of Mississippi, 2013); C. Gerald Fraser, "Harlem Response Mixed," *New York Times*, January 5, 1973, 65.

27. New York State, *Minutes of Transcript of a Public Hearing of the Senate and Assembly Standing Committees on Codes.*

28. Ibid.; Fraser, "Harlem Response Mixed," 65.

29. Robert McG. Thomas Jr., "New Drug Laws Scored in Harlem," *New York Times*, February 3, 1973, 30, emphasis added.

30. Ibid.

31. "Memo from Hugh Marrow to the Governor," January 9, 1973, Folder 347, Box 31, Series 21.2, Rockefeller Gubernatorial Records, Rockefeller Archive Center, Sleepy Hollow, New York; Clarence B. Jones and Stuart Connelly, *Behind the Dream: The Making of the Speech That Transformed a Nation* (New York: Palgrave Macmillan, 2011); Maurice

Carroll, "After Crime, Big Issues Are Prices and Fares," *New York Times*, January 17, 1974, A36; David Burnham, "Most Call Crime City's Worst Ill," *New York Times*, January 16, 1974, 113; Nathaniel Sheppard, "Racial Issues Split City Deeply," *New York Times*, January 20, 1974, 1.

32. "A Live Broadcast on WCBS/TV," February 25, 1973, Series 21.2, Box 33, Folder 350, Rockefeller Gubernatorial Records, Rockefeller Archive Center, Sleepy Hollow, New York.

33. Data provided to the author by the Bureau of Vital Statistics, New York City Department of Health and Mental Hygiene.

34. "Letter from Dr. Benjamin W. Watkins to Nelson A. Rockefeller," February 5, 1973, Folder 354, Box 34, Series 21.2, Box 33, Rockefeller Gubernatorial Records, Rockefeller Archive Center, Sleepy Hollow, New York; " 'Mayor of Harlem' Dies at Age 73," *New York Voice, Inc. Harlem USA*, September 6, 1995.

35. "Statement of Mr. Glester Hinds Testifying at N.Y. State Legislative Hearing at the Union Baptist Church," February 16, 1973, Folder 355, Box 34, Series 21.2, Rockefeller Gubernatorial Records, Rockefeller Archive Center, Sleepy Hollow, New York.

36. "Getting Serious about Drugs," *Amsterdam News*, February 24, 1973, A5; "Getting Serious about Drugs," *Wall Street Journal*, January 23, 1973, 18.

37. Francis X. Clines, "G.O.P. in Assembly Delays Drug Bill," *New York Times*, May 1, 1973, 86; *Report of the New York State Joint Legislative Committee on Crime, Its Causes, Control, and Effect on Society* (Albany: The Committee, 1967); *Report of the New York State Joint Legislative Committee on Crime, Its Causes, Control, and Effect on Society on the Drug Abuse Problem at the State University of New York at Stony Brook* (Albany: The Committee, 1968); *Report of the New York State Joint Legislative Committee on Crime, Its Causes, Control, and Effect on Society* (Albany: The Committee, 1971).

38. *The Voices of Organized Crime: An Educational Tape* (Albany: The Committee, 1968); *Governor Rockefeller's Conference on Crime, December 15, 1967* (Albany: New York State Crime Control Council, 1968); *Report of the New York State Joint Legislative Committee on Crime, Its Causes, Control, and Effect on Society* (Albany: The Committee, 1969), 306; M. S. Handler, "Harlem Officials Testify on Crime," *New York Times*, February 21, 1969, 50; "Mafia Is Reported Preying on Slums," *New York Times*, May 18, 1969, 77.

39. DiCarlo's bill would have also made possession of two ounces or more or the sale of one ounce or more of cocaine, morphine, heroin, or

opium a Class A felony, carrying up to a life sentence. Possession of one ounce or more or the sale of one-eighth of an ounce of dangerous drugs would be classified as a Class B felony and would carry up to a twenty-five-year prison term. Finally, DiCarlo's alternative would move the sale of marijuana to a person under the age of twenty-one from the Class B to the less punitive Class C category. William E. Farrell, "Mandatory Sentence Proposed for 2d-Felony Drug Offenses," *New York Times*, April 5, 1973, 49; Nick Ravo, "Judge Dominick L. DiCarlo, 71, Narcotics Fighter under Reagan," *New York Times*, April 30, 1999, C21.

40. Press Release, "Statement by Governor Nelson A. Rockefeller," June 12, 1973, Series 3, Box 4, Folder 19, Eliot Howland Lumbard Papers, M. E. Grenander Department of Special Collections & Archives, University at Albany.

41. William E. Farrell, "Governor Modifies Plan on Stiffer Drug Penalties," *New York Times*, April 13, 1973, 1; *Senate Debate Transcripts 1973, Chapter 278* (New York: New York Legislative Service, 1973); Farrell, "Legislators Seek a Compromise on Governor's Drug Penalties," 60.

42. "Governor's Bill on Drug Traffic Voted by Senate," *New York Times*, April 28, 1973, 69; William E. Farrell, "Revised Narcotics Measure Is Voted 80–65 in Assembly," *New York Times*, May 4, 1973, 77; William E. Farrell, "Senate Passes Assembly's Version of Antidrug Bill," *New York Times*, May 8, 1973, 28.

43. Amy Plumer, "Albany Notes," *Amsterdam News*, May 12, 1973, A6; Francis X. Clines, "Governor's Drug Bill Splits Black and Puerto Rican Legislators," *New York Times*, March 4, 1973, 38; William E. Farrell, "Governor Signs His Drug Bills and Assails the Critics Again," *New York Times*, May 9, 1973, 97; "Governor Nelson A. Rockefeller at the Bill Signing Ceremony, Narcotics Bills," May 8, 1973, Folder 265, Box 14, Series 12.3, Rockefeller Gubernatorial Records, Rockefeller Archive Center, Sleepy Hollow, New York.

44. Michael Javen Fortner, "Webs of Difference: The Social and Institutional Roots of Racial Politics in New York City and London," PhD dissertation, Harvard University, 2011; Paul Good, "A Political Tour of Harlem," *New York Times*, October 29, 1967, SM34; Alfonso A. Narvaez, "4 Puerto Ricans Will Take Seats In Legislature at Opening Jan. 6," *New York Times*, December 6, 1970, 51; "Assembly to Get a Black Woman," *New York Times*, November 19, 1972, 42; "Sidney A. von Luther, Former State Senator," *New York Times*, August 18, 1985, 36;

Monte Williams, "Samuel D. Wright, 73, Former Assemblyman," *New York Times*, February 1, 1998, 30; Edward Hudson, "Calvin Williams, 61, Car Service Operator and Ex-Legislator," *New York Times*, May 7, 1987, B20; "Sen. Galiber, Bronx Political Leader, Dies at 71," *Amsterdam News*, November 25, 1995, 49; "State Senator Joseph Galiber Dead at 71," *New York Beacon*, November 29, 1995, 2; David Stout, "Joseph L. Galiber Dies at 71," *New York Times*, November 22, 1995, D19; Louis Harris and Associates, *A Survey of Leadership Attitudes toward the Quality of Life in Harlem* (New York: Louis Harris and Associates, 1973), 15.

45. William E. Farrell, "Legislators Fire Questions at Governor on Drug Plan," *New York Times*, January 31, 1973, 89; Clines, "Governor's Drug Bill Splits," 38; "Dope Smear Sparks Jamaica Battle," *New York Age*, December 16, 1950, 7.

46. *Senate Debate Transcripts 1973, Chapter 278* (New York: New York Legislative Service, 1973), 1043, 4214.

47. Joseph E. Persico, *The Imperial Rockefeller: A Biography of Nelson A. Rockefeller* (New York: Simon & Schuster, 1982), 145; "Memo from Hugh Morrow to the Governor," August 6, 1973, Folder 347, Box 33, Series 33.1, Rockefeller Gubernatorial Records, Rockefeller Archive Center, Sleepy Hollow, New York.

48. For a discussion of institutional layering, see Kathleen Ann Thelen, "How Institutions Evolve: Insights from Comparative-Historical Analysis," in *Comparative Historical Analysis in the Social Sciences*, ed. James Mahoney and Dietrich Rueschemeyer (Cambridge, UK: Cambridge University Press, 2003), 208–240; Kathleen Ann Thelen, *How Institutions Evolve: The Political Economy of Skills in Germany, Britain, the United States, and Japan* (Cambridge, UK: Cambridge University Press, 2004).

Chapter 6: Race, Place, and the Tumultuous 1960s and 1970s

1. "Governor Nelson Rockefeller Addresses the '64 Convention," C-SPAN, August 1, 1988, online video clip, C-SPAN.com, accessed on February 20, 2014, http://www.c-spanvideo.org/clip/3807346.

2. George Gallup, "Kennedy Heads List of 'Most Admired Men,'" *Washington Post*, December 28, 1962, A5; George Gallup, "Johnson Heads Group Most Admired by Public," *Washington Post*, December 27, 1963, A2; George Gallup, "Johnson Again Named Most Admired Man," *Washington Post*, December 30, 1964, A2; George Gallup, "Public Picks

Johnson as Man of '65: Eisenhower, R. Kennedy Follow," *Washington Post*, January 2, 1966, A2; "Political Poll: Negro Publishers and Editors," May 6, 1964, Folder 3405, Box 107, Series 34.10, Diane Van Wie, Nelson A. Rockefeller Gubernatorial Records, Rockefeller Archive Center, Sleepy Hollow, New York.

3. Memorandum, "The Politics of 1948," September 18, 1947, Box 1, Clark M. Clifford Papers, Manuscript Division, Library of Congress, Washington, DC. It is important to note that the bulk of the memo was written by James Rowe Jr. "The Politics of 1948," September 18, 1947, from James Rowe Jr. to President Harry S. Truman, Kenneth Hechler Papers, Harry S. Truman Library and Museum, Independence, Missouri; Edward G. Carmines, *Issue Evolution: Race and the Transformation of American Politics* (Princeton, NJ: Princeton University Press, 1989); Samuel J. Eldersveld, "The Influence of Metropolitan Party Pluralities in Presidential Elections Since 1920: A Study of Twelve Key Cities," *American Political Science Review* 43, no. 6 (1949): 1189–1206.

4. Michelle Alexander, *The New Jim Crow: Mass Incarceration in the Age of Colorblindness* (New York: New Press, 2012). See Thomas Sugrue, *The Origins of the Urban Crisis: Race and Inequality in Postwar Detroit* (Princeton, NJ: Princeton University Press, 2005); Kevin M. Kruse, *White Flight: Atlanta and the Making of Modern Conservatism* (Princeton, NJ: Princeton University Press, 2005); Robert O. Self, *American Babylon: Race and the Struggle for Postwar Oakland* (Princeton, NJ: Princeton University Press, 2005); J. Anthony Lukas, *Common Ground: A Turbulent Decade in the Lives of Three American Families* (New York: Knopf, 1985); Ronald P. Formisano, *Boston against Busing: Race, Class, and Ethnicity in the 1960s and 1970s* (Chapel Hill: University of North Carolina Press, 2003); Loïc Wacquant, "Marginality, Ethnicity and Penality in the Neo-liberal City: An Analytic Cartography," *Ethnic and Racial Studies* 37, no. 10 (2014): 1687–1711, 1696.

5. Jonathan Rieder, "The Rise of the 'Silent Majority,'" in *The Rise and Fall of the New Order, 1930–1980*, ed. Steven Fraser and Gary Gerstle (Princeton, NJ: Princeton University Press, 1989), 243–268; James A. Stimson, Michael B. MacKuen, and Robert S. Erikson, "Dynamic Representation," *American Political Science Review* 89, no. 3 (1995): 543–565. See also James A. Stimson, *Public Opinion in America: Moods, Cycles, and Swings* (Boulder, CO: Westview Press, 1991); Robert S. Erikson, Gerald C. Wright, and John P. McIver, *Statehouse Democracy:*

Public Opinion and Policy in the American States (Cambridge, UK: Cambridge University Press, 1993); Robert S. Erikson, Michael MacKuen, and James A. Stimson, *The Macro Polity* (New York: Cambridge University Press, 2002).

6. Sam Roberts, "Infamous 'Drop Dead' Was Never Said by Ford," *New York Times*, December 28, 2006; Lawrence Gordon et al., *The Warriors* (Hollywood, CA: Paramount Home Entertainment, 2005); Robert A. Caro, *The Power Broker: Robert Moses and the Fall of New York* (New York: Knopf, 1974); Jonathan Mahler, *Ladies and Gentlemen, the Bronx Is Burning: 1977, Baseball, Politics, and the Battle for the Soul of a City* (New York: Farrar, Straus and Giroux, 2005); John H. Mollenkopf, *A Phoenix in the Ashes: The Rise and Fall of the Koch Coalition in New York City Politics* (Princeton, NJ: Princeton University Press, 1992); Kenneth T. Jackson, *Crabgrass Frontier: The Suburbanization of the United States* (Oxford: Oxford University Press, 1985); Ira Katznelson, *When Affirmative Action Was White: An Untold History of Racial Inequality in Twentieth-Century America* (New York: Norton, 2006); William Julius Wilson, *When Work Disappears: The World of the New Urban Poor* (New York: Vintage, 1997); Michael J. Bennett, *When Dreams Came True: The GI Bill and the Making of Modern America* (Dulles, VA: Potomac Books, 1999); Frances Fox Piven, "Federal Policy and Urban Fiscal Strain," *Yale Law & Policy Review* 2, no. 2 (1984): 291–320; John Mollenkopf, *The Contested City* (Princeton, NJ: Princeton University Press, 1983); Bruce J. Schulman, *From Cotton Belt to Sunbelt: Federal Policy, Economic Development, and the Transformation of the South, 1938–1980* (Durham, NC: Duke University Press, 1994).

7. U.S. Department of Justice, Federal Bureau of Investigations, Uniform Crime Reports, 1960 and 1968; Jameson W. Doig, "Crime, Police, and the Criminal Justice System," in *Agenda for a City: Issues Confronting New York*, ed. Lyle C. Finch and Annmarie Hauck Walsh (Beverly Hills, CA: Sage, 1970), 252; Stevens H. Clarke, *The New York City Criminal Court: Case Flow and Congestion from 1959 to 1968: Report to the Mayor's Criminal Justice Coordinating Council* (New York: New York City Criminal Justice Information Bureau, 1970).

8. Jill Jonnes, *South Bronx Rising: The Rise, Fall, and Resurrection of an American City* (New York: Fordham University Press, 2002); Kenneth Bancroft Clark, *Dark Ghetto: Dilemmas of Social Power* (New York: Harper & Row, 1965); David Burnham, "A Wide Disparity Is Found in Crime

throughout City," *New York Times*, February 14, 1972, 1. Data compiled by the Bureau of Vital Statistics, New York City Department of Health and Mental Hygiene.

9. Data compiled by the Bureau of Vital Statistics, New York City Department of Health and Mental Hygiene.

10. Daniel Glaser and Mary Snow, *Public Knowledge and Attitudes on Drug Abuse in New York State* (New York: Narcotics Addiction Control Commission, 1969), 11.

11. Daniel Yankelovich, "Voters in State Sampling Stress Moral Positions of Candidates," *New York Times*, October 30, 1970, 46.

12. Richard Reeves, "Poll Shows Political Views Unaffected by Union Membership," *New York Times*, October 15, 1970, 53; Richard Reeves, "Survey Confirms Politicians' Views of Attitudes of Ethnic-Group Voters," *New York Times*, October 25, 1970, 67. For example, Thomas Sugrue writes, "The 'silent majority' did not emerge de novo from the alleged failures of liberalism in the 1960s; it was not the unique product of the white rejection of the Great Society. Instead it was the culmination of more than two decades of simmering white discontent and extensive antiliberal political organization. The problem of white backlash in the urban North is longer-lived and far more intractable than recent analyses would suggest." Thomas J. Sugrue, "Crabgrass-Roots Politics: Race, Rights, and the Reaction against Liberalism in the Urban North, 1940–1964," *Journal of American History* 82 (1995): 578.

13. Martin Mayer, "The Full and Sometimes Very Surprising Story of Ocean Hill," *New York Times*, February 2, 1969, SM18. For discussions of racial and ethnic politics in postwar New York City, see Joshua Zeitz, *White Ethnic New York Jews, Catholics, and the Shaping of Postwar Politics* (Chapel Hill: University of North Carolina, 2007); Chris McNickle, *To Be Mayor of New York: Ethnic Politics in the City* (New York: Columbia University Press, 1993); Vincent J. Cannato, *The Ungovernable City: John Lindsay and His Struggle to Save New York* (New York: Basic Books, 2001); Jim Sleeper, *The Closet of Strangers: Liberalism and the Politics in New York* (New York: Norton, 1990). For discussions of the Ocean Hill–Brownsville school controversy, see Wendell Pritchett, *Brownsville, Brooklyn: Blacks, Jews, and the Changing Face of the Ghetto* (Chicago: University of Chicago Press, 2002); Jerald E. Podair, *The Strike That Changed New York: Blacks, Whites, and the Ocean Hill–Brownsville Crisis* (New Haven, CT: Yale University Press, 2002); Paul Ritterband,

"Ethnic Power and the Public Schools: The New York City School Strike of 1968," *Sociology of Education* 47, no. 2 (1974): 251–267; Richard D. Kahlenberg, *Tough Liberal: Albert Shanker and the Battles over Schools, Unions, Race, and Democracy* (New York: Columbia University Press, 2007); Bernard Weinraub, "Police Review Panel Killed by Large Majority in City," *New York Times*, November 9, 1966, 1; Jewel Bellush and Stephen M. David, *Race and Politics in New York City; Five Studies in Policy-Making* (New York: Praeger, 1971).

14. Albert J Reiss, "Studies in Crime and Law Enforcement in Major Metropolitan Areas," President's Commission on Law Enforcement and Administration of Justice, Field Surveys (Washington, DC: Government Printing Office, 1967); Seymour M. Lipset, "Why Cops Hate Liberals—and Vice Versa," in *The Police Rebellion: A Quest for Blue Power*, ed. William J. Bopp (Springfield, IL: Thomas, 1971), 34–36.

15. Maria C. Lizzi, "'My Heart Is as Black as Yours': White Backlash, Racial Identity, and Italian American Stereotypes in New York City's 1969 Mayoral Campaign," *Journal of American Ethnic History* 27, no. 3 (2008): 43–80.

16. *Trends in Narcotic Abuse in New York State* (Albany: New York State Department of Health, 1973); *Fourth Annual Statistical Report of the Narcotic Addiction Control Commission* (Albany, NY: Office of Fiscal and Management Services, Bureau of Management Information Services, 1971); *Third Annual Statistical Report of the Narcotic Addiction Control Commission* (Albany, NY: Office of Fiscal and Management Services, Bureau of Management Information Services, 1970); *Second Annual Statistical Report of the Narcotic Addiction Control Commission* (Albany, NY: Office of Fiscal and Management Services, Bureau of Management Information Services, 1969); *First Annual Statistical Report of the Narcotic Addiction Control Commission* (Albany, NY: Office of Fiscal and Management Services, Bureau of Management Information Services, 1968); Glaser and Snow, *Public Knowledge and Attitudes on Drug Abuse*, 5.

17. Drug Abuse Forum, Utica, August 26, 1970, and Drug Abuse Forum, Monroe County, September 9, 1970, and Drug Abuse Forum, Syracuse, September 17, 1970, Folder 345, Box 32, Series 21.2, Nelson A. Rockefeller Gubernatorial Records, Rockefeller Archive Center, Sleepy Hollow, New York.

18. Drug Abuse Forum, Utica, August 26, 1970; Testimony of Sheriff Michael Amico, Proceedings of State of New York Joint Legislative

Temporary Commission to Evaluate the Drug Laws, October 15, 1970; Drug Abuse Forum, Monroe County, September 9, 1970.

19. Thomas W. Ennis, "Industry Alters View of Suburbs," *New York Times*, March 17, 1957, R1; "City Official Sees Jobs at Dead End," *New York Times*, December 21, 1964, 34; Robert P. Goldman, "Dope Invades the Suburbs," *Saturday Evening Post*, April 4, 1964; *Trends in Narcotic Abuse in New York State* (Albany: New York State Department of Health, 1973); *Trends in Narcotic Abuse in New York State* (Albany: New York State Department of Health, 1970).

20. Glaser and Snow, *Public Knowledge and Attitudes on Drug Abuse*, 3; Letter from Frank G. Straub to Robert F. Kennedy, June 13, 1966, Series: Correspondence Subject File, 1966, Box 69, Folder: Narcotics, Robert K. Kennedy Senate Papers, 1964–1968, John F. Kennedy Library, Boston; *An Assessment of Drug Use in the General Population, Special Report* (Albany, NY: Narcotics Addiction Control Commission, Research Division, 1971); *Report of the State of New York Joint Legislative Committee on Narcotic and Drug Addiction* (Albany: Joint Legislative Committee on Narcotic and Drug Addiction, 1966), 22–23.

21. Leonard Victor, "A Cure for Young Addicts?," *Long Island Press*, January 11, 1966; Birchwood Elementary School PTA, Petition, and "Letter from Mrs. Charles Hubert to Bernard C. Smith," January 28, 1969, and letter from David Millman to Bernard C. Smith, January 15, 1969, Series 1, Box 6, Folder 7, Bernard Smith Papers, M. E. Grenander Department of Special Collections & Archives, University at Albany.

22. Leonard Victor, "Kids from Fine Families among Thousands Hooked," *Long Island Press*, January 6, 1966; Leonard Victor, "It Was Easy to Buy Deadly Pills on LI," *Long Island Press*, January 9, 1966; Leonard Victor, "Teen Addict's Arrest 'Saves' His Life," *Long Island Press*, January 8, 1966; Leonard Victor, "LI Dope Death Toll Still Soaring," *Long Island Press*, January 7, 1966.

23. Leonard Victor, "We Almost Clubbed a Man to Death," *Long Island Press*, January 4, 1966; Leonard Victor, "Why Teenagers Become Addicts," *Long Island Press*, January 10, 1966; "Quotes from Narcotics Forums," Folder 345, Box 32, Series 21.2, Rockefeller Gubernatorial Records, Rockefeller Archive Center, Sleepy Hollow, New York.

24. *Senate Debate Transcripts 1966, Chapter 192* (New York: New York Legislative Service, 1966).

25. Bill Kovach, "Governor Drafts Program on Teen-age Drug Abuses," *New York Times*, February 25, 1970, 1; "News Conference of Governor Nelson A. Rockefeller," February 24, 1970, Folder 3782, Box 136, Series 34.11, Diane Van Wie, Nelson A. Rockefeller Gubernatorial Records, Rockefeller Archive Center, Sleepy Hollow, New York; Thomas Nordegren, *The A–Z Encyclopedia of Alcohol and Drug Abuse* (Parkland, FL: Brown Walker Press, 2002); William E. Farrell, "State Senate Calls for Brooklyn Drug Hearings," *New York Times*, February 19, 1970, 1.

26. "The War We Have to Win," Position Paper of Paul L. Adams, Series 6, Box 1, Folder 10, Conservative Party of New York State Records, 1962–2004, M. E. Grenander Department of Special Collections & Archives, University at Albany.

27. "Pollster Finds Backlash Grows," *New York Times*, September 28, 1966, 26; Warren Weaver Jr., "G.O.P. Finds '68 Outlook Brighter As It Counts Election Successes," *New York Times*, November 10, 1966, 1; Lawrence E. Davies, "Reagan Elected by a Wide Margin," *New York Times*, November 9, 1966, 1; Gladwell Hill, "Reagan Emerging in 1968 Spotlight," *New York Times*, November 10, 1966, 1; Rick Perlstein, *Nixonland: The Rise of a President and the Fracturing of America* (New York: Scribner, 2008), xii.

28. "Meeting with Ad Hoc Committee to Discuss Problems of Negro Community," November 26, 1965, Folder 1722, Box 60, Series 34.06, and "Memo from Al Marshall to Wyatt Walker," April 4, 1966, Folder 1180, Box 43, Series 34.04, Danine Van Wie, Nelson A. Rockefeller Gubernatorial Records, Rockefeller Archive Center, Sleepy Hollow, New York.

29. Arlen J. Larges, "GOP Countdown: Rockefeller Pins Hopes on Southern Switches from Nixon," *Wall Street Journal*, August 2, 1968, 1; Tom Wicker, "Twisting Path to the G.O.P. Convention," *New York Times*, August 5, 1968, 19; Charles McCarry, "Win with Rockefeller," *Saturday Evening Post*, February 24, 1968, 3; Hal Burdett, "Rockefeller Draft Drive," *Evening Capital*, January 10, 1968, 1; Richard L. Maddens, "Supporters from 15 States Urge Rockefeller to Enter Race Now," *New York Times*, March 19, 1968, 37; "LBJ 'Vulnerable' Rocky Strongest, Rep. Laid Says," *La Crosse (WI) Tribune*, January 22, 1968; "To Pick Nominee with Eye on House," *Waukesha (WI) Daily Freeman*, February 19, 1968, 11; "Rockefeller Leads G.O.P. Poll for '68 Taken in Congress," *New York Times*, February 5, 1968, 20; James Marlow, "Poll on Vietnam Shows New Twist in American Politics," *Daily Freeman*,

November 11, 1967, 4; "On the Road," *Time*, November 3, 1967, 36; "Waiting for Rocky," *Time*, January 19, 1968, 20.

30. Theodore H. White, *The Making of the President 1968* (New York: Harper Perennial, 2010), 272–273; "To Burn or Not to Burn," *Wall Street Journal*, June 13, 1968, 10; "To Burn or Not to Burn," *El Paso (TX) Herald-Post*, June 13, 1968, 7; James Reston, "The Northern Vote: Nelson Rockefeller's Main Argument," *New York Times*, July 17, 1968, 42.

31. Richard Reeves, "Rockefeller's Strength and Weakness Are Analyzed," *New York Times*, March 30, 1970, 47; Richard Reeves, "Rockefeller's Strategy," *New York Times*, September 21, 1970, 37; Burt Glinn, "Making a Mensch of Arthur," *New York Magazine*, October 12, 1970, 38; Clayton Knowles, "Rockefeller Endorsed by Procaccino," *New York Times*, September 15, 1970, 1; "Memo from Joe Persico to the Governor," September 15, 1970, Folder 3177, Box 78, Series 33.FA372, Nelson A. Rockefeller Gubernatorial Records, Rockefeller Archive Center, Sleepy Hollow, New York.

32. George Gallup, "Agnew Has Lead for GOP No. 2 Spot," *Washington Post*, May 18, 1972, A19; "Survey Gives Reagan Clear Lead for 1976," *Los Angeles Times*, October 21, 1973, A1; "Reagan Picked in Survey of GOP Chairmen," *Los Angeles Times*, March 24, 1974, 5.

33. Joseph E. Persico, *The Imperial Rockefeller: A Biography of Nelson A. Rockefeller* (New York: Simon & Schuster, 1982), 144.

34. Gavin Wright, *Old South, New South: Revolutions in the Southern Economy since the Civil War* (Baton Rouge: Louisiana State University Press, 1996); Earl Black and Merle Black, *Politics and Society in the South* (Cambridge, MA: Harvard University Press, 1987); Earl Black and Merle Black, *The Vital South: How Presidents Are Elected* (Cambridge, MA: Harvard University Press, 1992); Earl Black and Merle Black, *The Rise of Southern Republicans* (Cambridge, MA: Harvard University Press, 2002); David Lublin, *The Republican South: Democratization and Partisan Change* (Princeton, NJ: Princeton University Press, 2004); Matthew D. Lassiter, "The Politics of Middle-Class Consciousness," in *The Democratic Experiment: New Directions in American Political History*, ed. Meg Jacobs, William J. Novak, and Julian E. Zelizer (Princeton, NJ: Princeton University Press, 2003); Matthew D. Lassiter, *The Silent Majority: Suburban Politics in the Sunbelt South* (Princeton, NJ: Princeton University Press, 2000), 250.

35. Kim Phillips-Fein, *Invisible Hands: The Making of the Conservative Movement from the New Deal to Reagan* (New York: Norton, 2009), xii; Lisa

McGirr, *Suburban Warriors: The Origins of the New American Right* (Princeton, NJ: Princeton University Press, 2001), 10.

36. John Mollenkopf, "Urban Political Conflicts and Alliances: New York and Los Angeles Compared," in *The Handbook of International Migration: The American Experience*, ed. C. Hirschman, P. Kasinitz, and J. DeWind (New York: Russell Sage Foundation, 1999), 421. See also Steven P. Erie, *Rainbow's End: Irish-Americans and the Dilemmas of Urban Machines, 1840–1985* (Berkeley: University of California Press, 1988).

37. Richard Norton Smith, *On His Own Terms: A Life of Nelson Rockefeller* (New York: Random House, 2014).

Conclusion

1. Leon H. Washington Jr., "Nation Watches as N.Y. Inaugurates Tough Drug Law," *Los Angeles Sentinel*, September 13, 1973, A6; "N.Y. Dope Law," *Afro American*, September 15, 1973, 4.

2. H. Carl McCall, "Looking Back," *Amsterdam News*, December 23, 1973, A5; H. Carl McCall, "Living with the New Drug Law," *Amsterdam News*, September 8, 1973, A5.

3. *New York State Felony Drug Arrest, Indictment and Commitment Trends, 1973–2008* (Albany: Division of Criminal Justice Research Services, Office of Justice Research and Performance, 2010), 4–5.

4. "Testimony of Robert A. Perry, on behalf of the New York Civil Liberties Union, before the New York State Assembly Committees on Codes, Judiciary, Correction, Health, Alcoholism and Drug Abuse, and Social Services regarding the Rockefeller Drug Laws," New York Civil Liberties Union, accessed March 8, 2014, http://www.nyclu.org/content/rockefeller-drug-laws-cause-racial-disparities-huge-taxpayer-burden; Rachel Porter, *Unjust and Counterproductive: New York's Rockefeller Drug Laws* (Boston: Physicians for Human Rights, 2004), 3.

5. Paul Pierson, "The Study of Policy Development," *Journal of Policy History* 17, no. 1 (2005): 34–51. For discussions of the temporal dimensions of policy development, see Paul Pierson, *Politics in Time: History, Institutions, and Social Analysis* (Princeton, NJ: Princeton University Press, 2004); Paul Pierson and Theda Skocpol, "Historical Institutionalism in Contemporary Political Science," in *Political Science: State of the Discipline*, ed. Ira Katznelson and Helen V. Milner (New York: Norton, 2002), 693–721. This book unites the insights of John W. Kingdon's theory of agenda setting and the insights of the polity-centered approach.

Although there are many commonalities between the two, Kingdon does not sufficiently stress the role that state capacity plays in periods of stability and periods of dramatic change in policymaking. The analysis in this book does not stop at the selection of policy ideas as it also interrogates the final design that certain policy ideas assume. It argues that, although issue networks could not beat back forces within the political stream, they used their ideas, organizational capacities, and political resources to shape the design of drug control legislation. John W. Kingdon, *Agendas, Alternatives, and Public Policies* (Boston: Little, Brown, 1984).

6. "Clean Out This Scum," *New York Age*, September 5, 1959, 6; Ghetto Testimony before Senate Draws Mixed Harlem Reaction," *Amsterdam News*, September 3, 1966, 1; Langston Hughes and Donna Sullivan Harper, *The Return of Simple* (New York: Hill and Wang, 1994), 126.

7. There is now a growing literature that documents the punitive preferences of African Americans. See James Forman Jr., "Racial Critiques of Mass Incarceration: Beyond the New Jim Crow," *NYU Law Review* 87, no. 21 (2012): 21–69; Michael Javen Fortner and Prentiss Dantzler, "Black Power, Black Pessimism: Federal Involvement in Law Enforcement in 1970s New York City," paper prepared for presentation at the American Political Science Association, Chicago, August 29–September 1, 2013; Michael J. Durfee, "'Get That Garbage Off the Streets': Black-lash and the Origins of Crack Era Reform," paper presented at the annual meeting of the Urban History Association, New York City, October 2012. For studies that claim that African Americans wanted more policing and social services, see Lisa L. Miller, "Crime, Punishment and Urban Governance in Contemporary American Politics," in *Urban Citizenship*, ed. Amy Bridges and Michael Javen Fortner (Albany: State University of New York Press, forthcoming); Peter Pihos, "The Local War on Drugs: Chicago, 1965–1989," paper presented at the annual meeting of the Social Science History Association, Chicago, November 21–24, 2013; Max Felker-Kantor, "'Kid Thugs Are Spreading Terror through the Streets': Juvenile Delinquency and the War on Crime in Los Angeles, 1968–1975," paper presented at the annual meeting of the Social Science History Association, Toronto, November 6–9, 2014; Michael Durfee, "48 Hours on Crack Street: How TV News and Congressional Politics Obstructed Grassroots Organizing," paper presented at the annual meeting of the

Social Science History Association, Toronto, November 6–9, 2014. Several contemporary national surveys bolster these propositions: Michael C. Dawson, *Behind the Mule: Race and Class in African-American Politics* (Princeton, NJ: Princeton University Press, 1994); Donald R. Kinder and Lynn M. Sanders, *Divided by Color: Racial Politics and Democratic Ideals* (Chicago: University of Chicago Press, 1996); Lawrence D. Bobo and Devon Johnson, "A Taste for Punishment," *Du Bois Review* 1, no. 2 (2004): 151–180; Tracey L. Meares, "Charting Race and Class Differences in Attitudes towards Drug Legalization and Law Enforcement: Lessons for Federal Criminal Law," *Buffalo Criminal Law Review* 1, no. 1 (1997): 137–174. This attitudinal evidence, however, shields the powerful politics of place and treats crime attitudes in static terms.

8. For Gramsci's discussion of hegemony and the "superstructures of civil society," see Antonio Gramsci, Quintin Hoare, and Geoffrey Nowell-Smith, *Selections from the Prison Notebooks of Antonio Gramsci* (New York: International, 1972). For Nancy Fraser's critique of a unitary public sphere, see "Rethinking the Public Sphere: A Contribution to the Critique of Actually Existing Democracy," in *Habermas and the Public Sphere*, ed. Craig Calhoun (Cambridge, UK: Cambridge University Press, 1992). For a discussion of the historical development of the black public sphere, see Aldon Morris, *The Origins of the Civil Rights Movement: Black Communities Organizing for Change* (New York: Free Press, 1984); Doug McAdam, *Political Process and the Development of Black Insurgency* (Chicago: University of Chicago Press, 1985); Michael C. Dawson, *Black Visions: The Roots of Contemporary African-American Political Ideologies* (Chicago: University of Chicago Press, 2001); Lawrence W. Levine, *Black Culture and Black Consciousness* (Oxford: Oxford University Press, 1978).

9. H. Carl McCall, "Looking Back," *Amsterdam News*, December 23, 1973, A5; David Garland, *The Culture of Control: Crime and Social Order in Contemporary Society* (Chicago: University of Chicago Press, 2001); Charles V. Hamilton, "The Patron-Recipient Relationship and Minority Politics in New York City," *Political Science Quarterly* 94, no. 2 (1979): 211–227.

10. Ann Shola Orloff and Theda Skocpol, "Why Not Equal Protection? Explaining the Politics of Public Social Spending in Britain, 1900–1911, and the United States, 1880s–1920," *American Sociological Review* 49,

no. 6 (1984): 726–750, 730–731; Kingdon, *Agendas, Alternatives, and Public Policies*. For a discussion of traceability, blame avoidance, and credit claiming, see R. Douglas Arnold, *The Logic of Congressional Action* (New Haven, CT: Yale University Press, 1990).

11. For a discussion of institutional layering, see Kathleen Ann Thelen, "How Institutions Evolve: Insights from Comparative-Historical Analysis," in *Comparative Historical Analysis in the Social Sciences*, ed. James Mahoney and Dietrich Rueschemeyer (Cambridge, UK: Cambridge University Press, 2003), 208–240; Kathleen Ann Thelen, *How Institutions Evolve: The Political Economy of Skills in Germany, Britain, the United States, and Japan* (Cambridge, UK: Cambridge University Press, 2004).

12. David Garland, *The Culture of Control: Crime and Social Order in Contemporary Society* (Chicago: University of Chicago Press, 2001). See also David Garland, *Punishment and Modern Society: A Study in Social Theory* (Chicago: University of Chicago Press, 1990). For a discussion of policy-feedback mechanisms, see Paul Pierson, "When Effect Becomes Cause: Policy Feedback and Political Change," *World Politics* 45, no. 4 (1993): 595–628; Paul Pierson, *Dismantling the Welfare State? Reagan, Thatcher, and the Politics of Retrenchment* (Cambridge, UK: Cambridge University Press, 1994); Andrea L. Campbell, *How Policies Make Citizens: Senior Citizen Activism and the American Welfare State* (Princeton, NJ: Princeton University Press, 2003).

13. Ann Swidler, "Culture in Action: Symbols and Strategies," *American Sociological Review* 51, no. 2 (1986): 273–286; Michèle Lamont, *The Dignity of Working Men: Morality and the Boundaries of Race, Class, and Immigration* (New York: Russell Sage Foundation, 2000); St. Clair Drake, "The Social and Economic Status of the Negro in the United States," *Daedalus* 94, no. 4 (1965): 771–814. For more textured and historically grounded assessments of black class categories, see Cathy J. Cohen, *The Boundaries of Blackness: AIDS and the Breakdown of Black Politics* (Chicago: University of Chicago Press, 1999); Evelyn Brooks Higginbotham, *Righteous Discontent: The Women's Movement in the Black Baptist Church, 1880–1920* (Cambridge, MA: Harvard University Press, 1993); Kevin Kelly Gaines, *Uplifting the Race: Black Leadership, Politics, and Culture in the Twentieth Century* (Chapel Hill: University of North Carolina Press, 1996); Hazel V. Carby, "Policing the Black Woman's Body in an Urban Context," *Critical Inquiry* 18, no. 4 (1992): 738–755;

Andrew Wiese, *Places of Their Own: African American Suburbanization in the Twentieth Century* (Chicago: University of Chicago Press, 2004); Michele Mitchell, *Righteous Propagation: African Americans and the Politics of Racial Destiny after Reconstruction* (Chapel Hill: University of North Carolina Press, 2004); Victoria W. Wolcott, *Remaking Respectability: African American Women in Interwar Detroit* (Chapel Hill: University of North Carolina Press, 2001).

Acknowledgments

Black Silent Majority goes against the grain, and while challenging conventional wisdom may be laudable, it is not always welcomed. Fortunately, many people kept an open mind, and this research benefited from their critical yet supportive feedback. They include Stephen Brier, Michael Durfee, Jennifer Fronc, Janet Golden, Christina Greer, Richard Harris, Drew Humphries, Kimberley Johnson, Penny Lewis, Stephanie Luce, Lawrence Mead, Lisa L. Miller, Lorraine Minnite, John Mollenkopf, Christopher Muller, Frances Fox Piven, Justin Rose, Joseph Spillane, Alan Tarr, Dorian Warren, Vesla Mae Weaver, Mabel Wilson, William Julius Wilson, and Stephan Wolff. I thank all the anonymous reviewers and journal editors who provided incisive and thoughtful comments on my articles on African American anticrime politics.

A few people deserve special mention. With great warmth and insight, Amy Bridges posed important questions and gave excellent editorial suggestions at various stages of this project. Jennifer Hochschild's generosity continues to leave me astounded and humbled. She kindly offered detailed comments on various sections of the book and provided substantial emotional support. I owe a great deal to Eric Schneider. His work on crime and drug addiction both informed and inspired my own thinking. Eric read most of my work and, at conferences, over email, and over drinks, helped me refine my arguments and bolster my historical analysis. Over the course of this project, I have learned that Robert Sampson's heart is just as impressive as his mind. In addition to sharing keen advice and useful references, Rob, at very stressful moments, always reminded me of our creed as social scientists: Evidence will out. This simple proposition fortified me and strengthened the book.

I could not have done this alone. Fortunately, I was aided by a small team of bright, energetic, and skilled research assistants, including Prentiss Dantzler, Kumar Ghafoor, Ashley Nickels, Jason D. Rivera, Daniel Stapelkamp, Jonathan Warren, and Zachary Wood. I was also aided by the amazing staff at the Paul Robeson Library at Rutgers University–Camden. I overwhelmed them with requests and they overwhelmed me with professionalism. I also received incredible assistance from archivists and staff members at institutions throughout the country: Rockefeller Archive Center; New York State Archives; Library of Congress; National Archives; M. E. Grenander Department of Special Collections and Archives, University at Albany; Special Collections Research Center, Syracuse University; Schomburg Center for Research in Black Culture, the New York Public Library; La Guardia and Wagner Archives, Fiorello H. La Guardia Community College; Special Collections and Preservation, Rush Rhees Library, University of Rochester; Special Collections and University Archives, Stony Brook University; Tamiment Library and Robert F. Wagner Labor Archive, Elmer Holmes Bobst Library; Spencer Research Library, University of Kansas; American Jewish Archives; Rare Book and Manuscript Library, Columbia University; Yale University Library; Sophia Smith Collection, Smith College; John F. Kennedy Library; Nixon Presidential Library and Museum; and the Gerald R. Ford Library. I am grateful to the staff of the New York City Department of Health and Mental Hygiene, specifically Regina Zimmerman, Berton Freedman, Gil Maduro, and Kelly Davis, for gathering and sharing their vital statistics.

This project required significant resources, space, and time. Luckily, I received substantial financial assistance from various sources. I benefited from a Rutgers University Faculty Research Grant and a Rutgers University Research Council Grant. Both the New York State Archives and the Rockefeller Archive Center graciously awarded me a grant to travel to and conduct research at their facilities. I am thankful to the leadership of Rutgers University–Camden, specifically Wendell Pritchett and Kriste Lindenmeyer, and my department chairs, Richard Harris and Marie Chevrier, for creating a supportive and rich intellectual environment to conduct this research and explore these heady issues. I thank the City University of

New York's School of Professional Studies, specifically John Mogulescu and George Otte, and the Murphy Institute, especially Greg Mantsios, for giving me a productive environment in which to finish the research and writing of this book.

Writing is a lonely process that I could not have survived without friends whose love, support, counsel, and jokes kept me going and helped me maintain my voice: June Arrington-Peña, Gwen Brons, Cynthia Dennard, Erick Espin, Jesus Franco, Cybelle Fox, Natalie Grizzle, Brian Grosz, Maria Guido, Sidnie Johnson, Rebecca McDonald, Randall Mish, Christopher Montepara, Rasaan Ogilvie, Jack Quinlan, Karthick Ramakrishnan, Matthew Robinson, Frankie Shipman-Amuwo, Juan Soliz, and Paris Tsangaris.

This book is a testament to the diligence, patience, skill, and support of Brian Distelberg, my editor at Harvard University Press. Brian helped me recover the voices of working- and middle-class African Americans suffering the ravages of urban decline and helped me find my own voice in the process. For that, I will be forever grateful.

Index